PRAISE FOR *FEARLES*

"*Fearless Tarot* takes the fright out of tarot. Thi card meanings and spreads designed to empower your life. If you want a book that represents the compassionate side of reading cards, then Elliot Adam's *Fearless Tarot* is your guide."

—Jaymi Elford, author of *Tarot Inspired Life*

"Everyone should read this book whether you are a novice or an adept. Elliot shares new twists with very helpful insights into each card. He shines the light on many situations through inner wisdom and allows you to discover all that is hidden. Elliot is a teacher with sharp precision who will guide you through the dark, the light, the good and the bad. *Fearless Tarot* is a great reference to keep by your side and a go to book, I guarantee you will be satisfied."

—Rana George, author of *The Essential Lenormand*

"Elliot has provided a masterclass in style. His book is a tarot resource that leads the student and adept through an approach to reading. He shares simple insights that are packed with positive truths."

—Seth Vermilyea, podcast host of *Coming Out of the Tarot Closet*

"Ever pull a scary-looking tarot card and freak out? At one point, we all have. In *Fearless Tarot*, Elliot Adam helps find the positive in the negative. That doesn't mean that you're ignoring the hard stuff. Instead, he's teaching you how to face the shadows in tarot—and your life—in a proactive way. If you've ever been nervous about a particular tarot card, this book will change your perspective."

—Theresa Reed, author of *Tarot: No Questions Asked*

FEARLESS TAROT

• ELLIOT ADAM •

FEARLESS TAROT

How to Give a Positive Reading in Any Situation

DARE TO PULL ANY CARD

Llewellyn Publications
Woodbury, Minnesota

First Edition
Second Printing, 2020

Cover design by Shannon McKuhen
Editing by Samantha Lu Sherratt

Library of Congress Cataloging-in-Publication Data
Names: Adam, Elliot, author.
Title: Fearless tarot : how to give a positive reading in any situation / Elliot Adam.
Description: First edition. | Woodbury, Minnesota : Llewellyn Publications, [2020] | Includes bibliographical references.
Identifiers: LCCN 2020026342 (print) | LCCN 2020026343 (ebook) | ISBN 9780738766690 (paperback) | ISBN 9780738766874 (ebook)
Subjects: LCSH: Tarot.
Classification: LCC BF1879.T2 A384 2020 (print) | LCC BF1879.T2 (ebook) | DDC 133.3/2424—dc23
LC record available at https://lccn.loc.gov/2020026342
LC ebook record available at https://lccn.loc.gov/2020026343

Llewellyn Publications
A Division of Llewellyn Worldwide Ltd.
2143 Wooddale Drive
Woodbury, MN 55125-2989
www.llewellyn.com

Printed in the United States of America

For my favorite artist Audrey Skott:
I miss you, Mom.

And to the many Gods and Goddesses she painted for me:
Pallas Athena, Delphic Apollo, Artemis, Aphrodite, Demeter, Hekate,
Hestia, and Hera of the Golden Throne.

Thank you, Athena, for finding that lost little boy in the library
so many years ago and teaching him the language of symbols and myth.

THE FOOL.
© 1971 U.S. GAMES SYSTEMS, INC.
IV
© 1971 U.S. GAMES SYSTEMS, INC.

Know thyself.

THE ORACLE OF DELPHI

VII
© 1971 U.S. GAMES SYSTEMS, INC.
XVIII
THE MOON.
© 1971 U.S. GAMES SYSTEMS, INC.

CONTENTS

PART 2: THE MINOR ARCANA

PART 3: HOW TO USE THE CARDS

Portions of this book originally appeared on the *Card of the Day* blog on the website ElliotOracle.com.

III
© 1971 U.S. GAMES SYSTEMS, INC.
VII
THE CHARIOT.
© 1971 U.S. GAMES SYSTEMS, INC.

FOREWORD

I'll never forget the time I walked into that tiny purple tea shop so many moons ago. I had heard rumors about a talented young tarot reader who worked there. At the time, I had an urgent situation and needed an objective set of eyes because I couldn't see the way ahead clearly. I was too emotionally invested.

A fresh-faced young man stepped out from behind the curtains, long hair gathered in a ponytail, and introduced himself as Elliot. He looked young enough to be my son, who was a teen at the time. While that might have made a few folks raise a skeptical eyebrow, I had no such qualms, for I had also started my own tarot career at a tender age.

I sat down at the little table, situated between books and fluffy pillows. Elliot poured me a tea and began to blow my mind.

As he laid out a version of the Celtic Cross that I had never seen before, he thoughtfully paused before each card. His interpretations were perfectly balanced between intuition and practicality. The anxiety I had about my situation was erased entirely, replaced with a hopeful forecast and actionable steps that put my future right in the palm of my hand.

That was my first introduction to Elliot Adam. I've been a fan ever since.

This book that you hold in your hands at this moment in time is special. Honed by years of experience and tempered with both wisdom and grace, *Fearless Tarot* will give you a peek into how an empowering tarot reader's mind works.

If I had to describe Elliot's approach to the tarot, I would say it is positive and uplifting. That doesn't mean anything is sugarcoated—he never does that. Instead, he's centered on being proactive, no matter what cards show up in the reading. Rather than viewing the tarot through the lens of fear, there is hope and a way forward. This turns tarot reading into more than divination—it becomes a problem-solving tool that can transform any situation.

In *Fearless Tarot*, you'll find empowering interpretations lovingly presented. A quick-start reference guide is included for those times when you need a fast glimpse (so useful when your brain is blank). A variety of spreads in the book gives you a layout for every situation (that extended Celtic Cross is here, too—finally, I learn the secret!). There is something in this book for everybody, from beginner to adept.

I cannot say this enough: you are so fortunate to have Elliot Adam by your side on your tarot journey. He not only talks the talk but walks the walk—he's a living embodiment of what it means to be a positive human being. *Fearless Tarot* will help you become not just a better tarot reader, but a more compassionate one.

Blessings,
Theresa Reed
The Tarot Lady
Author of *The Tarot Coloring Book* and *Astrology for Real Life*

INTRODUCTION

We've all been there. Sitting anxiously, you clutch your deck of tarot cards with a burning question in mind. You are desperate for an answer, a sign, some reassurance that there is a way forward. The fear of the looming decision you must make feels all-encompassing. Perhaps the cards will bring you clarity. You've always been an open-minded, spiritual person. Perhaps the Universe will finally give you the answer you need to get out of the pit of fear you find yourself in.

You take a deep breath. Trembling, you turn over the first card…

It's the Eight of Swords!!! This can't be good!

So many of the tarot books that you've read warn you about how awful this card is. Stagnation, fear, destruction, calamity, illness, the ruination of all your plans; the worst images of suffering cycle through your mind. You feel let down. This reading was supposed to make you feel good, to give you clarity. Instead you are more confused and even more desperate for reassurance. The Eight of Swords?! Are you kidding me?!

This just can't be. How could the answer be so hopeless? You think to yourself, "Perhaps I wasn't clear when focusing on my question." Aha! That's it! You just need to focus more—think positive thoughts! Law of Attraction, right?! If you think more positively, you can override your anxiety, and the next card will surely give you more uplifting news. Breathing deeply, you let go of the scary imagery of the first card. You begin to shuffle again. You focus on thinking happy thoughts. "Please be the Sun card… please be the Sun… be positive… happy thoughts… Ten of Cups would be good…" Your mind flashes the fear of the first card you drew. You still don't know if the Eight of Swords was a fluke or a real sign of problems to come. Whatever! Time for card number two…

The Devil reversed!!!

This is terrible!!!

This reading is a disaster! A sinking feeling of hopelessness prevails. Is the moon void of course? Maybe you just can't do a good reading because it's during a Mercury retrograde... maybe you are just a bad reader and don't know tarot as well as you thought you did... maybe you are a great reader, but your life feels like a complete mess with no hope, no way forward. How can the Eight of Swords and the Devil reversed be anything but horrible? Everybody seems to say so. All the books you've read, all the mini booklets that come with the cards—it's just more bad news. Even the sketchy fortune-teller you got that reading from on South 9th Street told you that the Eight of Swords and Devil reversed mean you must have a curse on you from a hidden enemy (and for nine hundred dollars she can focus all her magical prayers into removing it for you).

Let's face it: the tarot's symbolism can be downright scary when you are navigating alone in the dark with the fears you've brought with you. Some of the tarot's imagery, particularly in the Rider-Waite-Smith deck, can appear absolutely frightening! So many decks have evolved from this deck's iconic symbolism, and yet so many past interpretations of its "darker" cards leave little sense that life will improve—especially if you receive the Eight, Nine, or Ten of Swords to symbolize your outcome in a reading. Many of the interpretations available for the cards seem to pour kerosene on the flames of what we fear most. It's no wonder that there is an amorphous anxiety among the general public when discussing tarot card reading. For many, the cards seem linked to omens of bad news.

In popular culture, tarot is presented as "scary." We all remember the movies and soap operas in which the old woman with the raspy voice turns over the Death card, a sure portent for impending doom. Tarot is also presented as a scam. "Call me now for your free tarot reading!" Miss Cleo trumpets with her faux Jamaican accent. Unfortunately, tarot has been used by unscrupulous villains in the past to scare people with the tarot's imagery. After all, people who are afraid are easy to control.

The actual cards and their imagery are not the problem. The problem occurs when we look at those symbols through a lens of fear. In actuality, the tarot's symbols can uproot and highlight where our problems are originating from. If utilized to their full potential, tarot cards can be an extremely healing and transformative tool. Many of the problems in interpreting tarot can be found in our perspective. Not only in our thoughts while shuffling the cards, but in our immediate go-to definitions for what the cards mean. Tarot is subjective. It tells different stories to different people. Symbolism can be jarring, but it is *symbolism*. It is rarely meant to be taken literally. Even the most unsettling image has an important story to tell and a deeper place within your experience to illuminate. I have found that the cards we are most uncomfortable with are where we often find the biggest breakthrough and the greatest healing. After all, it's during our most challenging moments (not our easiest times) when we come into direct contact with what is best within us.

As a professional tarot reader for well over two decades, I used to hesitate when people asked me, "So what do you do for a living?" I always paused for a moment. What assumptions did this person have about what I do?

When I tell strangers that I read tarot, I get a range of reactions: Shock. Disbelief. Does not compute. Say what?! Many times, I've heard people say, "I would never do that; it's just too scary." I also get tons of skepticism. Then there is the reaction of smiling and nodding… basically as one does to humor a crazy person. I've even experienced some people who display anger and hostility toward tarot readings and readers. This is often a mask for their fears, too.

Why are people so afraid of tarot? I have come to find that they are afraid of what they don't understand. For my entire professional life, clients have come to me with their fears. They are looking for answers and for a way forward. In my experience, reciting the hopeless definitions of "bad cards" doesn't help people. I've seen many readers scare clients with "bad cards" to inflate their own weakened egos. Readers who receive a power trip by frightening people are not only inappropriate but unethical. It makes my stomach sink to see this sort of nasty manipulation.

I believe in using tarot for empowerment. I never use the tarot to exacerbate a client's anxieties. I prefer to help clients pinpoint what needs healing (especially with their inner perception of the situation) and reacquaint them with what is best within them. When interpreted in a manner that encourages people, the tarot's potent symbolism can illuminate a path to reclaim strength and restore personal power. This cannot be done if the individual is stuck in a fearful spiral, interpreting the tarot's symbolism with dark hopelessness. When people are reacquainted with their inner courage, they usually know just what to do.

TRANSCENDING SHADOWS WITH TAROT

The purpose of this book is to provide an empowering perspective as you journey through the imagery of the Rider-Waite-Smith tarot. Cards that appear frightening are symbolic wake-up calls. They are not meant to make you feel powerless or hopeless about the future. It can be argued that each card presents challenges. However, if you know where to look in the picture, the keys to overcoming the challenges can be found right in front of you.

This book will

- help you deliver empowering readings for yourself and others;
- aid you in transcending your shadows when interpreting your own cards;
- amplify what your inner wisdom has been whispering to you all along;
- increase your fluency with applying the details of tarot imagery to everyday life;
- challenge excessively negative interpretations of "darker" card imagery and view them in a new light; and
- reveal how to interpret reversed cards constructively.

Tarot is a powerful tool for inner transformation because symbols were our first written language. Images transcend words. We all know the saying "a picture is worth a thousand words." Tarot cards contain rich, archetypal imagery. People have been using symbols and archetypes to dialogue with their Inner Selves since the dawn of humanity. Originally, we were drawing these same primordial archetypes on cave walls. Tarot resonates because it speaks directly to the archetypes that collectively reside within us all. The symbolic figures depicted in the tarot are a powerful group. They encompass the full range of the human experience. The archetypes in the tarot are a mirror for the archetypes that are busily chatting away in the background of our consciousness.

This book will guide you through many hidden symbols within each card. In the case of darker cards, a hidden image in the card will be highlighted to reveal the way to overcome the challenge presented. Once you know where to look on the card, the solution to your present impasse can be quite simple.

Pamela Colman Smith's artistry is a testament to her genius. For over a century, tarot students have been reexamining these magical images. Like all great works of art, they speak to different individuals in diverse ways. The tarot interpretations on the following pages are my own observations, and I do not claim to recapture the original intentions of Pamela Colman Smith or Edward Waite. There are many wonderful books that can give you a historical perspective of the card's imagery, such as *Secrets of the Waite-Smith Tarot* by Marcus Katz and Tali Goodwin. This book delves into the history of the Rider-Waite-Smith tarot and extensively researches some of the original sources of inspiration for Pamela Colman Smith's artwork. As for the original card definitions of the Rider-Waite-Smith tarot, you could study *A Pictorial Key to the Tarot* by Sir Arthur Edward Waite. There are thousands of different perspectives on this iconic deck. Everyone who engages with these images ends up perceiving and applying them uniquely. I encourage you to let your own instincts and impressions inform your own unique interpretations of these amazing images.

An uplifting tarot reading can help you overcome external challenges by calling attention to their root causes within as well as the resources to overcome them. Everything you need to transcend your difficulties can be found reflected in these remarkable images. The tarot is an effective tool for illuminating pathways inward, through ancient archetypes and symbols, uncovering the place where your solutions were hidden. Tarot presents your situation in the context of the symbolic. This gives you the ability to reexamine your worries and fears with distance and perspective, thereby empowering you to act. Although tarot can be used as a predictive tool to reveal insights into a likely future, its revelations are not set in stone. You are empowered to change anything about your life you don't like. The future does not just happen to you, but rather is formed by every choice you make in the present. Your thoughts are the magic spells that manifest the reality you will experience. Tarot can help you focus those thoughts on what is best and brightest within you.

HOW TO USE THIS BOOK

This book can be a positive reference guide when providing readings to yourself and others. It is also intended to offer a constructive perspective when engaging with challenging tarot imagery. Many readers find that they are quite adept at offering uplifting consultations to others but find it difficult to retain their positive perspective when interpreting their own cards. For example, if the Tower appears in a client's reading, you probably wouldn't panic. You might see that the ground is metaphorically shaking, but there is still hope after the storm passes. However, if you are anxiously consulting your own cards and the Tower appears, you might feel defeated because it seems to contradict an outcome that you are attached to. Sometimes we are just too close to our situation to see it with a clear perspective. Other times, we may be so attached to the desired outcome that we are blind to the solution staring us in the face.

CARD OF THE DAY

Originally the descriptions for each card were written as *Card of the Day* blog posts on my website. They were intended to reveal areas of opportunity and to provide daily positive advice to my readers for empowerment. Many tarot readers pull a card every morning to center themselves and to see where their focus might best be applied for the day ahead.

To use the Card of the Day method for yourself, take a few moments in the morning to center and relax. Inhale slowly through your nose for eight seconds. Hold in your breath for another eight seconds. Slowly exhale through your lips over eight seconds, making a *pphhhhh* sound. Repeat this process two more times. Begin shuffling your tarot deck. Clear your mind and ask, "What opportunity is the Universe presenting me with today to grow and succeed?" With the cards facedown, allow your fingers to intuitively select the card that encapsulates the present message meant for you. You can't pick the "wrong" card. Try not to dismiss the card just because you don't like how it looks or because it wasn't what you expected. If you do feel resistant to a card's imagery, that should be a big red flag that the message is *definitely* for you. Human beings habitually avoid what isn't comfortable. However, the uncomfortable thing is usually what will get you to the next level if you can accept it.

The card you select may not be the card you expect, but there will be an important symbol found within it to provide you with new insight into yourself.

The Rider-Waite-Smith tarot is rich in symbolism. Some pictures appear uplifting, and some others appear rather jarring. For example, if you pull the

Ten of Swords as your card for the day, that does not mean you are doomed to have a terrible day. You are, however, being shown something important that needs your attention. In the case of the Ten of Swords, it might indicate that you are not facing something that is causing you to feel anxious. By facing the issue, you will feel stronger and will no longer feel like you are being chased or victimized by fear. Selecting a card with dark imagery does not guarantee bad news for you. In fact, the darker cards have the greatest propensity for catapulting you toward a huge breakthrough. As you will read in the following pages, there are various ways to apply even the harshest tarot symbolism in a positive and empowering manner.

REGARDING REVERSALS

One area of disagreement among readers is whether to interpret cards that appear reversed. There is no right or wrong way to interpret the tarot. There are many successful readers who don't care for interpreting reversals. This is totally fine. Tarot is not a fundamentalist pursuit. Its meanings are ever changing depending on who is engaging with the symbolism. I prefer to use reversals when providing readings, but in moderation. Usually I begin with all cards facing in the same direction before a consultation. While all the cards are facedown, I randomly select three to ten cards to turn in the reversed position. That way, if a reversed card appears in a reading, I know it is important.

Reversed cards have been mistakenly viewed by some as bad. Generally, I haven't found this to be the case in my interpretation. Also, a reversed card does not completely negate the imagery of its upright counterpart. I interpret reversals as still embodying the symbolic subject of its upright version, but with a twist.

Reversed cards can indicate

- that there is a challenge to be overcome by applying the card's strengths to your situation;
- that there is a blockage around the area of your life that the card describes;
- that the situation you are asking about needs to be viewed from an alternate perspective;

- that, in the case of challenging cards, you may find conditions are improving and you are finally freeing yourself from a personal struggle that is depicted in the imagery; and
- that balance needs to be reestablished in the sphere of life that the image is concerned with.

PART I
THE MAJOR ARCANA

The cards that compose the Major Arcana are a collection of archetypal images that symbolize the building blocks of the unconscious mind. Each card contains an archetype that speaks directly to the unconscious with clear, unvarnished clarity. When a Major Arcana card appears in a reading, it calls your attention to the inner workings of your situation. When several Major Arcana cards appear, it means you are confronting the "big stuff," the inner workings of your unconscious life that are having direct and indirect influences on your external situation.

The Major Arcana consists of twenty-two cards. They can be read sequentially as the "hero's journey." The hero in this case is the Fool, numbered 0, who confronts a powerful archetype along each step of his journey. The adventure through the Major Arcana is full of high and low points. There are times when the path feels smooth, and yet there are other times when the path places the Fool in direct contact with his greatest shadows and fears.

There is always another step to take, even when your pathway appears darkest. Nothing is ever truly hopeless. The Fool journeys across the brightest landscapes and into the darkest caverns. This journey mirrors our own lives. However, the Fool's journey always concludes with him returning to the light again. Arriving at the World, he completes one cycle and begins another.

THE FOOL

Risking looking like a fool.

The Fool is the archetype of freedom, humor, and positive new adventures. He is the wayward hero of the tarot, the embodiment of the young adventurer just getting started on his quest. He is the only card numbered 0 in the deck. This means that he is not attached to any identity that he must prove to others. He's not the "King of this," or the "Knight of that." He's just a fool: simple, unencumbered by worry, and completely free to go where he chooses.[1] The Fool's wisdom lies in his lack of pride and ego. He never despairs if he doesn't look competent. That's just another box he would hate to be suffocated in. He's not afraid if people laugh at him. He laughs at himself! This humor gives him an inexhaustible resilience. It also carries magical healing powers for himself and others.

Are you ever afraid of looking stupid? Can you laugh at yourself as you haphazardly try to learn something new? Is there an unrealized dream you still have, but you are too scared to go for it?

The Fool knows that people who buy into maintaining an image limit themselves to a self-imposed box to suffocate in. That's not living! The Fool is open and curious, journeying wherever he dares. The Fool can never be boxed in, kept, or defined by others. He represents the wild and rebellious part of your nature. He goes his own path. The sun is shining, and his spirits are soaring. He is wearing the ugliest pattern this side of creation. It brings him great joy to flaunt it. He loves to shock onlookers as he passes by. If he gets happiness from it, that's all that matters. After all, it's not like he's hurting anyone.

The Fool has packed his travel bag, emblazoned with the symbol of an eagle. Eagles represent Spirit and higher perspective. The Fool is on a spiritual journey. This is also reinforced by the color white, which appears so prevalently on the card. White is the color of purity, innocence, and spiritual light. The Fool's rose is white, his loyal dog is white, even the sun shining down on the Fool is white. The Fool prompts you to perceive the journey spread before you through the luminous eyes of your own Spirit.

The Fool doesn't seem to be paying any attention to the possibility of future calamities. His head is occupied with the thrilling possibilities of the day. Could he be in danger of going over the edge of the cliff? Possibly, but maybe that would be fun; he's never actually died before. The Fool knows an important secret: things are never as bad as they might appear. Somehow, he always manages to get back up unscathed. The Universe has a soft spot for fools and blesses them with the craziest luck. The Fool also wears a wreath around his cap. This symbol features prominently on the final card in the Major Arcana, the World. Although we begin the Major Arcana with the Fool, the wreath implies that he

1. Pollack, *Tarot Wisdom*, 18.

will go the distance and reach his destination. The Fool already possesses the symbol for victory and completion even at the beginning. Knowing this, you realize he really isn't in danger after all. You also have everything you need to achieve a victorious completion of your journey.

When the Fool appears, he is calling you toward a new adventure. It's time to escape from the confines of ruts and routines. What are you afraid of plunging into? What would make your life feel lived? The Fool represents the need for taking risks. Even if others might think you are foolish for trying, it's time to throw your hat in the ring for your dream. Take an action toward your goal and don't overthink it. Just begin, and momentum will follow. Leap into the unknown landscape of possibility.

Release your inner Fool, for your heart's desire awaits! Abandon the self-consciousness that prevents you from appearing too enthusiastic in public. Release thoughts of "I really should do this," or "What will so-and-so think?" from your consciousness. Learn to laugh at yourself and the world. Remember that after all the work and worry of crafting an image for others, you are still a primate. Let go of fears that stem from the ego and concerns about how you appear to others. Find the sunny, warm, funny, innocent, and optimistic spark that waits deep within you, and set it free! You will be much more fun to be around. When the Fool appears, approach your situation with optimism and humor.

The Fool gleefully whispers his words of wisdom to you: "Let go and cast off your fears of trying, of dying, and of looking stupid. They're cheating you out of a full life."

The Fool Reversed

If the Fool appears reversed, he asks you to release your fear of failing before you begin. The fear of failure is a crippling companion. It can completely halt your momentum. Errors are our best teachers. We need them to grow. When the Fool is upright, his instinct is to begin his new journey unselfconsciously. When the Fool appears reversed, he represents the need to release limiting self-consciousness, which can keep you feeling stagnant.

The Fool often appears reversed when we feel lost, confused, or like we are being pulled by an overwhelming life full of unknowns and uncertainties. What "future unknowable" feels scariest to you currently? What avoidance mechanism is holding up your success? The Fool is only a fool because of what he doesn't know. Anyone can gain more knowledge to solve any difficulty. When you challenge yourself to learn new things that are out of your comfort zone, you build self-esteem and become empowered.

The Fool reversed can also indicate a sense of imposter syndrome. This is the fear that others will find out you don't know everything about a position you hold or a subject you are studying and therefore you must not belong. The fear that others will discover you aren't somehow qualified is very common, even among the most successful people.

Ask yourself what you need to learn more about to empower yourself. Challenge yourself to take a risk and learn something new. This will ultimately put you on a direct path to reaching your goals. Don't be afraid of doing it wrong, looking stupid, or not knowing what's ahead. You will find that the choice to act will give you great power. The Fool safely finds his way through openness and trust. Be brave and take the steps you are afraid to take.

THE MAGICIAN

Your thoughts are magic spells that create your reality.

Each of us is a magician, and our predominant thoughts are the magic spells that produce the life we are experiencing. All the situations you see in front of you can be changed, but first you must change where your mind is fixated. The Magician is in complete control of his environment. He represents the power of your mind's focus, which creates the reality you are living in.

What predominant thoughts do you harbor during the day? Are your thoughts generally positive or negative? Do you feel in control of your thoughts, or do they run uncontrollably on automatic?

The Magician stands before his altar. Before him are four objects: a cup, a pentacle, a sword, and a wand. Each represents the different elements of his external environment: his emotional life, monetary life, predominant thoughts, and ambitions. The Magician has the power to move the objects on the altar any way he chooses. This symbolizes your ability to affect your external environment by choosing to focus your thoughts and intentions. The Magician's white wand is raised high, channeling his Higher Self. He also wears a white diadem. When you are channeling your Higher Self, you can manifest marvelous things as if by magic. The garden symbols of the white lily and the red rose are also significant. The white lily shares the color of the Magician's wand and robe (transcendent spiritual awareness). The red rose represents passion. It takes passion to manifest your loftiest goals. The red rose reminds us of the color of blood and vitality. The Magician blends the energies of his Higher Self (lily) to manifest what he is passionate about (rose) in the real world.

Your Higher Self is the part of you that feels limitless. The Magician taps into this infinite power symbolized by the infinity sign above his head and the Ouroboros serpent biting its own tail around his waist. When you invoke your limitlessness, you will you feel energized, motivated, and confident. Unfortunately, we live in a society that barrages us with images of how we don't measure up. This affects our unconscious mind, which will run on autopilot until it is challenged. Once self-doubt takes the megaphone, your Higher Self can feel all but drowned out. If your predominant thoughts are "I'm too fat," "I'm not good enough," "I can't do this," "I don't know how to make this work," "Guess that's just life," "I'm a fraud," "I know I won't succeed at this anyway," then you are tuning out the voice of your Spirit.

To reconnect with the limitlessness of your Spirit, remember a time in your life when you felt truly powerful. Recall when you stood up and did the difficult thing. Hold that courageous feeling. That person of your memory is still you. No matter what's transpired, this is still the true essence of who you are.

When the Magician appears, you must take responsibility for where you allow your mind to dwell. It's totally controlling your reality! Challenge negative thoughts instead of letting them run on autopilot. If your focus is on the negative, place it instead on something that makes you feel good. You can make your life so different if you just change your mind to do so.

The Magician Reversed

If the Magician appears reversed, he calls your attention to thoughts that feel out of control. The Magician teaches, "As above, so below," meaning that your inner beliefs about yourself shape the reality you are experiencing. The reality that you see in front of you can be changed, but you must take ownership of your thoughts and beliefs about yourself. The Magician (upright or reversed) is a messenger from your Higher Self. The message is that you can change what you are experiencing by altering how you think about your current circumstances and your power over them. Are the hidden beliefs uplifting and empowering, or fearful and self-sabotaging?

Remember, your thoughts are like magic spells. They create your life experiences.

The Magician reversed encourages you to clean out your mental attic. It's time to throw away the clutter that appears in the form of negative, self-limiting thoughts that make you feel powerless and small. You are so much more powerful than you think! If you want proof, just look back at all the challenges you have overcome without giving up.

To throw out negative thoughts, stop yourself when you are having them. Hold that thought in your mind. Does it make you feel tight, anxious, worthless, or afraid? If it does, tell that thought, "You are garbage, and I'm taking out the trash. I don't need you anymore. You aren't true, and I'm better than this." Then shift your thoughts to something beautiful about yourself or your life. Acknowledge a hard-fought achievement you've made. Have a few thoughts handy that always make you smile to shift gears.

You are the magician of your life. Be mindful of what spells you are casting.

THE HIGH PRIESTESS

Trust your inner knowing.

The High Priestess is the personification of wisdom and inner knowing. If you've ever trusted your gut instincts, then you were trusting her. You know far more than you think you know. To access your instincts and inner wisdom, you need to push aside the veil of the endlessly chattering, "rational" mind. The High Priestess guards the realm of your deeper feelings. When you access the deepest core of your being, you will often find you already know the answer. You just might be too distracted (or too afraid) to trust it.

Do you trust yourself and your instincts? Is it hard to access your inner knowing because you are distracted by anxiety? Do you confuse fear with your feelings, causing you to not trust your instincts?

The High Priestess is the mistress of what lies beyond the veil. She is the keeper of your deepest wisdom. She challenges you to look past the thin shroud of your rationality and experience the deep sea of your inner knowing. She is crowned with the moon in its three phases: waxing, full, and waning. The High Priestess sees the big picture and knows the beginning, the middle, and the end.

The High Priestess sits between two pillars: one black, and one white. This symbolizes that life's answers are hardly ever black or white but, like the Priestess's position, are found somewhere in between. The pillars are decorated with the letters *B* and *J*. These are the initials for Boaz and Jachin, which were the names of the two entrance pillars to the ancient temple of King Solomon.[2] Like the High Priestess, King Solomon is an archetype of wisdom. The High Priestess sits before a veil decorated with pomegranates, the fruit of the Underworld. This symbolizes her answers are found beyond the anxious fears of death and change. Peeking from beyond her veil is the vast sea of the unconscious. All the answers to your questions can be found in those primordial waters.

The High Priestess appears today to guide you back to your instincts. Instead of throwing your hands in the air and yelling, "I don't know what to do," go further within yourself. The Priestess knows that feelings of helplessness are just superficial exclamations of fear on the surface. She asks you to summon the courage to pull back the veil blocking your vision and access your deepest self for the answer. The answer is right there, beyond the veil of fears, and you already know what to do.

Trusting your instincts can be difficult. The what-ifs begin to emerge from your fears. "What if I'm wrong?" "What if this is just a big mistake?" "What if I don't really belong here?" "What if I fail?" These fears are as thin and superficial as a skimpy veil attempting to block the vast sea. Your fears are not your instincts.

2. Pollack, *Tarot Wisdom*, 45.

To know the difference between your fears and your instincts, check in with your body. Fears will make you feel tight and anxious. Instincts, on the other hand, make you feel sharp, clear, and empowered to act. Your instincts can be found in the place beyond the tightness, deeper within your core, deeper within your Spirit. Your inner wisdom is an instinct that will guide you, like an infallible compass, whenever you feel lost.

The High Priestess Reversed

If the High Priestess appears reversed, she asks you to notice any recurring signs or symbols you are receiving. The High Priestess is a teacher. She alerts you to a lesson you are learning. When the High Priestess appears, she tells you that the issues you are experiencing are deeper than they may at first appear. She is also calling your attention to the language of signs and symbols. Like an abstract painting, the High Priestess reversed asks you to examine the situation from different perspectives to understand it. There is deep wisdom to be gained from recurring signals.

The High Priestess speaks in a language of pictures, signs, and symbols. This language is not literal and cannot be understood by the rational mind alone. Trust your feelings to illuminate what the message is. There is nothing to fear when the High Priestess appears, upright or reversed. There is magic afoot. The Universe is communicating with you in serendipitous and synchronistic ways. It is encouraging you to find the answers to your questions by accessing your inner wisdom. Today, notice any unusual signals you receive. Is there a bird or an animal that finds its way onto your path? What could that animal be teaching you? Is there a color or something that catches your eye? Ask yourself what this means to you. Is there a card from your tarot deck that keeps emerging? What could it be telling you? Today, look on the grand design of the world with the wise eyes of the High Priestess. The answers will be found within, but the Universe will always provide clues in the form of recurring signs.

THE EMPRESS

You are nurtured and safe and have everything that you need.

When the Empress appears, worries can no longer exist. The Empress is the ever-loving Great Mother who encourages, nurtures, and protects all her children. The Empress reassures us that we are safe and protected and have access to all the abundance we need. She lovingly holds out this truth even when you are unable to feel it, see it, or believe it.

The Empress archetype has gone by many names throughout human history. She's appeared in every land and in every culture since the dawn of time. There have been many attempts throughout history to repress her, discredit her, or forget her completely. However, after every dark age in human history, she always reemerges with a gentle smile. The Empress appears today to tell you that there is something important in your life that needs to feel loved, nurtured, and protected to thrive. She advises you that self-love will be your strongest shield moving forward.

Are you feeling safe, reassured, and abundant right now? What part of your life needs nurturing, love, and protection currently? Are you able to access the fearless place within you where love resides?

The Empress sits in her abundant garden. She looks kindly at you as you approach her throne. She wears the sparkling Crown of Twelve Stars, signifying her status as the eternal Queen of Heaven. The crown symbolizes her ability to see the big picture, or the eternal context of every situation. The Empress also wears a second laurel-leaf crown, which corresponds to the final card in the major arcana, the World. The crowns give her the ability to see the time before, the beginning, the middle, the end, and the great beyond. Seeing situations in the context of the eternal is a great remedy for fear. The Empress reminds us we have so much more purpose in our existence than our fears would have us believe. The Crown of Twelve Stars also reminds us of the months of the year—the signs of the zodiac—and represents all things growing at their appropriate time. The crown of leaves (which we will see again on the Chariot) represents victory within the world, while the crown of stars represents the perspective of the heavens.

The robes of the Empress are covered with images of fruit, representing her power to bring prosperity and abundance to everything she nurtures. A shield in the shape of a heart lies at her feet, emblazoned with the symbol of Venus, the Goddess of love. This symbolizes that the Empress uses love to protect what she cares for. Her field of wheat signifies her ability to feed and nourish her children. She reminds us that there is more than enough for everybody. The Empress embodies comfort, love, and understanding. She is the nurturing face of Mother Nature, who gently guides you back to your Authentic Self. She patiently waits with open arms to unburden you of troubles and wipe away all tears. The Empress can always be felt in the part of your heart that transcends fear and glows with love.

The Empress makes all things grow with the power of gentle patience. This loving force is always busy at work. It can be seen in our major life events and rites of passage. The Empress is also busy in the background of our lives, making the trees blossom, the grass grow, and the generations pass on their torches. Her loving energy is present when a mother holds her baby for the first time and when an old man calls out to his mother before he is about to pass on. The Empress reminds you of the power of your highest ideals. This energy allows you to manifest whatever dream you are trying to create. When the Empress arrives, she unburdens you of worries because she places issues in the context of the big picture. The Empress reminds you that all that really matters is love. Therefore, you can believe her when she whispers, "Everything is going to be okay."

The Empress Reversed

If the Empress appears reversed, she gently asks you to consider which area of your life is feeling neglected. The Empress represents love and nurturing, so if there is an area that feels abandoned, it is time to make it a priority. Ask yourself, "What have I been neglecting within myself?" Your instincts will probably be shouting the answer as you're reading this. The Empress is a comforting card, upright or reversed. When reversed, she asks you to shower a neglected part of your life with your love, care, and attention.

The Empress is the Great Mother archetype. When she appears reversed, she could be providing insight into your current situation through the lens of your own experience with your mother. Relationships with mothers are complicated, but they always reveal interesting patterns. What behaviors did your mother figure model when confronting similar situations? Sometimes this card brings healing to learned behaviors from parents. As an adult, you get to choose which parental traits you wish to exemplify, and which are not working for this situation.

The Empress reversed might also appear when there is a fear that there will not be enough of something. This could be love, money, understanding, or safety. The Empress archetype does not understand the concept of scarcity. Upright or reversed, the Empress assuages your fears and reminds you that you exist in a Universe of plenty. There are a plethora of good experiences still waiting for you out there, no matter what past issue is being healed. The Empress reminds you that love will protect and shield you. So often, just giving yourself a little more love is all that is needed to make a huge breakthrough. Therefore, the Empress carries the shield in the shape of a heart, inscribed with the symbol of Venus. This symbol represents opening your heart and allowing love to be the solution. The shield also symbolizes protecting your heart by viewing your current situation with unconditional love.

Look at your plans, projects, and priorities as your children. They need attention, consistency, love, and discipline to grow and thrive. The Empress bestows all forms of prosperity whether she appears upright or reversed. When reversed, abundance may seem a little more elusive, but it is still there. When looking for answers, this card reassures you that the solution to insecurities will not be found out in the world or from another person. The Empress will open the pathway forward when you nurture the part of yourself that's been neglected.

THE EMPEROR

Establishing strong foundations and boundaries.

The Emperor is the archetype for assertiveness and initiating a firm foundation for success. He teaches you that feeling secure can only exist when you establish strong boundaries. If you don't stand up for yourself, you are metaphorically wearing a sign that tells others they can take control of your life and its direction. To the Emperor, this is the same as ceding his crown to a lesser king. The Emperor's personal honor code forbids victimization. The Emperor is the personification of the voice within that urges you to speak up assertively when something feels unjust. If you continually feel resentful that others aren't treating you with respect, it's probably because you haven't been letting your inner Emperor speak up.

Do you feel respected by others and that your personal boundaries are honored? Do you have trouble saying no without an apologetic excuse or a fib? Do you want to "be nice" and think that assertive people are somehow mean, selfish, and don't care about others?

The Emperor is seated on his throne, which is decorated with rams. Rams charge forward, assertively defending their territory and mates. The Emperor wears armor under his robes. This symbolizes that he is ready for action at any time. He is not afraid to stand up and protect his realm. His beard symbolizes his wisdom gained from experience. The Emperor is never aggressive just to prove his masculinity. He acts only when his realm needs to be stabilized and protected. The mountains surrounding him are protective barriers. They are also his seat of power. From their peaks, he can survey all his realm and swiftly act to protect his personal boundaries. The Emperor wields the scepter and the orb. The scepter is a symbol for masculine energy, and the orb is a symbol for the feminine. The Emperor holds both in balance and understands that each are equally indispensable. The Emperor is relaxed and at peace with his masculinity and femininity. If you look closely, there is even a stream emerging from his mountains in the distance. The Emperor does have contact with the sensitive element of Water. This spring will flow down his mountain and feed the Empress's waterfall far below.

The Emperor appears as a firm figure, the compliment of his soft-featured wife, the Empress. The Empress sits relaxed in her garden, dispensing love, peace, and nurturing to her children. However, the Empress's garden can only exist because the Emperor protects its borders, giving her this safe space to do her important work. Within you, there is not only an Empress, but an Emperor as well. Both are vitally important to be a balanced human being. If one archetype is ignored, inner turmoil often results.

American society is obsessed with gender roles. It brainwashes children into believing that life is a series of "boys are this" and "girls are that." Boys should act more aggressive and assertive; girls should be nicer and more accommodating. The truth is we all have both the Empress and the Emperor archetypes within us, regardless of what gender we are. Both archetypes must be respected for inner and external balance to occur. Too much Emperor can make you overly aggressive, combative, and belligerent. Too much Empress can make you passive, a doormat, and a victim.

Today the Emperor is calling you to be assertive. You don't need to justify your right to be, but you do need to stand up for it. Respectfully asserting your position is very empowering if you've been overly passive. This card also portends the need to create structure to aid in the achievement of a goal. Take responsibility for yourself and your dreams. Stand up and protect your realm. Stop meekly saying yes when your inner Emperor is bellowing "NO!"

If you honor your inner Emperor, you will feel secure in yourself and your place in the world.

The Emperor Reversed

If the Emperor appears reversed, he may be asking you to identify what feels unstable in your realm at this time. Often this instability results from procrastination on pressing matters that require confrontation. Sometimes this card alerts you to embodying too much passive Empress energy. Confrontation can seem like an uncomfortable concept. We often would much rather avoid the conflict. In truth, avoiding and procrastinating lead to a perpetual sense of inner turmoil and anxiety that is much more difficult to exist with. Confronting issues or projects that have been avoided will revitalize and restore your sense of order, control, and self-confidence. Take responsibility for all that is under your charge. It's time to lead, not follow. The Emperor's role is to defend, promote, and protect all that he cares for.

When the Emperor appears reversed, he also reminds you to step into your majesty. Stop fooling yourself into thinking you can't do this. Instead of avoiding that which needs to be reinforced, dive in and change it. Take charge and create the stability you wish to see. Face the issues confronting you and act. The Emperor is the archetype of pro-activity. Meet your deadlines and take charge of your life. Confront your finances, take care of that cavity, dust off your to-do list. The Emperor exemplifies not only control of his empire, but self-control as well. Your self-esteem will skyrocket when you summon the courage to do what is right.

THE HIEROPHANT

Revealing the Sacred Mystery.

The Hierophant archetype symbolizes seeking the Sacred. Every culture since the dawn of human history has had a concept of (and instinct toward) spiritual awareness. Some names for this awareness are God, the Universe, the Gods, Higher Power, Spirit, the Goddess, Nature, Angels, the Higher Self, the Great Mystery… the name is different depending on whom you talk to. Nobody's really right or wrong because no one can perceive the complete scope of this infinite thing. Each of us is part of a divine collective, describing the same "Holiness" from different vantage points. What is sacred to one may hold no meaning for another. However, the part of our psyche that prays and wishes is universal. Spirit transcends cultural identity and imperfect human perceptions of religion.

Even most atheists concede that humans evolved with a biological component in the brain that developed into an instinct toward spiritual belief. Whatever your personal beliefs are, the Hierophant symbolizes one important thing: we humans have an instinct to commune with an awareness bigger than ourselves.

Does religious baggage prevent you from connecting with the Divine? Are you skeptical that a Goddess/God/Awareness/Spirit even exists? When was the last time you prayed for something and felt truly heard?

The two monks pictured on the card are seeking wisdom from His Holiness the Hierophant. One wears a robe of roses, while the other wears a robe of lilies. The Monk of Roses represents your heart. The Monk of Lilies represents your soul. The Hierophant knows how to reconcile the needs of your heart and soul to overcome your worldly troubles. The Hierophant raises his hand in a gesture of blessing. He is the guardian of rites of passage that *you* choose.

The Hierophant archetype is the awareness within that knows your whole story. This awareness reflects the radiant divinity within you. He balances the concerns of the earth with those of the heavens. This Holy Awareness exists deep in your Spirit and patiently waits for you to ask for what you need. The Spirit that inspires the Hierophant can find the quickest path to transcend whatever challenge you are experiencing. The Hierophant's unwavering faith can make him appear stubbornly fixated on his own beliefs. Try to embody the tenacity and faith of the Hierophant without becoming dogmatic.

In ancient Greek language, the *hierophantes* is the one who teaches the rites of sacrifice, traditions, and worship.[3] For miracles to take place, a personal sacrifice of some sort is usually required. The Hierophant unlocks the gateway toward answers. He can tell you the "why" behind what you are experiencing. He will also reveal what you need to sacrifice in order to pass through this gate-

3. Liddell and Scott, *Greek-English Lexicon*, 377.

way. The keys at the Hierophant's feet represent the need to unlock the sacred place within. Reaching out to the sacredness within can assist in releasing burdens that feel bigger than you. If your prayers are true, they are always heard. You may not get what you expect, but you will receive a sign pointing the way forward.

What has been feeling so heavy, so unsolvable, and so hopeless? You're being heard right now. The Hierophant encourages you to ask for whatever your heart and soul need. If you are willing, he will safely guide you through this spiritual rite of passage.

The Hierophant Reversed

If the Hierophant appears reversed, he warns against inflexibility. Many people turn away from cultivating their spirituality because of the inflexible examples of dogma in religions and religious leaders. When the Hierophant appears reversed, he asks if there are beliefs in your own life that are keeping you in a state of rigidity.

Where might you need to bend more? Are your assumptions calcifying a once open mind? Is there an inflexible person who is irritating you right now, reflecting a part of yourself that is also intransigent?

Try to approach your current situation with open-mindedness. Sometimes the Hierophant reversed represents an inflexible situation that you must find your way around. When two inflexible and immovable objects are about to collide, it often leads to suffering. Be the bigger person by embracing the part within you that can transcend needing to be right. Allow yourself to ask for help when needed. The Hierophant is the messenger of the Great Mystery. Perhaps all that is needed is more time for meditation and reflection. Take a time-out from controlling behaviors. Allow all answers to reveal themselves to you on your path. Look on this situation with the same magnanimity as your better angels.

THE LOVERS

The formula for unconditional love, inner peace, and balance.

The Lovers represent love in all its forms. This includes relationships with lovers, friends, family, and, most importantly, yourself. The Lovers symbolize inner balance and peace. They represent the different aspects of you that must be brought into harmony in order to regain perspective. The Lovers card also represents choices. They remind us that we can heal any situation and free ourselves from suffering by viewing the matter through the eyes of authentic love.

Do you have difficulty truly loving yourself? Are you able to open your heart and be completely honest about who you are and what you feel? Are you able to look at your place in life right now with acceptance and inner peace?

The Lovers are brought together in a state of harmony under the acceptant gaze of the Angel. They are naked and feel no shame for it. They don't need to cover up or put on a front to impress each other. A mountain separates the Lovers, creating a barrier. However, the Angel transcends all barriers and allows the Lovers to relate to one another, no matter what obstacles are present. The male gazes at the female. She in turn gazes up through the fog at the Angel. When these different aspects of yourself are brought into balance, you can then experience the most fulfilling relationships with others.

The male represents your worldly, conscious self.[4] Behind him is the Tree of Life.[5] This fiery tree is a symbol for vitality and external awareness. He is the part of you that operates in the real world. The male part of the self wants to mentally figure everything out with a rational explanation. He fears the unknown and yet is strangely attracted to the mysteries embodied by the female on the card. Status, strength, and reason matter to him. However, by himself, he is incomplete. He needs to connect with something much deeper than what he finds in the world. He sees this in the female. He gazes at her beauty and is mesmerized by her. She is the part he is missing. She is very precious to him and reminds him of what really matters in life. The male looks to the female for clues on what kind of person he should present himself as in the world. If the female is wounded, it alters his perception of his value.

The female represents the psyche, your unconscious awareness, and your capacity to feel.[6] Behind her is the Tree of Knowledge.[7] The snake of transformation and wisdom coils around its trunk. The snake represents the transformation that occurs when you tap into your inner wisdom. The woman takes what happens externally and creates change by incorporating these experiences into her inner knowledge. She is sensitive and kind. She loves beauty and comfort. She

4. Pollack, *The Complete Illustrated Guide to Tarot*, 78.

5. Fiebig and Burger, *The Ultimate Guide to the Rider Waite Tarot*, 34.

6. Pollack, *The Complete Illustrated Guide to Tarot*, 78.

7. Fiebig and Burger, *The Ultimate Guide to the Rider Waite Tarot*, 90.

feels compassion and wants all things to go smoothly. And yet, on her own, she is incomplete. She has the tendency to avoid conflict at all costs. Without conflict, there is no growth. She needs the male on the card to bring balance, healing, protection, and growth. She also feels too much sometimes. This makes her forget that there is a wider world outside of her feelings. In order to heal the wounds in her sensitive heart and find peace, she must look to the Angel.

The Angel represents your Higher Self: your superconsciousness.[8] He looks down on the different parts of the self with compassion, acceptance, and perspective. He bathes the male and female aspects with an unconditional, loving light. There is no judgement in the Angel's face—only love and acceptance. He does not judge them for how they look, what they do, how much they have, or what may have happened in the past. The Lovers are below a misty cloud. This represents that it is not always easy for the different aspects of the self to see things from a spiritual perspective.

The gazing figures on the Lovers card show a formula for inner peace. The external worldly self (male) must know his real feelings (female) to find peace and harmony. He must make peace with his feelings by being honest about them. The nakedness of the figures means baring it all, releasing feelings of inhibition that keep you covering things up to maintain an image. But stopping at the realm of feelings isn't looking deep enough. To heal the wounds that all people eventually acquire, one must go even deeper within for harmony. This is the realm of the Spirit (Angel). Only the Angel can see things from a vantage point of complete perspective. No mist covers the Angel's eyes. Only the Inner Spirit can truly validate the self. When you look on the naked truth of who you are with the eyes of the Angel, there is nothing but love.

We fall out of harmony by attaching ourselves to only one aspect of our lives and losing the perspective of the Angel. By ruminating with emotions too much, we lose sight of the world's unlimited opportunities. Concern for status or how we appear to others can bring an equal measure of suffering. The only way to free yourself from suffering is to love yourself enough to go within and seek your light. Seek your Higher Self. Look on yourself with wise, radiant, luminous eyes. The Angel resides deeper within, beyond the pain.

8. Pollack, *The Complete Illustrated Guide to Tarot*, 78.

When the Lovers appear, it's time to love yourself. You may have to dig deep within to find love, but it's there, patiently waiting. Reflect on yourself through the eyes of your Inner Angel. Then look at other people in the world with those same eyes. This perspective will reveal a lot to you. Instead of feeling wounded by the actions of incomplete people caught in their own suffering, you can see how they have unfortunately forgot to be their own better angel that day. Just like you occasionally do. Look on yourself and others with the love of your Inner Spirit. This frees you from all suffering and will restore harmony every time.

The Lovers Reversed

If the Lovers appear reversed, it is time to restore harmony and tend your relationships (romantic, professional, and familial). This card represents healing the connections you share with others. It also reveals that the things that are driving you crazy about someone else may be highlighting an imbalance or disconnected part within yourself. Notice the three figures on the Lovers card. They are all aspects of you. They all need to communicate with one another. If they are not in harmony, imbalance occurs. This disharmony will most likely surface in your relationships with others. It may be simpler to think that *they* have the problem; however, the Lovers reversed ask you to reflect on your own part to play in the drama.

This card asks you to look at where disharmony may be occurring between you and another. Instead of getting angry at this individual, ask, "What is this relationship challenge teaching me about myself? How am I putting myself in a state of suffering?"

Challenging people and situations are teachers. Frustrating people get on our nerves because they highlight what we have difficulty accepting or facing within ourselves. People who annoy us can illuminate our shadow. Everyone has a shadow. It is the amorphous thing within us all that we have a hard time loving or accepting.

The Lovers hold the secret to solving all internal imbalance and external drama: love. Love begins with acceptance. You cannot heal your own heart if you are busy blaming another (past or present) for your imbalance. Being miserable because of what someone else did in the past is a choice. You don't have control over the past, but you do have control over presently creating harmony within your own heart. Once you decide to love and let go of the source of internal imbalance, you will begin to see even the most irritating people in a new light. They are teachers for you, too. What are you learning about yourself through others?

When the Lovers appear reversed, it is time to fall in love with your life again and to let go of anything that is prolonging a sense of suffering. What part of yourself used to give you the greatest joy, making you feel empowered, full of possibility, and awake? Don't romanticize the past, but do look at the truth it holds. When the Lovers appear reversed, they signify that the shortest route toward inner peace will be engaging with the neglected parts of your heart, talents, and abilities.

Heal your relationships by understanding yourself first.

THE CHARIOT

When you choose courage over fear, you've already won.

The Chariot symbolizes courage in the face of uncertainty. It represents taking risks and stepping toward what you really want out of life, even when there are no guarantees. The Chariot illustrates that victory does not come from the attainment of a goal, but instead occurs at the exact moment you choose courage instead of fear.

Do you avoid making decisions that could lead to your happiness because you are afraid of failing? Have you ever stayed in unhealthy situations longer than you should have because you feared an unknowable future? Is there something you would like to change about your life right now, but you are too scared?

The Chariot is led by two sphinxes, one black and one white. They face in opposite directions, representing two possible futures. The sphinxes are creatures of riddles and mysteries and represent the unknown. The man in the chariot is taking a risk and letting the mysterious sphinxes lead him. He doesn't know what lies ahead, but he has taken the risk anyway. The sphinxes both hold their tails. They reveal that accessing the wisdom that is behind you will give you the courage to face the unknowable future.

In the background of the card, there is a large castle surrounded by stable walls. This represents leaving the safety of the home to go out into the world. A large moat surrounds the castle and has also been crossed. This represents bypassing emotional decision-making, which usually favors comfort over self-improvement. The Chariot is covered by a veil imprinted with stars. Stars are eternal and ancient. They symbolize that the charioteer is seeing the big picture. His Higher Self is directing his path.

Look at the Charioteer's armor. The mantle covering his shoulders is decorated with two moons. This symbolizes that trusting his instincts is his best defense while he is out in the world. The two moons could also indicate that the success you seek could manifest in about two months.

The charioteer is still advancing toward his goal, and yet he is already double-crowned (like the Empress) and sceptered. He has already won. He made the decision to have courage—instead of a need for comfort, assurance, and security—direct his path.

The Charioteer advises you to take risks to improve your life, even if there are no guarantees. Choosing courage empowers you and already makes you a winner.

The Chariot Reversed

If the Chariot appears reversed, it warns of indecision, which can rob you of feeling in control of your life's direction. This card will often accompany a feeling that you are being pulled in two opposite directions. Fear of committing to a choice can lead to a sense of being stuck. Avoidance of taking ownership of your life's direction and making a choice will only make things feel more out of control. The Chariot driver reminds you that you are in the driver's seat of your life. You get to choose whether to respond assertively or reactively to the situation confronting you. Once you make the choice you have been avoiding, you can reclaim your self-confidence and self-esteem.

The only wrong decision for you currently is making no decision at all. Be bold and proactive. Take charge. Even when this card is reversed, it reminds you that you still embody the powerful qualities of the brave charioteer. The Great Mystery symbolized by the sphinxes will lead you to safety every time. You can still be victorious, but only if you have a horse in the race. There is no need to fear mistakes. Even if mistakes happen along the way, they will prove to be your best teachers. Success comes from action, not avoidance. Reclaim your personal power and make the decision you've been too scared to make!

STRENGTH

You are stronger than the challenge before you.

The Strength card is a symbol of inner fortitude, which helps us prevail in the face of life's challenges. Strength is something that needs to be reinforced every day. Just as muscles need to be continuously used to maintain their power, so too does inner strength need to be habitually exercised. Every time you act in your own best interest despite your fears and inner weaknesses, you are developing strength. Strength is a choice. You can either buckle to what keeps you stuck and afraid, or you can choose excellence.

At what time in your life did you feel you were strongest? Do you sometimes forget you are that same person? Do you need to get back on track by standing up to inner weaknesses that have been keeping you stuck and afraid?

The woman on this card does not sport bulging muscles, but she is the epitome of inner strength and confidence. The lion on the card represents her lower impulses, such as fear, anger, bad habits, belligerence, and other out-of-control behaviors. She confronts her lion by gently closing its mouth, thereby not allowing it to consume her. She loves the lion and it loves her, too. You can see the lion licking her affectionately. Your Higher Self appreciates when you focus your passions constructively. The infinity symbol above the woman's head shows that she is eternally confronting the lion. Her strength is part of her now. It has been habitually reinforced by confronting and overcoming weakness every day. The lion's tail is between his legs, symbolizing submission to the part of you that knows best.

Strength is not manifested by large displays of power, but by gentle, compassionate, self-directed corrections in the form of good decisions. Strength is also not just used once and then you're done! It is a daily routine that becomes much easier with practice and time. It's also important not to make self-corrections because of how guilty you feel. Inwardly directed corrections should come from a place of self-love and compassion, or they won't work (later the lion will rebel and revert if it has guilt or shame to latch on to).

You are more powerful than you may give yourself credit for. Human beings get stuck in ruts, and sometimes it feels that we can't change something because we've been acting that way for so long that it is just part of who we are. If a certain behavior has been running amok like a wild lion and you feel it can't be self-controlled, think again. Every day you have the power to be excellent. You have the choice to direct your own life or leave it to the shadows. Being strong in the face of your inner beast can feel difficult at first, but with continued positive action, the lion is always tamed.

Commit to three choices you can make today to rein in the beast. This will affirm your strength.

Strength Reversed

If the Strength card appears reversed, it usually comes at a time when you are starting to doubt your courage, personal power, and abilities. Don't let this happen! A good way to remind yourself of your strength is to keep a courage journal. This invaluable little book is where you will record your victories, great and small, each time you faced your fear and prevailed. Every time you meet a challenge you are afraid of and persevere, write it in the courage journal. Every time you make a huge life achievement, write it in the courage journal. This special little book can be taken off the shelf anytime you are facing a frightening challenge. It will immediately remind you of your personal power.

The courage journal is written proof that you can accomplish what you once thought impossible. It will be a repository of hard evidence, proving that you can handle the issue confronting you. To begin your journal, start with the five most pivotal turning points in your life where you kept going, even when you thought you couldn't. That is where your courage and character are found. Write about who you were before the event and who you became after. Remember that you have come so far and can go even farther. Add pages to your courage journal each time you choose bravery instead of fear. In time, you will see written proof of your excellence. Your record book of strength will be there to pull off the shelf anytime you need it.

Strength reversed can also indicate that you are being too hard on yourself in the quest for self-improvement. The woman on the card is making gentle self-corrections. She isn't beating the lion up. Today, be kinder to yourself when taming the unruly parts of your experience. It is important that you aren't just courageous, but that you are also respecting who you are and what makes you strong.

THE HERMIT

Seeking answers within.

The Hermit symbolizes that the answers you seek to any problem can always be found if you look within. If you make time to center, feel your real feelings, and quiet mental chatter, your inner wisdom will guide you out of any rut. Sometimes the biggest block to hearing your Spirit's inner wisdom is the fear of feeling something uncomfortable. Many people distract themselves from the discomfort and avoid resolving the imbalance. The Hermit represents the need to periodically withdraw from the world and reconnect with your deeper awareness.

Do you take time to regularly reconnect with the wisdom residing within your center? Do you habitually distract or numb yourself from what is causing your discomfort rather than looking at it? Are you conscious of the Wise One who resides within?

The Hermit takes his lantern into the dark, uncomfortable places to examine what's there. His staff and beard symbolize the stability and wisdom that you can always find within. If you examine the card, you'll notice he's traveling over snow. This symbolizes feelings that you have "put on ice." The snow can also represent freezing or numbing pain. The gentle Hermit comes with his warm, illuminating lantern and his sturdy staff of wisdom. These can melt the cold ice that metaphorically forms around the heart, allowing feelings to be resolved and released. Under his gentle guidance, he can show you the hidden lesson beneath the ice. Does your heart feel like it's keeping something frozen? Can you feel the feelings within your heart, or does it feel numb?

The fear of discomfort is just a mask, preventing you from accessing your deeper wisdom. One error many people make with the lesson of the Hermit is mistaking "wisdom" with "thinking." "If I just sit here alone and think about this uncomfortable thing for a long time, I will figure it out." Thinking about problems just leaves the anxiety in the background to go unchecked as your mind frantically races from one hollow solution to another. Thinking about the discomfort doesn't really resolve it. Feeling it does. Many times, people are so scared of feeling that they pull out their phone, have a drink, or binge-watch television, thinking, "That will get that inner chatter to shut up for a while!"

Avoidance freezes the feeling for a time, but the unfelt feelings remain under the ice and grow in strength until they finally burst through. This process takes longer for some people than others, but it always ends the same… with a twitch, a feeling of being hollow, or a nervous breakdown.

If you are courageous enough to go within, seek your discomfort, pull the mask back, and feel the feelings you are avoiding, you will discover that this discomfort is a wise teacher and friend. The deeper awareness residing beneath the fear will calmly tell you what you need. This is your inner Wise One. The inner Wise One will show you how to resolve and release what is troubling you.

Today, reflect on what is going on within you. Is there something making you anxious? Are you dulled, numb, or frozen? Take time to connect with the sacred hermit within. He will safely guide you to what lies beneath the ice. There is nothing to fear with the Hermit guiding you. Take the time to light a sacred candle in a quiet place. Be brave and melt any ice that may have formed around your feelings. Pull back surface fears. Look beneath the ice. Examine what the Hermit is guiding you to understand. Another card drawn may illuminate the issue that needs healing. You will know that you have found the answer when you say, "Aha! That's what I needed to resolve within myself."

The Hermit is an old man walking through snow. This symbolizes slow movement. Take your time to find your way. The lamp of your inner Hermit will guide you out of darkness every time.

The Hermit Reversed

If the Hermit appears reversed, it indicates that it is time to reemerge from your inner landscape and share yourself with the outside world again. After a period of introspection and self-work, you have gained new insights and wisdom. Now the demands of the external world may be calling you back. Duties will multiply, and events may pick up speed. The Hermit is the "way-shower" from within. Don't be surprised if you become a way-shower to others now that you have made your own journey. It is time to engage with the world around you and share your unique wisdom and experiences.

The Hermit reversed also indicates that you may possess something important that can contribute to the world around you. However, you cannot share it if you are hiding. It is so important that you don't hide, avoid, or become shy about what you offer. The Hermit represents the authentic place within you. Have the courage to reveal your Authentic Self to others. Your challenges and introspective journey have given you valuable wisdom. Reconnect with the world and share that wisdom with others. When the Hermit appears reversed, he reminds you that you are not alone. It is time to seek the company of others who have also done the inner work to know their Authentic Selves. Sometimes this card simply means that you are not as isolated as you think. New friendships, partnerships, and connections will appear. A breakthrough will happen if you are open and reconnect with others at this time.

WHEEL OF FORTUNE

Making peace with life's unpredictability.

The Wheel of Fortune symbolizes unpredictable events, both fortunate and unfortunate. These are the events that occur with seeming randomness. They leave you feeling as if you have no control over them. The figures on the turning wheel illustrate that life moves in cycles; during some periods you feel on top of the world (like the sphinx), and during others you feel down and out (like the descending snake and Anubis, the God of the Egyptian Underworld). Chaotic and unplanned things do occur in life. The rim of the wheel represents the external world with all its chaotic unpredictability. The center of the wheel represents your center: the seat of your best self. If you can find your way home to your center, then the random things that occur in the world outside of your control will not feel as disturbing.[9]

Are you stuck at the rim of the wheel, rising or falling with each unexpected event in your life? Can you take unexpected events in stride, or are you rigid and inflexible? Do you panic when something doesn't go exactly according to plan?

The Wheel of Fortune floats amid the clouds, the domain of the element of Air. The sphinx, symbolizing all that is mysterious and unknowable, is seated on top of the wheel wielding a sword. The sword and the cloud imagery represent the element of Air and symbolize the powers of the mind to find the patterns in seemingly random occurrences. We do this every time we chaotically shuffle tarot cards and identify the patterns laid out in front of us. The mind organizes data through patterns. Amid the Hebrew letters around the wheel are four English letters: T-A-R-O. If read clockwise, starting and ending at the top of the wheel, they spell TAROT. If you begin reading the letters at the bottom of the wheel clockwise, they spell ROTA (Latin for "wheel"). The Wheel of Fortune can reveal patterns in seemingly random occurrences.

In her book *Following Your Path*, Alexandra Collins Dickerman perceived the rim of the Wheel of Fortune as a metaphor for the changeable external world.[10] If you wrap up your whole identity and self-worth with what everybody out there thinks at the rim of the wheel, then you will be doomed to emotionally rise and fall with each acceptance or rejection you receive. However, if you can reconnect with your center (symbolized by the hub of the wheel), you can remain centered without taking the chaotic ups and downs of life personally. When you operate from your center, life no longer feels random, and you can control the direction of the wheel of your life.[11]

When the Wheel of Fortune appears, it is time to get off the emotional roller coaster and detach from external dramas. Staying fixed at the edge of the

9. Dickerman, *Following Your Path*, 131.

10. Dickerman, *Following Your Path*, 137–39.

11. Dickerman, *Following Your Path*, 131.

wheel can get emotionally exhausting rather quickly. The truth is we don't have complete control of every life event that occurs. Sometimes bad or unfair things just happen. Other people have free will and can also act unpredictably. Good things can happen to awful people, and terrible things can happen to good people. Some people win the lottery without having done anything to deserve it. Others get hurt through no fault of their own. In life, events rarely go exactly according to plan. These occurrences are outside of our control. However, you do have the ability to control how you respond to life. You can choose to let either your wise Spirit handle the situation, or your fear.

The Wheel of Fortune appears when it's time to take unexpected things in stride. Good or bad. Fair or unfair. Don't take random events in life personally. All you have control over is you and your chosen response. Choose to respond with excellence. Reclaim your connection with your wise center. Sit peacefully within the eye of the storm. View your current situation with the higher awareness that resides within you. If you are centered, you will operate from a place of great personal power. The Wheel of Fortune foretells good luck for those who find their way back to their center.

The Wheel of Fortune Reversed

If the Wheel of Fortune appears reversed, it illuminates repetitive cycles, patterns, and recurring life lessons. Just as a wheel that moves in reverse brings a vehicle backward, so too the Wheel of Fortune reversed can take you back to an old life lesson that seems to be repeating itself over and over. Getting frustrated at the repeated lesson is fruitless. The lesson is recurring because it holds the key to moving forward. Once you accept the lesson and do the work on self-improvement, the wheel will begin to move forward once again. Surrounding cards may illuminate what this life lesson is rooted in. Human lives are governed by cycles. Sometimes you are up, and sometimes you are down. The key is to not link your whole identity with the place on the wheel where you find yourself at this moment.

It can feel frustrating when you eagerly wish to move forward only to find that you seemingly keep moving backward. However, success is hardly ever arrived at in a straight line. The journey toward success bends and curves and spirals. Like a spiral, it sometimes loops back over itself. Sometimes you will feel like you are back where you started with no progress being made, but this is an illusion. Wisdom is accumulated with each cycle. Each time you revisit a challenge, you know it more intimately and can see dimensions that were not apparent before.

The wheel is more than just its outer rim (a symbol for the external world); its source of strength is its center, the hub (a symbol for the divine center within you). Don't get angry at recurring cycles, for there is an important pattern revealed in them. The Universe is always showing you ways to move forward through patterns. Sometimes you do need to go back and pick up an important part of your center that was left behind.

Don't allow your feelings to be hurt by the ever-turning Wheel of Fortune—whether it is upright or reversed or if you find yourself rising or falling. Ask yourself what the Universe is teaching you through the cyclical patterns you are experiencing. Are you learning about your true worth? Perhaps you are remembering how to reclaim your courage. Often, revisiting the place where you are stalled to reclaim the part of you that seems lost is just the remedy needed to begin progressing forward again.

JUSTICE

Honesty.

Justice is the archetype of honesty, which is essential for restoring balance and harmony. Lady Justice grasps her mighty Sword of Truth. Her goal is to restore order and equilibrium, symbolized by the golden scales she holds in her left hand. The Justice figure in the tarot is not blindfolded. She sees the situations confronting her clearly. The sword she wields represents that assertive action is needed to cut away the source of our imbalance. Imbalance often occurs when we aren't being 100 percent honest with ourselves. Lady Justice restores balance and clarity through facts.

Does your life feel balanced right now? What do you need more or less of? Do you need to speak your truth to yourself or to another, even if the thought of it makes you uncomfortable?

Justice personifies that little voice within us that is observing the truth of any given situation, no matter how inconvenient that truth might be. The figure of Justice is flanked by two gray pillars. The color gray is associated with neutrality. Whenever Justice appears, it is helpful to look at all the facts in an unbiased, neutral manner. To be neutral requires that you not let your emotions and expectations distort the facts. Wanting to believe something is true even when the facts prove otherwise will place you on a collision course with reality. If you look closely, you'll see that Lady Justice has a square clasp at her neck and a square jewel in her crown. Squares are associated with honesty and strong foundations. We've all heard the expression "fair and square." In astrology, squares aren't considered *easy* aspects, but they are considered responsible for the development of character and strength. The squares decorating Lady Justice symbolize that truth may not always be easy to confront initially. However, if you choose to proceed with integrity and honesty, you will find yourself on a stable pathway toward happiness, harmony, and success. Secrets and buried truths have the potential to create feelings of guilt or shame. Justice asks you to face the hidden things so that they can be released.

Lady Justice reminds you to be clear with yourself and others to restore harmony. Be warned, however: honesty may require you to add the word "N-N-N-N-N-N-No!" to your vocabulary. Justice advises you to approach the source of your imbalance dispassionately. The scales of justice symbolize the need to weigh all the facts before deciding how best to act.

If you've already been doing the work of facing your life honestly, Lady Justice arrives to declare, "Good for you! Isn't the sensation of balance derived from honesty wonderful?" It takes courage to be honest with yourself. This is especially true if you are attached to a certain outcome. Other cards that appear around Justice can highlight which areas of your life require honesty at this time.

Justice Reversed

When Justice appears reversed, she symbolizes periods when your life feels lopsided. This sense of imbalance occurs when we are so focused on one part of our lives that we neglect other important aspects. Perhaps it's time to step out of your routine to gain some clarity and perspective. Which area of your life is demanding too much of your energy? What part of yourself could you invest in to remedy this?

Justice reversed can also appear in the guise of situations that seem unfair or unjust. You may be tempted to blame someone or something for a sense of imbalance, but, ultimately, you are the one who is responsible for restoring order in your life. Not everything in life is fair. Sometimes you must make the best of what you are presented with and proceed with excellence regardless. The situation may not seem fair, but a larger universal order and balance are always working behind the scenes. This concept is known as the Law of Karma. Perhaps you need to detach from a desire to teach someone a lesson. Step out of the drama and let Karma take care of it. If the source of the injustice originates from another person, they'll reap what they sow eventually. Sometimes a seemingly unfair situation will illuminate how you are being unfair to yourself. Are you tolerating something that violates your personal honor code? Upright or reversed, Lady Justice supports you in taking a clear-eyed look at the facts to restore your personal power.

THE HANGED MAN

Sacrificing for the greater good.

The Hanged Man represents making a temporary sacrifice to achieve a greater goal. This could mean sacrificing time, energy, comfort, resources, old habits, or an outdated attitude. For success to be achieved, a sacrifice is often required. By pooling your best energies and resources into your goal, you will ensure that it manifests.

What changes would you like to see in your life? Do you have a goal that requires a lot of work? Is making a sacrifice scary for you because it means that everything will change?

The Hanged Man is suspended from the branches of the Tree of Wisdom. He is seeking to improve himself. By hanging upside down, he is gaining a new perspective, and he looks at the world from a different vantage point. All the blood rushes to his head. All his energy is being pooled into his mind. He is temporarily sacrificing the use of his legs and arms. This represents sacrificing the desire to walk away. The Hanged Man is suspending his normal routines to focus his energy. His face is calm. Although he is not comfortable, he is not suffering. He knows that sacrificing his usual stance of keeping his feet firmly on the ground will free his mind to new solutions. The Hanged Man is looking ahead. The position of one leg crossed behind the other mirrors the final card in the Major Arcana, the World. The World represents completion and attainment. The Hanged Man symbolizes temporarily enduring discomfort to ensure the achievement of your greatest goals.

If you want to achieve anything of lasting value in this life, you will need to make sacrifices. The currency of the Universe is exchange. What you put in, you will get out. It is comforting to know that if you make the sacrifices and do the work, you can alter the course of your destiny. Any goal you have can be achieved, but it does require that something must be given up. At first, sacrifice may feel like you are losing something. This is an illusion. Investing time and energy into what empowers you can release you from habits and attitudes that have been keeping you stuck.

For example, if you want to lose weight, you may have to sacrifice eating after 8 p.m. and cut your calorie intake. To get a wonderful new job, you may have to sacrifice some of your leisure time to look for a job and meet with the people who can open doors for you. To foster a talent, you may have to sacrifice a lot of time to refine your skills.

The appearance of the Hanged Man is often a good sign. He represents looking at your life through the lens of transcendent wisdom. Viewing your experience from a different point of view leads to breakthroughs that will lead to a glorious new you. You can achieve your goal if you are willing to be courageous and make the proper sacrifice.

To free yourself from dissatisfaction, you may have to sacrifice your routines, habits, and the status quo, just like the wise Hanged Man.

The Hanged Man Reversed

If the Hanged Man appears reversed, he is back on his feet again! After spending considerable time suspended upside down from the Tree of Wisdom, he is now ready to walk out into the world with valuable new insights. He has made tremendous sacrifices and has surrendered his ego's assumptions of how life *should* unfold. He has given himself over to the greater wisdom of the tree he spent so many years suspended from.

When this card appears reversed, it is as if all that felt upside down is turning right-side up again. You may also feel more grounded and surer of your path. You have been suspended from your own metaphorical Tree of Wisdom, and now it is time to engage with life using the wisdom you've gained. All your sacrifices up until now have been indeed worth it. This is because you are perceiving your experiences within a wider context. Be proud of the things you have achieved and sacrificed for. When you look on the world with the wisdom you've earned through your many sacrifices, it no longer appears upside down.

DEATH

Accepting inevitable change.

The Death card is the tarot's most notorious symbol for change and transformation. Many people are afraid to sit at a tarot reader's table because the dreaded Death card might show up! We've all seen the movies in which the dark and mysterious fortune-teller turns over the Death card to foretell someone's ghastly end. In actuality, the Death card is an invaluable card to get in a reading. It indicates that you are undergoing vitally important changes, *for your own good*. Although not always welcome and sometimes shocking to experience, the changes before you are the next step in your personal evolution. Although Death outwardly appears frightening, he is *always* accompanied by rebirth. Like the legendary phoenix, you too will rise from the ashes to live a joyful new life, revitalized and renewed.

Do you struggle with accepting change? Does the fear of death keep you from living your life? What old, unneeded part of yourself are you resistant to letting go of, even though you know releasing that part would set you free?

Death appears astride his white horse, heralding an end to old ways. His steed marches over kings and commoners alike. No one is immune from his power. All must change. Everything that lives must die. Death's banner is a white rose on a black background. This is a stark symbol of a truth that is black and white. Light and life (the white flower) always emerges after darkness and death (the black background). Although his skeletal face looks scary, Death is not a monster. Nobody wants to see Death, even though he has the thankless job of kindly ending suffering. Death cannot be bargained with and eventually visits us all. The king under the horse found that out. No amount of money could put off this day for him. The adolescent girl in the card averts her gaze, unable to look Death in the face. The priest has been preparing for Death his whole life, and yet even he kneels uneasily. The priest reminds us of the fixed quality of the Hierophant card. Death shows us that change is coming, whether our own fixed beliefs allow for this eventuality or not.

Only the fearless little child in the foreground holds a flower up to Death. Children don't get scared of change the way adults do. Children don't fear Death because they don't understand a fear of the realm beyond. It's a land filled with infinite light where they were just residing not too long ago. What's so scary about a realm of infinite peace, release, joy, and laughter?

Look closely at the background of the Death card, past the river, way up in the distance where the two towers form a gate. A realm of light lies beyond, represented as either a rising or setting sun. Whether the sun is rising or setting is unimportant, for as the sun is setting here, it is simultaneously rising there.[12] Could that be a shining city illuminated in the sun's radiance?[13]

Overcoming your fear of change is the requirement of this card. I find it fascinating that the card we associate with change in the tarot is also the card that elicits a twinge of fear whenever many of us see it. This illustrates that change, no matter how positive the promised outcome, is still scary. And yet change is inevitable. Much like the boat in the distance crossing the river Styx, you need to cross over into the next phase of your life. In nature, that which cannot change and adapt becomes extinct.

The changes occurring for you are leading you to new life. Other cards that surround the Death card will indicate what part of your life is undergoing change at this time. Have courage and let go of all that you no longer need. The light of rebirth awaits you.

Death Reversed

If the Death card appears reversed, it asks you what changes you are resisting. Often the answer can be found in what you are avoiding. It's time to challenge any form of denial. You know what needs changing. You know what needs your courage right now. The question is if you are going to approach your personal transformation with passive or assertive energy. Passive energy is going to make you dread change. You will say to yourself, "Why is this happening to me?"

When you approach difficult changes and life challenges with courage, then you have some control over your response to the situation. Facing fears gives you great power over them. You no longer find yourself running and hiding from reality. Death reversed brings you in touch with the very things you've been avoiding. This is where you will find the next steps toward your personal evolution.

Death reversed asks you to step out of the shadow and back into the light. Confront and let go of all that no longer serves you. What has been keeping you stuck and in a state of fear or immobility? This card is very healing for clearing out energy blockages. Death (upright or reversed) is always accompanied by rebirth. Rebirth is the yang to Death's yin. As the sun sets here, it is

12. Dickerman, *Following Your Path*, 167.

13. Fiebig and Burger, *The Ultimate Guide to the Rider Waite Tarot*, 48.

simultaneously rising elsewhere. Do not fear what is changing right now. Often the fear isn't of *something*, but rather of stepping up, taking your power back, and allowing yourself to grow past this lesson. The "old and familiar" can often seem comfortable even if it's killing you inside. Joseph Campbell used to say, "We must be willing to get rid of the life we've planned, so as to have the life that is waiting for us."[14]

Have courage; the transformation you are resisting will lead to a better you. Let your changes happen. Your sun will rise again.

14. Osbon, *A Joseph Campbell Companion*, 18.

TEMPERANCE

Finding the right recipe for balanced living.

Temperance signifies balance, moderation, and slowing down. This card represents your inner stress barometer, which notifies you when your mind and body are under too much strain. When Temperance appears, it is time to give your body more of what it needs right now in order to restore your equilibrium. The card encapsulates finding the right balance between two opposing forces to restore harmony.

Does your body act up when you're stressed? Do you get strange sensations that make you worry you might have something seriously wrong with you? Do you listen to your inner needs when you are spread too thin, or do you power through, depleting yourself further?

The Angel on the Temperance card represents your Higher Self, which knows just how much of anything you can endure. The Angel is pouring just the right amount of water from one cup to replenish the other. This represents your need to replenish what has been depleted. The Angel also has one foot on dry land and the other foot in the stream. This symbolizes that although he is operating in the real world (the dry land), he keeps one foot in contact with his intuitive inner world (the stream). The path behind him leads to a bright destination. If you follow the Angel's example and look after your equilibrium, you will also find a healthier, happier future awaiting you. The iris flowers call to mind Iris, the Messenger Goddess. Your body, mind, spirit, and the Universe surrounding you are constantly offering messages of how to best heal.

Temperance is sandwiched between the Major Arcana's most challenging cards: the Hanged Man and Death, and the Devil and the Tower. It is an oasis in this leg of the journey. Temperance represents a place of self-care and restoration before getting back in the ring. The many Angels that appear in the tarot represent your Higher Self. The location of Temperance in the Major Arcana symbolizes the need to reconnect with a transcendent big-picture perspective while amid difficulties. Stressful situations can deplete you quickly. It's like holding your breath underwater and endlessly swimming. The symbol of Temperance can be described as returning to the water's surface and replenishing yourself with a fresh breath of sweet air. Temperance enables you to go within and return to the surface renewed and revitalized.

You may think that life is just too demanding and busy and that you don't have the time for self-care. Many people give all the energy they have and wonder why they feel strained, stressed, and even crazy. The answer is simple: they are burning the candle at both ends. Temperance reminds you to listen to your body, quiet your mind, and come up for air. No matter what demands are being placed on you currently, you need to replenish yourself.

Not wanting to disappoint others makes us jump through impossible circles and hoops, attempting to be Superman or Superwoman. All the while, we slowly deplete ourselves to the point where we need rescuing! Temperance gently guides you to protect your own health and well-being first. In this way, you will have plenty to share with others.

To restore your balance, what is your body signaling that it needs? More water? More rest? Some quiet time? A vacation? A break? Time with your favorite books? A reading?

Wrap yourself in the Angel's wings and lovingly give your body some attention. The Angel of Temperance is guiding you back toward what you need for balance. Taking the time to restore your equilibrium will ensure that you have an abundance of energy to invest in all the people, goals, and improvements that are waiting for you.

Temperance Reversed

If Temperance appears reversed, it signifies depletion and a need for restoration. You may be literally or symbolically dehydrated. Temperance reversed calls your attention to areas of your mind and body where knots of tension have formed and asks you to release them. The Angel on the card symbolizes the need to surrender current stress to the Divine. You are being called back to reconnect with what is personally sacred to you. The imagery of flowing water on the card signifies the healing properties of water. An easy way to restore equilibrium is to give your body more water. This will do wonders for your mood and energy level. Perhaps it's time to reconnect with the bodies of water in nature. Rivers, lakes, and oceans naturally have a soothing effect that can release accumulated stresses that are disturbing your mind and heart.

Temperance is all about balance and moderation. When this card appears reversed, you will find that it is necessary to release *excessiveness*: excessive worry about a stressful situation, excessive focus on only one area of your life, excessive consumption of something that depletes your energy, excessive escapism, excessive obsessions. Your personal energy field needs to be cleared to move forward at this time. If you find yourself excessively doing one thing, shift your energy to focusing on another aspect of your life that would benefit from your attention. Know that where you are today is just where you need to be. Be okay with areas of your life being works in progress. Other cards in a reading may illuminate what the source of your depletion is.

THE DEVIL

Confronting your inner saboteur.

Nobody likes to confront the Devil. The Devil can be a jarring image to face. This is because he represents our shadow self, the inner saboteur. This is the insidious voice within that tells us we aren't worthy, that we can't be successful, and that we are stuck with our lot. Often this voice pipes up just before we are about to make a huge breakthrough. This voice comes as a final test to see what we really believe about ourselves. The Devil is known by many names, but by far the most fitting is the Prince of Lies. The biggest lie the Devil tells is that he is more powerful than we are. Each day you have a choice to believe the voice that tells you you are garbage or to hear your better angels who remind you that you are worthy.

How does your shadow manifest in your life? Do you struggle with self-esteem? Do you feel trapped in a situation that feels beyond your control?

When you look at the image of the Devil card, you can see a man and a woman chained to his throne. They are a corrupted version of the innocent and pure man and woman who appear on the Lovers card. The trees that were featured on the Lovers card now appear in the form of unnatural tails sprouting from the pair. This shows how applying life and knowledge solely toward materialism and external gratification leads to corruption. The two figures also sport horns, symbolizing their enslavement to the animal parts of their nature. The animal nature is only concerned with survival and protection of itself. It is not enlightened and manifests in the form of fear, excess, jealousy, anger, hatred, addiction, unforgiveness, and the pursuit of personal comfort over all else.

Look closer at the figures chained to the Devil's throne. The chains represent the falsehood of being stuck; the chains the figures wear are quite loose. In fact, they could step out of them at any time! This shows that despite the fearful size of the Devil, one can be free of him whenever they choose. When the Devil appears, he calls your attention to the self-limiting thoughts and behaviors that are keeping you imprisoned. You can be free at any time, but you must stop rationalizing these behaviors and confront them honestly. Written on the Devil's right hand is the symbol for Saturn. In astrology, Saturn rules limitations, setbacks, and self-improvement over time. This implies that honestly confronting your inner shadows will compel you to improve over time, even if the process feels uncomfortable.

The Devil highlights any untruths you may be telling yourself that are keeping you from being the best version of yourself. The shadow is real, but you are more powerful.

The best way to transcend shadows is to embody love. Be loving to yourself and others. Don't get hooked into defending yourself in the face of someone else's shadow. Lovingly help someone else. Be of service. Be kinder. If you are feeling fear, help someone else feel braver. Challenge the lie that you are stuck.

Send light and love to those people you can't quite seem to forgive. Unhook yourself from the Devil's chains.

By embodying your better angels, the Devil will lose all power.

The Devil Reversed

If the Devil appears reversed, then the loose chains on the upside-down figures will easily fall away from gravity alone. Old habits that once kept you stuck are no longer the insurmountable challenges they once were. You are letting go of these outdated, self-limiting beliefs. You may find that you outgrew them and that they no longer hold you in bondage.

Often, habitual cynicism will rush in to justify why it's important to hang on to past negative beliefs. The familiar, even when destructive, is far more comfortable than the unknown. The ego's cynical aspect hates not knowing things, so it looks for something to attack. The Devil reversed represents releasing the negative habits and assumptions that keep you in a pessimistic hell.

When the Devil appears reversed, your shadow's power is fading. It is time to challenge any remaining unconscious attitudes of fear, anger, or sadness that you have been carrying. Bring it all into the sunlight. Each day you work on your best self, you become less stuck than the day before. It's time to remember your strengths, talents, and abilities. These are who you truly are. You are not the awful things your shadow wants you to think you are. Be kinder to yourself and be on your own team!

The Devil reversed also means that you have received your "Get Out of Hell Free" card. Let the chains of negative thinking slip off and fall away. Know that when these chains manage to hook you, they are born from fear and old shadows from the past. Choose to step back into the radiant light of your limitless Spirit. Your power is in the present, not the past. You are so much more than what the shadow wants you to believe. The light within you is stronger than the darkness, and it's time to affirm it. As always, sunlight is the best disinfectant.

THE TOWER

Coming back to earth.

The people falling from the Tower were prisoners of their own making. They built walls around themselves that grew taller and taller. These walls separated them from feeling reality. The Tower gained in size and made them numb. Being numb kept them "safe" from being hurt by the past and the present. In the Tower, they could pretend there was no loss, change, or death happening outside. They would say things like, "I'm great! No sad things ever happened; what are you talking about?" The lightning on the card represents the inevitable crisis the Universe always sends to cause those in denial to wake up and to heal what needs healing. One falling figure is crowned, while the other is not. This symbolizes that being in a state of denial is unsustainable, whether you are a commoner or a king.

Are there unresolved hurts from the past that you need to heal, surrender, and clear? What would you rather not deal with right now? Do you zone out to deny reality? Is there a fear that, if you open yourself to feeling it, it will hurt too much and won't stop hurting?

Despite the destructive imagery, the Tower is one of the most healing cards in the tarot. The Tower snaps us out of pretending we are not hurting. It is a cathartic card where old pains are finally felt and released for healing. In that way, the old pains no longer keep us a prisoner escaping reality. When you reflect on your life, you'll realize the moments that made you strongest are often the hard times. Avoiding challenges doesn't make us strong—dealing with them does.

Denial of truth is unsustainable. Spirit, God, or the Universe always sends along a proverbial lightning bolt to snap us out of delusion. The breakdown moment is surprisingly a blessing. Lightning bolts symbolize flashes of divine magic and epiphanies at play in your life. Once reality is accepted, it can then be healed. The people falling from the Tower are returning to earth. Not only are they returning to reality, but they are returning to their true nature as well. The crowned roof of the Tower is also being ejected, symbolizing a need to get out of the rationalizations of your head and get back to reality.

When the Tower appears, it's time to stop avoiding something that you know needs to be felt. Don't deny your feelings another day or they will continue to keep you imprisoned. Give yourself some privacy and space to really feel something that hurts. Release it through tears or even yelling. A wise teacher of mine told me that if you can't scream in the house because there are people around, do it in the car. People will just think you're singing.[15] It's time to be honest with yourself and feel your real feelings. The Tower represents freedom from feeling trapped.

15. Retzlaff, *Cinderella Doesn't Live Here Anymore*, 90.

The Tower Reversed

If the Tower appears reversed, you may have just undergone a period where everything felt shaky, uncertain, and full of volatile changes. Although the Tower indicates a transformative period that can be deeply healing, it always accompanies feelings of instability. Old, outdated structures in your life are being swept away. This clearing is making room for positive new beginnings. If you cooperate with your life changes at this time, you will feel electric—as if there is divine momentum propelling you forward on your path. Although you may not feel very sure about where your path is heading, the Tower reversed indicates that there's nowhere to go but up.

This card position often feels like a hurricane just ran through your life, and now you are charged with the duty to clean it all up. The thing you must keep in mind is that *the storm is over*. It is time to move forward and not be fixated on what has just changed. There will be time enough in the future to emotionally process your recent transformation. For now, you must stay clear and focused on your present priority.

Upright or reversed, the Tower advises you to allow what you don't need to crumble away. The changes you are experiencing will only feel traumatic if you resist them. The sun is peeking through the clouds again, and hindsight will reveal the necessity of the storm's passing.

THE STAR

Transcendent wisdom.

The Star is a symbol of renewed hope after turbulent times. The hope comes from seeing your life transcendentally. From this higher vantage point, you can see the big picture and your real-life purpose. The Star asks you to follow your proverbial North Star, the compass point that leads you back to your Authentic Self—the best of who you really are. In fact, the eight-pointed stars depicted on this image resemble the points on a compass. When the Star appears, then you will find your way. The Star is associated with the eternal, immortal part of your Spirit. This authentic essence continues long after your body has gone. By tuning in to the eternal aspect of yourself, you can transcend any challenge you confront in the mundane world.

What is the meaning of *your* life? Have you lost perspective, becoming consumed with something that really isn't that important in the long run? When was the last time you felt clear about your purpose?

The woman on the Star card has drawn from the healing waters of the universal pool of the collective. She is pouring some of these waters on the parched earth beside her, symbolizing a replenishment of her world and the neglected parts of herself. What feels dry and parched in your world? What needs replenishment and watering? The woman is taking some of the water for herself. She knows she is worthy and that it is wise to do so. By taking the gifts of the Universe to replenish herself, she will be able to share more of herself for the benefit of all.

The woman is also pouring some of the water back into the universal pool. She is giving something back to the collective to improve and enrich it. To whom much is given, much is required. If she keeps returning some of the water to the pool, she will ensure it never dries up and that she'll be able to draw future blessings from it when needed.

The Major Arcana in the tarot can be interpreted as a path laid out in symbols toward a deeper understanding of the self. In the Major Arcana, the Star is numbered XVII and occurs immediately after the most challenging cards (XII The Hanged Man, XIII Death, XV The Devil, XVI The Tower). After accepting sacrifice and death, confronting the shadow self, and returning to her true nature, the superficial layers of the ego are stripped away. The Star represents the imperishable light within you that transcends the fears of the ego. This is the eternal starlight of Spirit. Each of us possesses this light. This light is always sparkling within us. However, sometimes it is so buried beneath burdens and layers of ego and fear that it is hard to feel or see. Some people forget this light exists altogether—until they see a laughing baby or are moved by pivotal (sometimes traumatic) life events. The Star card reminds us that our inner light exists. When we draw from this eternal source, we can bounce back from death and defeat, transcending all challenges. Knowing this, we come to understand there is really nothing to fear.

In the background sitting in a tree is an ibis bird. The ibis was very sacred in ancient Egypt. It is the emblem of the God of wisdom, Thoth. The ibis calls us to the wisdom we need in order to fly above our present challenges. The ibis, high on his tree, grants the perspective of the big picture. He is the God of the moon and writing. Perhaps it's time to journal your deeper revelations.

The Star reminds you to replenish yourself by accessing the transcendent light within. When you have drawn from the power of this light, pass along its blessings and reinvest in the universal pool. Open your eyes to where you are truly needed in your world. If you've ever helped the homeless or sat with an old, lonely lady who needed to talk or left a huge tip and a sweet note for a hotel maid or waitress going through a rough patch, then you've been doing the work of the Star. You've been replenishing the waters of the collective good. The Star is all about restoring hope in yourself and others.

Follow your North Star back to the best parts of you and your true purpose. If you continue to pass on blessings to others, you will always be blessed.

The Star Reversed

If the Star appears reversed, it signals a need to balance practicality with transcendental spiritual concerns. Upright or reversed, the Star encourages balance. It is important to give consideration to your spiritual needs while also remembering to invest time and energy in the practical. Many spiritual people need to be reminded to face the external world and its challenges without getting too carried away by the higher planes. When this card appears reversed, it can indicate a neglect of practical concerns. These earthly concerns include money, financial planning, taking care of your physical body, or experiencing life outside of your ivory tower. The Star is a very spiritual card with an emphasis on the eternal, otherworldly, and mystical. The appearance of the Star reversed can also indicate that you have been swimming in the universal pool for too long and may be ignoring some important practical matters. Look at how the woman on the card takes water from the pool and spreads it on the dry earth. You may need to invest some more of your energy into something mundane yet necessary.

Conversely, the Star reversed can indicate a neglect of what is eternal within you. By pouring all your energy on the dry earth, you may be forgetting to look at the situation from a transcendent place. It may be time to draw inspiration from the pool, reclaim your wisdom, and step into an awareness that you are a luminous and eternal Spirit in human form. It may also benefit you to invest time in activities that make your Spirit feel inspired, vital, and engaged.

We are all children of the stars. The same atoms that make up the cosmos are present in you. Your creative contributions to the planet are part of a larger universal pool. Today, it is not all or nothing. You can be a practical person who remains connected with your Spirit. You can also be a spiritually evolved individual who pays their bills on time! After you have balanced your inner and outer worlds, the Star (upright or reversed) requires you to give something of yourself back to the universal pool—something to benefit all. Share your gifts without expecting a return. This will ensure that the eternal pool within remains full.

THE MOON

Unconscious influences.

The Moon symbolizes your instincts and unconscious emotions. These deep undercurrents can alter your perception of the world around you. If you harbor habitually negative emotions, you will look at the world and constantly see evidence of negativity. Likewise, if you are brimming over with positive energy, you will see a world full of joy. The Moon reminds you to check in with your unconscious moods and feelings. These emotions are coloring your perception of the good or bad things you are seeing in front of you.

What color would best describe your emotions today? Are your emotions a healing blue? A depressive gray? A heartfelt pink? A sunny yellow? An emerald green or a dirty yellow-green? Have you been feeling a bit moody lately?

The moon beams brightly in the sky, pulling on the instincts of the animals on the card in very mysterious ways. A wolf appears in the image, howling at the moon. The wolf represents the primitive, instinctual side of your nature. A domesticated dog also appears alongside the wolf. The dog represents your civilized self.

What is the dog doing in the card? He is howling at the moon just as loud as the wolf is! This represents that no matter how rational and intelligent you may like to think you are, you will still be pulled by mysterious and irrational forces. The moon is a force of nature that tugs on your deepest instincts and emotions.

A lobster is drawn out of the deep waters, pulled from its lair by the power of the moon. Lobsters have hard shells to protect them from the world. However, there is no armor that can contend with the moon's power. This symbolizes that no matter how much you try to wear hardened armor over your own vulnerabilities, you will still be influenced by your habitual, sensitive nature. A pathway winds up the mountain in the distance and past the gate made by two towers. This shows that when you take the time to look inward, your pathway of ascension will be revealed.

Nature *feels* the moon, because the moon tugs on the earth's gravity as it orbits. The moon's great weight pulls on the oceans, lakes, and rivers as it circles, creating the tides. Humans are made up of about 65 percent water. It is probably safe to say that our bodies are unconsciously affected by this rhythmic, cyclical pull each month.

The moon tugs on our instincts. When this card appears, it is time to listen to your deepest feelings and let them guide your path. Tune in to your intuitive hunches. Trust yourself when something doesn't feel right. Reconnect with your wiser, magical self. Like the lobster emerging from the depths, let your deeper wisdom rise to the surface and bring valuable insights to your conscious mind.

When the Moon appears, it reminds you to trust your impressions, hunches, and instincts. With time and practice, your intuition will grow sharper and guide you through any challenge. Many people in our modern society would like to think the rational mind is the only foolproof way to experience reality. However, it is undeniable that we are creatures of nature and instinct. Sometimes people don't act rationally. Sometimes there is no logical explanation for why something occurs. Sometimes signs do present themselves on our path. Sometimes we need to tune in to the undercurrents that are shaping the realities we experience. You possess great depth. It is time to allow it to emerge.

The Moon Reversed

If the Moon appears reversed, it indicates that you may have been neglecting your deeper instincts. More recently, you may have had to conform to the demands of the external world to survive. Conformity is sometimes necessary to function in the world, but it should not come at the expense of your deeper feelings and instincts. The Moon reversed calls you back to your instinctual self. It's time to ask yourself how you really feel. It's time to reconnect with the natural world, with magic, with the changing seasons, and with your deeper wisdom.

When your instincts are neglected, they begin to act up. In Latin, the moon is called *luna*, which is where we get the word "lunatic" from! Neglected instincts will often make you feel crazy. The Moon reversed can signify illusions created from unresolved feelings. If you have felt unlucky, are imagining terrible things, or feel psychically lost, the Moon reversed asks you to look deeper within and feel what is trying to emerge. If you keep encountering the same cycle or problem in the external world, the reason could be linked to what you still need to resolve within. The other cards that appear around the Moon reversed can give you a glimpse into what those unresolved feelings are about.

When the Moon appears reversed, it can also indicate a time when mysterious forces are working through the undercurrents of your life. Be open to magic and listen to your deepest hunches. Destiny may be calling. This could be a time when doorways begin to open and the creative potential that was beneath the surface suddenly emerges. Most importantly, trust the voice of your intuition. You unconsciously know more than you think you do. Your instincts will guide you toward the right action every time, but only if you are tuned in to them.

THE SUN

The best card in the deck!

The Sun is considered by many to be the best card in the deck. It signifies success, optimism, and everything generally working out as it should. The Sun is life, light, and vitality. The truth is, the sun's energy (figuratively and literally) is present not just for today, but every day. We just get so wrapped up in our dramas and inner turmoil that we forget to remember this. Every day the sun rises.

Every day there is a new opportunity to feel grateful for existing, to make good choices, and to celebrate living.

Is your life presently feeling sunny? Are you approaching this moment with joy or dread? Do you know you can instantly change your feelings by changing your perspective?

The imagery of this card is vibrant and joyous. The Sun Baby riding the horse represents the dawn. He wears the optimistic red plume, just like the Fool. Innocence, joy, and positivity are returning to your world. The child reminds you to look at the magic of existence with wonder, not as a problem that always needs solving. You don't need to be in control of everything. You don't need to run the solar system—that's the sun's job! The Sun Baby is having a blast riding his horse. Horses symbolize assistance. These are the animals that aided humanity in the growth of civilization. Horses made it possible to cross once vast and impossible distances. Horses symbolize that the help you need will come when you need it. It may not seem possible now, but solutions to the impossible will find their way to you every time!

Why am I so confident everything will work out? Because it always does! Don't you remember all the other times it did? If you can't trust this truth, then you may as well believe that when night comes, it will stay dark forever. Sounds preposterous, doesn't it? The light will always return. That's just common sense.

The sun is always up there in the sky, blessing us with life. We wouldn't be here without it. Even when it is hidden behind the clouds, it always reemerges. Even when light leaves our world each day, the sun promises to come back with the dawn. This is a fundamental truth for all of us. Light will always return, even after your darkest moments. Sometimes this card appears when you must surrender a situation that you can't solve alone. Look to the symbol of the horse. Magical assistance will find its way to you when you choose to step into the light.

The Sun arrives to tell you to lighten up! Stop being so negative about life's snafus as they appear. It may get dark periodically, but it won't stay that way for long. Like the sunflowers, turn your face toward the light. Everything is working out just as it should.

You can be as sure of this as the sun rising in the east.

The Sun Reversed

Upright or reversed, the Sun is always the best card in the deck. This card refuses to be a buzzkill! The Sun reversed may be indicating that you have had your share of cloudy setbacks up until this point. However, now things are beginning to brighten up. Express your vitality, move, and brighten the lives of others by exuding joy. The horse on the card is a reminder to ask for and seek out assistance when you need it. Look at your possibilities with the magical eyes of a child—with wonder, excitement, and promise. There is so much good stuff still ahead for you! Do you truly believe this? If not, it's time to start! Positivity is a choice. Don't dull your enthusiasm to gain the acceptance of snarky sarcastic people or Debbie Downers. Stay true to your joy.

A new day has dawned, and you can choose your life's direction from this point forward. Proceed with confidence as the sun illuminates your golden path.

JUDGEMENT

Rebirth.

Judgement symbolizes rebirth, renewal, and restoration. It represents reawakening and returning to life after loss. Often when people see this card, they are afraid that somehow this means they will be judged. The only judgement this card decrees is that you are worthy to rise again and make your life as joyful, healthy, and full as it can be. Judgement represents your ability to abandon the thoughts, habits, and attitudes that keep your mind in "death consciousness."

Fear, hopelessness, avoidance, procrastination, self-limiting behaviors—these are all mental graves that it's time to step out of now!

Do you wish you could break away from the depressive feeling that you are slogging through life like the walking dead? Have you been avoiding a personal goal that promises to make your life better because you are afraid of failing? Have you forgotten that you still have the power to make your dreams come true?

A luminous Angel emerges from the clouds, blowing the golden trumpet of life. Its brazen notes resonate across the whole earth. Angels throughout the tarot symbolize your Higher Self. The notes blown from the trumpet symbolize that you are going to be hearing your Higher Self loud and clear. All that appeared dead, lost, and forgotten will rise again, reborn and revived. A new day has dawned. The graves are cast aside. Judgement declares there is still life to live!

All the figures on this card represent the different facets of you. The Angel is your Higher Self, calling the long-dead parts of yourself to return to life. Dreams abandoned, goals forsaken, hopes crushed; all these trials were necessary to make you the strong person you are today. It wasn't for nothing. The Angel is the voice in your head that says, "What am I doing? I deserve better! I am ready to get the most out of life!"

When Judgement appears, your best self is giving you a wake-up call. It's time to get up and step out of the self-imposed grave your mind has been confined to. Today it's time to push past self-limiting behaviors about your potential and worth. Breathe new life into projects and dreams long thought dead. You can start living the life you want now, today, at this moment, if you summon the courage to step up and live consciously. Rise up like the fiery phoenix out of the ashes.

Everything in nature changes and dies. It can be sad to look back at the times when something important felt lost and you felt forsaken. But remember, *everything* in nature reflects rebirth. This includes you. This is the divine and natural law. This is the benevolent judgement of the Universe.

Judgement Reversed

When Judgement appears reversed, it asks if you are sleepwalking through life. Upright or reversed, Judgement represents awakening and transformation. Judgement reversed indicates that in order to progress, you must be fully conscious about what is occurring at this time. Only by being awake and alert can you choose to establish new conditions.

Periodically, we wake up to realize we've become entranced. A whole day or week or month has gone by without a sense of awareness, memory, or vitality. Procrastination is often a side effect of this; however, at the root of procrastination is detachment. It's as if there is a disconnect between the mind and the heart. Ask yourself today, "Am I feeling my heart? Do I recognize the sensations of feelings like love and joy in my chest?"

There are all sorts of reasons to allow yourself to become entranced. Many times, it's because of fear. Fear of pain, fear of discomfort, fear of taking responsibility, fear of letting yourself down—the list goes on and on. The Angel of Judgement represents your Spirit, which needs to periodically blow bombastic notes from its trumpet to give you a wake-up call. If you can tune in to the sensations in your heart, you will gain valuable information about what you need to do next. Allow yourself to feel your real feelings, especially the neglected or difficult ones.

Judgement reversed asks you to alert your Higher Self if you have been sleepwalking through life. Renew your passion for your goals, projects, and interests. If you feel dead toward them, try to do a little work on them anyway. Even fifteen minutes can be enough to rekindle the flames of creativity.

If you don't like the sleepy direction your life is heading in, you can choose to wake up now. The phoenix within your soul is restlessly stirring. Set her free!

THE WORLD

Completion.

The World represents the successful completion of a life cycle. This card encourages you to finish what you've started. The old is being completed, and loose ends are now being tied up. When the World appears, you are crossing an important threshold. The World symbolizes that you aren't just completing a chapter of your life, but an entire volume. This card also rules important rites of passage. Magical new possibilities are opening to you now. Take a deep breath, summon your courage, and boldly cross the finish line.

What are you working on finishing? What world have you been creating for yourself? Are you aware of new opportunities currently opening to you?

The World card is the zenith of the Major Arcana. The figure depicted on the World card has faced all the wonders and perils of the previous twenty-one cards. This image depicts her graduation. To mark this rite of passage, she has been given not just one white magical wand, but two. The two wands symbolize total empowerment, perspective, and mastery. The right hand symbolizes assertive, outwardly directed energy. This is the hand the Magician uses to hold his white wand. The left hand symbolizes receptive energy, directed inward. The wands symbolize that the figure on the World card has mastered both the active and passive parts of her psyche, the left and the right brain. She can give and she can receive.

The figure on the World card is a powerful sorceress and knows it. Some tarot readers view her as an intersex being who has synthesized the polarities of both sexes, becoming enlightened. This could be the case as her genitalia is obscured. Her left leg is bent behind her right, just like the Hanged Man. This shows that the sorceress has achieved all that she has sacrificed for. She is not afraid of her future because she sees herself in the context of the universal. She is past the fear of death, having faced it along with her shadows to be born anew. She is aligned with her Spirit's authentic purpose. She knows who she is.

The World reminds you that you can create miraculous changes in your life when you remember your Spirit. Only by honoring your whole journey with all its losses, successes, and disappointments will you be able to accept wholeness. The sorceress on this card can send her energy out into the world to effect change, just like the Magician. They both hold magical white wands in their right hand. However, this sorceress has also done her inner work. The wand in the left hand symbolizes her mastery of the unseen, darker pathways on her journey. Acceptance of her entire path opens her to receiving. Not just the joyful, successful times, but the hard times as well.

Think back on your life's journey. What hills and valleys did you pass through to arrive at this moment? Breathe in the magnitude of your presence and perseverance! If you are here, you still have new purpose and new work to do.

Completion can be frightening. It requires you to commit yourself to unknowable new experiences. When the World appears, allow yourself to feel excited about this rite of passage! Be proud of your accomplishments and your total journey. You now *know thyself*... and through you, the Universe is conscious of a precious part of *itself*, too. There is powerful magic in remembering that you are infinite and limitless.

The World Reversed

If the World appears reversed, it asks you to stop procrastinating and complete that which remains unfinished. If your world feels upside down, it may be linked to resistance to change. Are you hanging on to something you no longer need? Do you keep confronting the same issue again and again? It's finally time to grow and allow yourself to graduate to the next level of development. Close the door on a pattern that continuously prevents you from moving forward. You will know what needs to be released because there will be a twinge of resistance to letting it go. Often, the thing you are afraid to let go of also makes you feel comfortable.

Procrastination is often fear in disguise. By putting off completing one phase, you still hold on to the past, pretending that you need more time to let it go. Pivotal life changes are rarely made with 100 percent assurance that everything will work out. Often, your best transformations come from having the courage to let go of old tired patterns and commit to a new way of seeing your life.

The definition of insanity is doing the same thing over and over while expecting a different result. The truth is, when your world gets turned on its head, it offers you the opportunity to release outdated perspectives about yourself and what you think is possible. Stop the insanity and do something new!

To help you get off the hamster wheel, you may have to reach out for the perspective of another. A trusted loved one can often offer you an understanding assessment of your experience if you ask for it. To escape from entrapping mental patterns, sometimes you need to get out of your own head. Go for a walk. Get *into* the world. Other cards may reveal clues as to what patterns need to be released. If you make a choice to move on from the old and tired ways of doing things, boundless possibilities will await you.

PART 2
THE MINOR ARCANA

Traditionally, the Minor Arcana addresses external concerns—the issues we must grapple with in the real world. The Minor Arcana is separated into four suits: Swords, Cups, Pentacles, and Wands. Each suit is associated with an element: Air, Water, Earth, and Fire. These elements are symbols for the four ways in which we can interact with the external world around us.

In the Rider-Waite-Smith tarot, Swords are associated with Air, and Wands are associated with Fire; however, different deck creators are more comfortable with Wands being associated with Air and Swords being associated with Fire. I think this makes perfect sense since Wands usually derive from tree branches that blow in the wind and Swords are forged in fire. However, for this book, we will follow the imagery created by Waite and Smith and view Swords as linked to the Air element and Wands to the Fire element.

The element of Air is associated with the mind. It is symbolically linked to rationality, the law, thinking, mindsets, reason, brilliance, communication, logic, and oftentimes a need for a dispassionate perspective. When Swords appear in a reading, they call your attention to your mental state or the thoughts of the people around you. Swords may also illuminate mental blockages that must be resolved to regain your personal authority and power.

The element of Water is symbolized by Cups in the tarot. Cups are associated with feelings, emotions, love, relationships, memories, illusions, creativity, sensitivity, and all matters that affect the heart. When Cups appear in a reading, they reveal what is being felt. Cup cards lead you inward to understand your heart and feelings about particular people and situations. Cups also show pathways forward when working on relationships with others.

The element of Earth is presented as Pentacles in the tarot. Pentacles have also been called "coins" and are often linked to issues of money, finances, stability, prosperity, jobs, security, wealth, instability, manifestation, poverty, caution, and real-world practical action. When Pentacle cards appear, they call your attention to your finances and the security of your home, self, and career. Many times, Pentacles will reveal where you have an opportunity. Pentacles are rooted in practicality and hard work. Pentacles will also reveal *worth* and how worthy you feel.

The element of Fire is linked to the suit of Wands. Wands are associated with ambition, creativity, boldness, dynamism, vitality, growth, awakenings, brilliance, charisma, action, movement, ego, and actions that must be taken quickly. Wands reveal areas of personal growth and opportunity. When Wand cards appear in a reading, they often reveal what you are striving for. The little leaves sprouting on each of the wands symbolize personal growth and progress.

When giving a reading, be mindful of what suit seems to dominate. It will reveal what issues you are working on and where to look for pathways forward. Just as importantly, look at which suit seems to be missing. If other cards are providing a message that you are experiencing imbalance, the missing suit can reveal where you need to invest your energy to restore harmony.

THE SUIT OF SWORDS

Your state of mind.

The Swords suit addresses your mindset and what predominant thoughts are currently at work. As such, they are associated with the element of Air, which is linked to logic, intellect, reason, and thoughts. Some of the most difficult cards in the tarot appear in this suit. This is because our minds are repositories of information. All the good and bad things that have ever happened to you are stored away in your brain. These thoughts eventually sink in to the unconscious where they dictate your perspective, whether you are aware of your thoughts or not. Sword cards reveal how your thinking has been affected by past experiences, especially trauma. When Swords appear, do not be afraid or feel defeated. Important issues are being worked out in your mind. An abundance of Swords in a reading does not necessarily mean that you will have only bad things on the horizon. The Swords suit is where some of the most meaningful pathways toward healing can be found. Each of the Court cards in the Swords suit reveals an intelligent figure.

Before you can achieve anything, your mind must be made up to do so. The Swords suit can help you regain dispassionate clarity, thereby giving you the ability to achieve your goals in a sensible manner. Swords also highlight the negative thoughts you harbor, which could be blocking your progress.

Some people fear that the scary images of the Swords suit will signify terrible calamities that could happen to them. Tarot is a collection of images that symbolically reflect real-world situations and attitudes. Some of the images are meant to be jarring. They serve as psychic wake-up calls to alert you to harmful or destructive thought forms. Mastering the lessons embodied in the Swords suit is extremely empowering. Its archetypes and symbols can arm you with the ability to defeat mental shadows, thereby reclaiming the power and potential of your brilliant mind.

ACE OF SWORDS

Reclaiming your personal power.

The Ace of Swords symbolizes reclaiming your personal power by taking charge of your life. Like all Aces, it symbolizes that a new beginning is at hand. Your personal power is much like a sword, waiting to be drawn from a scabbard. When you grasp what makes you powerful, you can transform your energy from victim to victor. The Ace of Swords cuts through trancelike states of mind. It flashes with dazzling light, awakening your self-confidence.

Do you feel your personal power has been depleted somehow? Are you avoiding something that you know will make things better if you just get the ball rolling? Are you overwhelmed by anxiety, causing you to feel uncomfortable with confronting an area of your life?

A mighty hand grasps the flashing sword. Six sparks crackle from its blade. In numerology, sixes represent an ideal balance and the restoration of harmony. The sword represents your vitality, life force, and personal power. The sword is crowned. This symbolizes that when you grasp your power, you become fit to rule your life. You are the king or queen of your own world, vested with the divine authority to make it as successful as you dare. The mountains symbolize the great heights you will ascend to—if you decide to act.

An olive branch dangles from the left side of the crown. This symbolizes that your life will feel more at peace when you act. This seems counterintuitive to our fears, which tell us to avoid things that might create stress. However, inner turmoil comes from the avoidance of confrontation, not from taking responsibility.

A palm branch graces the right side of the crown. Palm trees are primordial, tough, and hearty. They can endure desertlike heat and torrential hurricanes. The palm branch symbolizes your resilience. You can endure much more than you may be giving yourself credit for.

Today, a new beginning is at hand. Don't dwell on yesterday, last year, or what might lie ahead. Your personal power is crackling in the present, right now. Where will you send that energy? Channel this energy toward the place in your mind where your power resides. Act on something that you have been avoiding. This will restore confidence in your mind and its ability to make better decisions.

Ace of Swords Reversed

If the Ace of Swords appears reversed, it represents defending positive new ways of thinking that are still in their infancy. When the blade of a sword is depicted upright, it symbolizes that it is at the ready. When a sword is upraised, it is ready to fight or to act. An upraised sword can respond to any anticipated action. When a sword is depicted with its blade lowered (as in this case), it symbolizes that the sword is in a state of peace, rest, and that it is *guarding* something.

When the Ace of Swords appears reversed, it can mean that you need to stay vigilant and protect something that is just getting its start. This could be new habits, a new mind frame, a new perspective, or a new creative project. Aces always represent new beginnings, and the Ace of Swords reversed can indicate that you need to take special care of something fragile that is still in its beginning phase. This card could also mean that you need to protect yourself during a sensitive time of change. For these positive new developments to take root, you must protect them until they are strong enough to stand on their own. The Ace of Swords reversed can also symbolize the need to protect yourself from the negative thoughts, comments, and actions of others.

The Ace of Swords (upright or reversed) indicates the necessity to change your perspective from feeling powerless to feeling powerful. You can indeed triumph, but first you must rediscover confidence in yourself and your abilities. Like the palm branch, you are far more resilient than you think. Have courage and protect the empowered person you are becoming.

TWO OF SWORDS

Making peace with "in-between."

The Two of Swords symbolizes making peace with the feeling of being "in between." In between life stages, in between jobs, in between relationships, in between projects, in between moving situations, in between friendships, in between career goals, in between big plans, and so on. This card advises you to find your center amid the transformations swirling around you. The truth is, we are always in a state of in-between somewhere in our lives. The Two of Swords illuminates that the place in your life that feels unresolved is precisely where life's greatest magic is happening.

What feels uneasy or unresolved in your life? Is this in-between situation making you anxious about the future? Can you be at peace with not having everything completely figured out right now?

The figure on the Two of Swords is also in between. She is in between the land and the sea. In between the new moon and the full moon. In between the two swords she is holding. Yet, she is in a pose of complete balance. The Two of Swords is the Minor Arcana complement to the Major Arcana's Justice card. However, the woman depicted here *is* blindfolded. This symbolizes that she can't see what is coming and may not possess all the facts yet. But look how calm and centered she is. She has accepted not seeing with her eyes because she is at peace with her center, with the core of who she really is. She's okay with not having everything figured out. She's accepted being between the worlds. She knows that the *in-between times* are when the magic of the natural world happens.[16] Symbolism of distance and isolation pervade this card. The woman confidently wields the powers of her own inner sight.

In nature, the in-between time is at dusk or dawn, and it is magical. At dusk, all the animals get ready for the transition to night. The birds excitedly chirp for their companions to come roost for the night. The quiet deer come out of hiding to drink at the pond. The owls rise and call to one another. The light in the sky transforms. The atmosphere at sunset stirs and the winds begin to gust. The clouds glow in shades of violet-pink and golden-orange. If you witness this, there is an indescribable sense of peace and tranquility during this in-between time. This is how nature illustrates in-between. Nature guides us to experience serenity amid transition.

The Two of Swords asks you to make peace with the area of your life that is still in-between. This card reflects nature, where twilight leads to night, which is then followed by dawn. The in-between time is where your Higher Self is most alert. The lessons you are currently learning are making you wiser, stron-

16. Andrews, *Enchantment of the Faerie Realm*, 24. Ted Andrews often wrote about the magic that occurs during what he called the "'tween times." These include dawn, dusk, noon, midnight, equinoxes, and solstices.

ger, and more aligned with the center of who you really are. Your best potential is manifesting.

You are exactly where you need to be, and everything is transitioning perfectly.

Two of Swords Reversed

If the Two of Swords appears reversed, it is time to boldly step out of limbo. If an aspect of your life has been suspended for too long, then it's time to get things moving again. The Two of Swords reversed usually appears after a period of incubation, a time spent making peace with yourself. It is a card of precarious balances between the needs of the world and the needs of the self. Now that a truce has been made with your deepest creative self, it is time to act. Commit your energy to completing projects, tasks, and goals. Step out of indecision and reveal your vision.

This card is always a reminder that we are all in a perpetual state of in-between. Once you have found peace within yourself, it is time to engage with the world. After stillness, action must follow. Take the blindfold off and see how things in your world have magically transformed. Step out of limbo and seek closure.

THREE OF SWORDS

Forgiveness.

As you might imagine, the Three of Swords symbolizes the wounded heart. Everyone experiences betrayals, cruelty, unkindness, and even abuse to varying degrees. These traumatic events can feel like swords driven into the heart. Like any penetrating trauma, the shrapnel must be extracted for the injury to heal. Likewise, the swords pictured on this card need to be drawn out and released from the heart so that it can heal. Sounds easy, right? Well it's not! This is because the only thing that can give you the power to release the sword from the wound is *forgiveness*. What?! Forgive that bastard?! Never!

Are you unable to forgive individuals from the past who betrayed you? Do you still get angry and feel victimized? What emotions do you feel when you conjure up the image of this person … hatred, revenge, rage, sadness?

The heart on the card is the victim of a devastating injury. Three large swords symbolize wounds inflicted by three past traumatic events. The swords are weighing the heart down beneath gray clouds. There are three complete clouds depicted in the image, yet one cloud in the background is incomplete. The three completed clouds could refer to the negative thoughts brought on by the three swords. The incomplete cloud could symbolize future thoughts—still unformed, but potentially influenced by past trauma. Perhaps it's time to at least think of the *possibility* of future happiness instead of being defeated by the same old tragedies of the past.

Rain continuously pelts down on the sunken heart. And yet, look at the proportions. The floating heart is quite large when compared to the swords. This symbolizes that the heart is stronger and more resilient than any wound to it. It also symbolizes that the wounds can weigh down a normally buoyant heart. This negative energy prevents the heart from rising above the clouds to bask in joyful sunlight.

The Three of Swords reminds us that even though another may have put a metaphorical sword in our heart through a past betrayal, we perpetually betray ourselves by not letting go and releasing the resentment. So, if the only thing that will unburden the heart is forgiveness, then why is there such resistance to letting the swords go?

Swords represent power. Righteous indignation is seductive and can give a false sense of empowerment. The heart may want to hold on to the swords because it feels that somehow it now possesses more power. Although it gives an immediate illusion of being the moral victor (we are not the bad one, after all), it also leaves us feeling hollow and empty. This sense of power is held on to for dear life so that we aren't suckers caught off guard again! And yet, the heart remains heavy and isolated, and we miss the joy of the sunlight above the clouds.

Practicing forgiveness allows for releasing the negative energy within so that you are not carrying it with you everywhere. Each day you refuse to forgive, you are deciding to continue carrying all that toxic poison within you for another day. There is an anonymous quote that says, "Holding on to anger is like drinking poison and expecting the other person to drop dead!" Think about our world affairs and how lack of forgiveness perpetuates war, hatred, and conflict.

Forgiveness does not mean condoning the reprehensible behavior of another. It doesn't mean that you need to call your abuser over for tea and pretend nothing happened. Forgiveness is less about them and more about you. The wound happened, but it's not still happening today unless we choose to hurt ourselves with it. This means that you also must forgive yourself for holding on to this garbage for so long. Forgiveness gives you the power to let the painful past go, allowing you to move on with your life unencumbered and free.

The Three of Swords indicates that it's time to let go of any painful people or things that are weighing your heart down. Forgiveness often doesn't come overnight! It takes time and continual affirmation before the swords are released. An opportunity for major healing is being presented to you now. Like the rising phoenix, let your heart ascend above the rain clouds and into the realm of light.

Three of Swords Reversed

If the Three of Swords appears reversed, it calls your attention to any self-inflicted wounds that are being perpetuated through negative thinking. Holding on to negative expectations is a form of self-betrayal. The clouds that appeared in the sky are now on the base of the card. Clouds symbolize the element of Air, and Air represents your thoughts. The Three of Swords reversed can indicate that the negative thoughts you are holding on to are affecting your outlook. This includes thoughts that project catastrophes into a future that hasn't even happened yet or replaying past traumas mentally and anticipating that they will happen again. Your anxieties aren't harbingers of disasters to come. They are merely fears, and they rarely resemble the future that will actually come to pass.

When the Three of Swords reversed appears, it's best to avoid "borrowing trouble." Negative projections into the future will cause you to miss out on being joyful in this moment. If you are anxious about what hasn't even happened yet, then you are harming yourself with your thinking. Catch yourself when you notice you are falling into this. Release harmful thoughts and know them for what they are: *thoughts*. Choose to focus your thinking on something that really interests you or brings you joy. Remember, the heart on this card is much larger and stronger than any wound it's experienced. Your heart is stronger than your fears and wounds from the past. Transcendent love is always a viable answer when this card appears.

FOUR OF SWORDS

Restoring inner peace.

The Four of Swords symbolizes our need for inner peace. It encourages rest and recuperation. The appearance of the Four of Swords gently reminds you to call your attention to your body and any areas where tension has been building up. You may need to give yourself some peace and quiet to rejuvenate your body, mind, and Spirit. You could also find that it's time to let go of whatever is preventing a sense of peace and causing inner suffering.

Do you feel inner peace, or have you been suffering? When is the last time you gave yourself a relaxing midday nap? Do you need a break from the stress that's built up?

Hidden in the upper left corner of the stained glass window in the Four of Swords is the word *pax* (Latin for "peace"). Aside from encouraging rest, this card asks if you are feeling inner peace. Often the cause for suffering in our lives is the attachment to things that need to be surrendered. Trying to control outcomes and hanging on to a path that no longer brings rewards are examples of this. Identify anything that is interfering with your inner peace. Is it a life path that you honestly aren't happy with? Is it a fixed attachment to a specific outcome? Wouldn't it be a relief to finally let the source of your suffering go and see what new wonders await you? We are often very good at rationalizing why we need to suffer, but there is no real rationalization for it. You can choose inner peace and let go of whatever you've outgrown that keeps preventing you from being at peace within yourself.

Prayer imagery is also prevalent on this card. The figures in the stained glass are praying, as is the effigy on the sarcophagus. The scene depicted takes place in a church. This reminds us of the Hierophant card and the rebalancing that occurs when seeking assistance from the Divine. Perhaps the peace you are seeking will be obtained through reconnecting with what is most sacred to you. Feel your stress dissipate as you ask Spirit for what you need.

Another way to bring a sense of inner peace is deep breathing. Secure ten minutes for yourself when you won't be disturbed. Sit back and relax in a comfy chair. Bring your awareness to your body. With your mind, slowly scan the sensations of your body from head to toe. Is there an area with tightness built up? Find the area of tightness and relax the muscles surrounding this area as much as you can. When you identify where the tension has built up, it's time to breathe into that area. Empty all the air from your lungs. Take a deep breath, slowly inhaling through your nostrils over an eight-second count. Fill your body with revitalizing air. Let your stomach expand with the inhalation. Inhale the revitalizing oxygen into the place of tension. Hold the air there for eight seconds, right in the tense spot. While holding the air, purse your lips as if you were about to drink from a small straw. Exhale all the air over eight counts through this aperture slowly. It should sound like a dolphin's exhalation (*PPH-HHHHHHHH*). Use your abdomen to press all the old air out of your body.

Let all the tension escape with the breath. Feel the muscles around the tense spot relax even further. Repeat this breath exercise with two more healing inhalations and exhalations (eight counts in, hold eight counts in the stressed spot, release through pursed lips over eight counts). With each exhalation, allow your body to let go of all the accumulated stress of the week.

People in Western culture often need to be reminded to breathe, relax, and let go. Modern humans are always being stimulated by tasks, media, and demands. Breathing is the easiest way to release tension, but there are so many other ways to relax. Take a nice hot bath with candles and scented water. Sip a cool refreshing drink or soothing herbal tea. Take a relaxing nap for an hour just to rest your brow. Read your favorite book with snuggly blankets and a cup of cocoa. Take a breather in a cool, darkened room.

When the Four of Swords appears, you must allow yourself rest and recuperation. Perhaps it's time to plan a vacation or even a walk in nature. You don't need to suffer. Blessings will always come to those who are at peace within themselves.

Four of Swords Reversed

If the Four of Swords appears reversed, it indicates that there is a restless energy about. Restless energy is not always bad. It can motivate you to accomplish goals and get events moving again. It can also indicate excitement and motivation toward action. Restlessness becomes unhelpful when it turns into anxiety. The Four of Swords reversed may indicate that you may have to stop the flurry of rapid thoughts barraging your mind and remember to breathe.

This card encourages you to reject frantic thinking. Take a time-out. Remember to breathe. Take a break from problem-solving. If you allow yourself some time to rejuvenate your mind, you will be able to return to the task at hand with clear perspective. Everything is falling into place. Like the word "pax" on the stained glass suggests, allow yourself peace of mind. There is no need to get anxious, tight, or stressed. Tune in to your body as a barometer for what you currently need. Avoid excess and extremes today. Strive for inner peace.

If there is still accumulated restless energy, channel it into something constructive. Don't ruminate. Let your restlessness become fuel for your greatest goals.

FIVE OF SWORDS

Know your limits.

The Five of Swords warns you to not take on more than you can handle. Its message is that of pacing yourself. Less gets accomplished (not more) when you are spread too thin. Procrastinating will not help you manifest your dreams, but neither will inundating yourself with the present task (which is the opposite extreme). The Five of Swords encourages you to get organized in your thinking and break down your larger task into smaller achievable pieces that can be accomplished over time. This will aid you in replenishing self-esteem and personal power.

Is there a huge issue looming in your mind that is giving you anxiety? Are you already so overwhelmed with current tasks and to-do lists that it's hard to see how it will all get done? Do you feel spread too thin?

The Five of Swords depicts three squires all trying to secure the job of assisting a brave knight. The two squires in the background are defeated. They are focused on the sea, the element of Water, which is a symbol for their feelings. They couldn't lift all five heavy swords at once, and the knight's horse, and the knight's armor, and the knight's demands, and, and, and...

Aggghh! It's just too stressful! They quit!

A fresh breeze blows through the red hair of the squire in the foreground. The red hair can symbolize the element of Fire, which is fueled by Air. The squire initiates action (Fire), as a result of the idea brought by the fresh breeze (Air). The brisk winds are dispersing the gray clouds in the sky above. This symbolizes the element of Air, which in turn represents reason, logic, and intelligence. This redheaded squire finds that he can easily complete the tasks required by taking the initiative. Instead of seizing all the swords at once, he will collect only the amount he can carry. He can come back to the other two heavy swords lying on the ground once he gets the first task completed. In this way, he will do each task well. The reds and oranges depicted on this card symbolize the element of Fire and taking initiative. It's time to start—wherever you are.

The Five of Swords advises you to not waste another minute resisting your tasks with avoidance, exasperation, or procrastination. Get organized in your thinking! Pull out your calendar. Partition off one sacred hour a day, for seven days, to plug away at the task. Keep your commitment to yourself. Once it's in the calendar, it must be done! This is a sacred contract with your integrity and will systematically help you regain self-esteem. If something comes up in life (as sometimes happens), schedule a makeup hour to keep your commitment to yourself. Open yourself to the fresh breezes of action to break up the gray clouds of indecision.

As you keep your commitment to yourself, a strange thing will happen. You will look forward to working on your task, because confronting it will continue to make you feel powerful. You can achieve your dreams, but first you must schedule the time to work on them.

The Five of Swords also warns you not to take on too much of other people's issues. You may have to let others do their own work without coming to their rescue. Maintain healthy boundaries.

Five of Swords Reversed

If the Five of Swords appears reversed, it carries a similar meaning to the upright position but to an even greater degree. Often this card appears when there is a looming deadline or heavy expectation placed on the self to succeed. This card also appears when you have been pushing hard for something over and over, only to feel like you are hitting a wall. Events may feel overwhelming, so you must pace the tasks in front of you to avoid burnout. Learn from the mistake of the discouraged squires in the background of the card. They tried to collect all the swords at once and were quickly overwhelmed by the weight. Instead, do a bit of the task now, leave it, and schedule consistent times to come back to finish the task gradually. Patience and consistency will help you win; don't get flustered or overwhelmed.

The Five of Swords reversed can also represent times when your energy feels scattered and unfocused. Perhaps you've been getting burnt-out lately. What can you do to restore a sense of calm and clarity? What could you give yourself at this time to feel better?

The Five of Swords reversed asks you to take control of your stress level by taking control of your time. Be patient with yourself and stop cracking the whip over your own back. Break up larger tasks into smaller ones. Often, our best work emerges from taking breaks, taking our time, and returning to projects rested and clear-minded. If your thoughts are muddled, then there may be emotions that need to be heard right now.

The task before you will not prove to be as overwhelming as the other big trials you've faced in life if you approach it systematically.

SIX OF SWORDS

Moving on.

The Six of Swords represents moving on from one place in your life to another. This card can indicate travel, changing careers, leaving relationships, or even moving. The Six of Swords can also signify an elevation to the next level in your professional life. When this card appears, the changes you are experiencing are for the best. The Six of Swords suggests that you go with the flow rather than fight the current. If you surrender to where life's momentum is currently flowing, you will speedily arrive at a safe harbor.

Where is the energy of change flowing in your life? What destination do you have in mind? What must you leave behind?

The ferryman is guiding two refugees—a mother and her child—to a new life. Ferrymen represent situations that carry us from one life to the next. Ferrymen are harbingers of change. The skies are gray, and the mood is somber. The mother's first duty is to protect her child. The refugees are leaving behind the past for the promise of a brighter future. The waters behind them are rough, but the waters ahead are smooth. In order to reach the safe shores, they must leave behind past troubles. Although the boat is not very comfortable, it promises to lead them toward a happier life.

Change is happening in your life, too, and this change is usually accompanied by temporary discomfort. You may be unsure of your footing, and simple challenges may seem magnified. A small inconvenience can seem like a momentous stress when navigating life's transitions. However, know that the changes occurring in your life right now are truly for the better. Don't fight to stay in the old lands, for the metaphorical boat is taking you to new shores. The Six of Swords heralds an exciting time of movement. This card can also herald a trip or a journey. Distance will aid you in acquiring perspective and awareness of your new opportunities.

Any discomfort you feel during these current transitions is normal and will soon pass. A better life is opening to you now. Try not to fixate on the discomfort you are experiencing. Channel any feelings of anxiety into excitement instead. Ride the waves toward progress. Go with the flow.

Six of Swords Reversed

If the Six of Swords appears reversed, it directs your attention to what currently feels stuck. People get stuck when they habitually avoid the discomfort that naturally accompanies change. Don't allow the discomfort of growing pains trick you into avoiding changes and taking risks toward your goals. *Discomfort does not mean something is wrong, it means something is growing or changing.*

Imagine that you are the ferryman in the card. On your journey, you need to propel the boat forward by placing your oar into the river. Anticipate moments when the oar will periodically feel stuck in the mud. Your strength and determination can pull the oar free, allowing you to propel the boat forward. Getting the boat moving again after being stuck is the tough part. However, once it gains momentum, the journey becomes easier.

The Six of Swords reversed urges you to pull your oar free. It may feel like things are stuck, but this is an illusion. Stop fighting the waves and allow your best transformation. Sail over the temporary choppy waters. The promise of a safe harbor lies ahead. Anything in your life that feels stuck can become *unstuck*. However, you must accept the temporary discomfort of change.

SEVEN OF SWORDS

Outwitting your obstacles.

The Seven of Swords represents using your wits to overcome obstacles in your path. It suggests that you not *fight* life's challenges, but instead use your intelligence to bypass what appears fixed or immovable. The Seven of Swords reminds you that it's not over until it's over. There is usually a way to succeed if you don't give up. You are cleverer than your current challenges, but you must think smarter and not work harder!

Do you give up easily when life sends you setbacks, or do you find a way around them? Have you used your wits to outsmart a situation that looked hopeless? Are you tired of fighting against one life barrier after another?

Don't get mad—get smart!

The thief depicted on the Seven of Swords is a brilliant tactician. In the background, you see an army has invaded his homeland. They have set up camps and are conferring with one another about how they will divide the invaded territory. Instead of fighting the whole army by himself, the trickster on the card uses his wits to outsmart them. While the troops are distracted, he creeps in and steals five of their seven weapons, greatly diminishing their strength. Instead of fighting or retreating, he uses his mind to find a brilliant solution to the present impasse. The Seven of Swords also depicts a golden sky. In the Rider-Waite-Smith tarot, golden skies usually appear on cards that imply eventual success or joy. However, the thief is grasping the sharp ends of the swords while tiptoeing, indicating that you must handle this situation with care.

Not every challenge in life needs to be approached with the fight-or-flight instinct. Sometimes all that is required is to use your mind and systematically review the challenge from all angles. Often you can find a way *around* the obstacle with much less frustration and angst.

The Seven of Swords suggests that you apply a different perspective to what currently appears hopeless. Ask experts for advice. Get more information. Really know the details of the situation you are grappling with. Understanding the challenge in its entirety will give you power over it. Use the internet! Everything you need to know is at your fingertips. Are you arming yourself with enough knowledge, or are you just hoping everything will work out?

Sometimes we avoid the solution because it means we must commit to our decision and risk change. New can feel scary. The man on the card is taking a risk by invading the enemy camp. There is a risk involved, but he knows that being proactive is better than futilely hoping the army might retreat.

The Seven of Swords suggests that rather than aggressively ramming your head into a current life challenge, you can choose to be smarter than it. Apply strategic thinking and do some research. Don't give up when life screams, "NO YOU CAN'T!" Respond with, "Hmm, I bet I can find a way around that!"

Using your wits will give you immense power over any obstacle you are currently confronting.

Seven of Swords Reversed

If the Seven of Swords appears reversed, it represents changes in luck. If an unlucky black rain cloud has been following you around, then this card could indicate that it is finally dissipating. The trickster on the card announces that unexpected events are currently swirling around you. Lucky meetings and encounters may take place. However, you may also need to be on guard for unscrupulous individuals. Read between the lines in any agreements; there is always an unpredictable (and sneaky) quality to this card.

When the Seven of Swords appears reversed, it also suggests you can change your own luck. A former teacher of mine used to recite a well-known saying: "Luck is what happens when preparation meets with opportunity." Think ahead and prepare for what you are trying to accomplish. Use your resilient wits, and good luck will find you.

The Seven of Swords reversed asks that you pay attention to details. The thief on the card could indicate the need to review current payment plans to ensure that you aren't being robbed by a corporation or even another individual. Upright or reversed, the Seven of Swords asks you to get smarter. Preparation of the details will give you the ability to change your luck and overcome your challenges.

EIGHT OF SWORDS

Freedom from fear that binds and blinds.

The Eight of Swords illustrates the kind of fear that blinds us, causing us to not see the present. It paralyzes us as we wait for bad things to come to pass. The Eight of Swords symbolizes fear that relies on past evidence to validate it. Something traumatic happened to the woman in the card. She was blindfolded, bound up, and abandoned. The people who brought her to this place are gone.

Her fear that she is worthless has convinced her that all that remains is to wait for the tide to come and swallow her whole. She has been shunned.

Has a traumatic experience from your past made you feel damaged or worthless? Is fear blinding and binding you somehow? Are you so focused on potential catastrophes that you can't see your many opportunities? Do you rationalize your fears, using past traumas to validate their existence?

The Eight of Swords uses gray imagery that makes the woman's situation look hopeless and bleak. But always with the tarot, you must look closer...

She can free herself! So easily!

Wait—what?!

She could use any one of the abandoned swords that flank her to cut the ties around her hands. With her hands free, she could quickly remove the blindfold. Her legs obviously work, so she could still run for safety. Perhaps she could seek sanctuary in the large castle behind her. Why is she not focused on fighting for herself or her survival? Why is she accepting the shame cast on her by others without fighting?

It's because she really believes she is worthless.

Feelings of worthlessness are lies that will keep you scared and bound. Today you must see your worth! If you are having trouble seeing your worth, look at the people who love you most. How would they feel without you in their lives? How sad would they be if they never experienced the special memories you made together? Reflect on your irreplaceable light today. Your light is so special, so uniquely you. In the whole cosmos, there is only one like it.

The Eight of Swords challenges you to see if there's still some fight left in you. Cut away the fears that bind you, and rip away the blindfold! The tide depicted in the card could symbolize the turning of the tide. How are you going to turn the tide toward empowerment? Stand up to what is scaring you. Feel your mighty worth. The past can't get you now, so don't let it continue to overthrow your mind. Do not give in to the illusion that you are trapped.

You are a survivor. You are worthy. It is time to turn the tide.

Eight of Swords Reversed

If the Eight of Swords appears reversed, it means you are escaping from once powerful self-limiting thoughts. Old fears that once had a great hold over your life are now losing their grip. Reversed cards can indicate that inwardly directed healing is occurring around the issues that the symbols of the card portray. In the case of the Eight of Swords, its reversal indicates that the metaphorical blindfold is coming off, allowing you to see your *true self* with clearer perspective. You can choose to see the whole you as opposed to only seeing the worries, fears, or limitations that surround just a small part of you. The Eight of Swords reversed represents *escape.* Like Harry Houdini, you are wriggling out of the mental traps that used to bind and blind you. You are becoming more adept at seeing yourself clearly, without the outworn blindfold. You can see more of your opportunities and gifts. You can begin to see what *really* makes you happy in this life. Without the blindfold, you can see the light and your worth again. You can see that you are so much more than your worries.

What are all the various roles you play in life? Are you an artist? Lover? Mother? Writer? Musician? Brother? Sister? Teacher? Wise One? Healer? Collector? Best friend? Scholar? Expert? Gardener? Father? Daughter? Tarot reader? Your roles change depending on who it is you are interacting with. Also, each role is only one small piece of all that you embody. Don't feel trapped by limiting yourself to only one role, blindly worrying about one aspect of your life that fails to encapsulate the whole you. You are not one-dimensional. Look at all the complex roles you play in this life. Write them down. Remember all that you encompass. Take off the blindfold and cut away your bonds. See the value of the *whole* you with eyes wide open. This will cause the fears surrounding only one part of your life to look small by comparison to your totality. Reclaim the gift of perspective. You will be free whenever you choose to be.

NINE OF SWORDS

Transcending your inner shadows.

The Nine of Swords has been called the "worst card in the deck."[17] Although the imagery isn't as jolting as some of the other cards, it is called the "worst" because it represents the potential of mental shadows to attack you from within. Fear, shame, guilt, feeling utterly alone—these are all tools our inner shadow uses to sabotage us. The brighter the light you shine, the greater the shadow

17. Hollander, *Tarot for Beginners*, 191.

you cast. Sensitive, kind, and creative people who bring light into the world must be especially strong when facing their shadows. Inner shadows are like nightmares: they are scary, but they don't *really* exist. You are stronger than your inner saboteur, but you must stand up to it when it tries to overtake your mind.

Have you ever encountered your inner saboteur? Have people ever told you that you are a talented, amazing person, and yet you can't believe it? Have you been letting your shadow sabotage you and thwart what you think is possible for your future?

The man on the card just can't sleep. His mind has been overthrown by shadow thinking. He's in the dark—the realm of anxiety. His mind has been racing all night, cycling from fear about the future, to guilt about his past, to self-loathing for not having control in the present. His shadow is holding him hostage, making him forget his light and how valuable he is.

Look closely at the paneling on the bed. He is submitting to his attacking inner saboteur. But even now, there is still hope. He just can't see it because he is covering his eyes. The pointed, sharp ends of the swords are cut off at the edge of the image, neutralizing their threat. Also, look closely at his quilt.

Blankets are shields. They can comfort us and remind us that we are safe. His blanket is covered with roses. The roses symbolize that he is still vital and still has a wonderful life ahead of him, despite what the shadow tells him. His quilt is also covered with the signs of the zodiac: the star patterns of the Universe. This symbolizes that he can free himself from fear if he remembers to view himself in the context of Spirit. The man pictured here is a thread in a greater universal tapestry. He is a vital part of a bigger (universal) plan. To escape the fear, he must view himself from a higher, universal perspective. This card reminds you that you do deserve to live and thrive, but you must *know yourself* and see the truth of your light that exists beyond your shadow.

Everyone is given a security blanket when they're born. It's also the first thing they pass out to aid in disaster relief. Hold on to the knowledge that you are not alone and are a vital part of a greater design. You wouldn't exist if there weren't something important that you were here to do. Life is school for the soul. You are not garbage and never will be.

The inner saboteur is like anything—it wants to survive and continue to exist. The more you affirm it with self-loathing, guilt, shame, and fear, the more it thrives. Turn off the spigot and transfer your attention to loving yourself and respecting how far you've come. Affirm your value to yourself, and the shadow will lose all power.

Today, stand up to shadow thinking. When your inner saboteur says you can't do something, you do it anyway. When it says you should feel like crap, do something good for someone. If it seizes you in the shadows, light a candle and go to a mirror. Remind yourself that you are luminous, loving, and have a life purpose that doesn't include shooting yourself in the foot.

If you periodically struggle with shadows, it's just proof that your Spirit radiates a unique and luminous light.

Nine of Swords Reversed

If the Nine of Swords appears reversed, it indicates that you are waking up from the nightmare of thinking you are less than you are. Life has been presenting you with challenges that have tested your faith in yourself. You may have had to accept that it's okay to walk away from something that is toxic and be true to your path. Fears and nightmares aren't facts. They do not rule you, and neither do superstitions and omens.

Free yourself and shift your perspective. Remember the Sun card with the child on it? To escape the dread of fear, look on life with the wondrous eyes of a child. See the magic in existing at this moment in time. Remember the vastness of the Universe and all its wonders. It is so much bigger than what you are afraid of. See the radiant light and love that protect and assist you every day. Switch mental gears. If you can't sleep, get up and shift your thoughts for a bit. Read something that always brings you comfort. Remember your source of joy. There are even more joyful times to come. The light always returns. Day always follows night. Every time you choose to stand up to fear, you become more aligned with the light of your Authentic Self. Everything is going to turn out better than you fear. It always does.

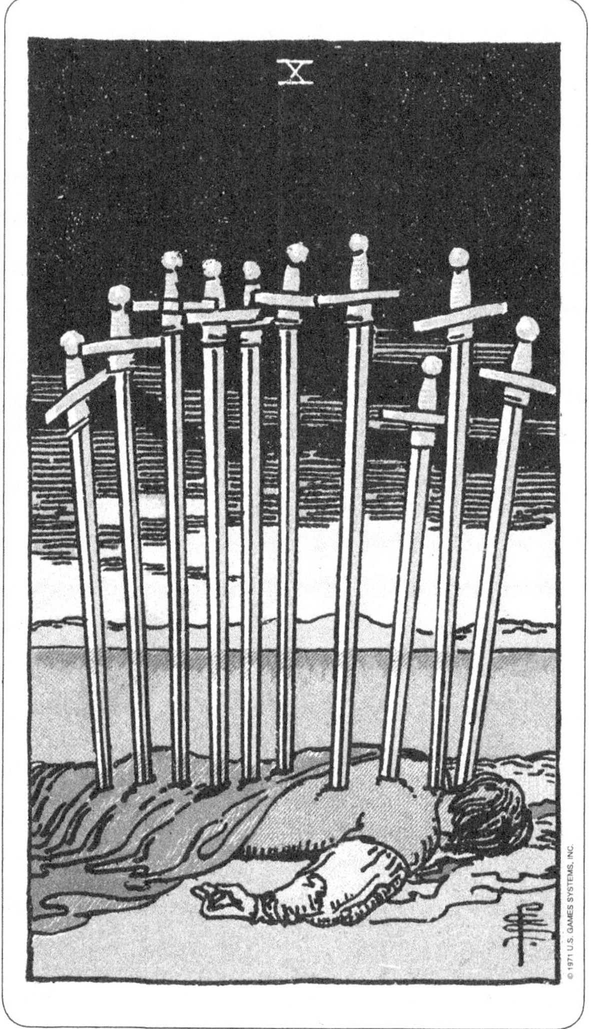

TEN OF SWORDS

Face the source of your anxiety.

Help! The Ten of Swords looks scary! Are we all going to die?!

Absolutely not! The tarot has done it again, using potent symbolism to get us to wake up and pay attention to something very important.

The man on the card is facedown. All the swords are in his back. Whatever got him was chasing from behind. He was running away. The swords in his back symbolize his irrational fears. They finally caught up with him. But look closer. In his last moment, he finally learned to surrender his fears to Spirit. This is symbolized by his right hand signaling a gesture of blessing, just like the Hierophant. Whereas the Hierophant represents rites of passage *you* choose to undergo, the Ten of Swords represents challenging rites of passage that you may not have chosen. The gesture of blessing on both cards indicates that the transformation you are undergoing is meant to be. This rite of passage will serve to make your Spirit stronger; its sacred meaning has yet to be revealed. It is time to stop avoiding the threshold you must cross. Surrender and have faith.

What fears are you constantly trying to keep ahead of? Is your day filled with thoughts of terrible things that might happen? Do you try to just keep busy so you don't have to face the source of your unease?

Ignoring fear is the same as running from it. It's still there. Lurking about as usual. Often the thing we fear (horrible illnesses, death, poverty, loss) is a distraction from going deeper and listening to our Inner Self. Spirit does not want suffering for you. But the only way to be free from needless suffering is to surrender. You aren't surrendering *to* fear, you are surrendering *the* fear. Surrender to feeling the fear and then let it go.

The Ten of Swords asks that you turn around and face the fears coming from behind. The spilled blood could represent that a sacrifice is needed. Where would your blood, sweat, and tears be better spent? Certainly not on more anxiety. When you show up in life as a victim, you will be doomed to be victimized. This card asks you to sacrifice and surrender the parts of your identity linked to victimhood.

Although black clouds may have gathered, the light will return. Tell your fear, "I'm not running from you today." Give yourself five minutes to feel all the scary things fear is trying spook you with (illness, aloneness, poverty, loss, failure). Set a timer. When the alarm goes off, that's it. The fear doesn't get any more of your energy today; it's already taken five valuable minutes. Let go of amorphous fears and enjoy something about being alive *at this moment*. Focus on the colors around you. Witness something beautiful. Fear is like the dog who chases the car. When the car stops, the dog doesn't know what to do. Fear thrives when you ruminate. Switch mental gears. Reach out to a trusted loved one. Speak your fear aloud. Sometimes speaking the fear to someone who supports you is the first step toward truly letting it go. Take your fears out of the shadows and into the light. Sometimes bad things do happen, and we have no control over them. However, you do get to choose if you face your challenges with courage or run away only to become a victim. Running away from problems never works. Just look at the man on the card. If you can face your challenges, you can finally surrender them. Remember the gesture of blessing on this card. The darkest times are when Spirit will help you, making Itself known.

Ten of Swords Reversed

If the Ten of Swords appears reversed, the sunlight now appears at the top of the card. The clouds are parting, and light is returning once again. This card reminds you that the light will always return, no matter how many dark days you've experienced. There is a quality of resignation to this card. When it appears, life will no longer feel like a breathless sprint to avoid difficult inevitabilities. The storm has happened, and now it is time to assess where to go from here. Pick yourself up, dust yourself off, and stand tall once again. The Ten of Swords reversed symbolizes that you have accepted reality instead of rationalizing it away.

Challenges in life do not present themselves to destroy you, but rather to motivate you to grow beyond your current limitations. Look on challenges from a different perspective, with the wise eyes of Spirit. You will always see the way out of the maze when viewing it from high above.

When the Ten of Swords reversed appears, you're learning that the source of your anxiety is merely a puzzle to solve. Stop avoiding your growth by keeping busy. The Ten of Swords (upright or reversed) asks you to accept truth so that you can finally be released from feeling metaphorically chased. The light on this card symbolizes that sunlight is the best disinfectant. Raise your shadows into the light, and they will no longer haunt you.

PAGE OF SWORDS

Lowering unnecessary defenses.

The Page of Swords represents unnecessary defensiveness. These defenses guard a wounded area of the heart that needs healing. The Page of Swords guards himself from the feedback others give, which stunts his development. He often pretends that he is *fine*, and that it's *everyone else* who has the issue. If the Page of Swords could lower his unneeded defenses, he would experience a huge breakthrough. His openness would get him past the blockages he keeps experiencing. He would then ascend to the next level.

Do you ever get defensive? (If you rush to say "No!" then this card is for you!) Is it difficult to hear honest critical feedback from others? Is fear of people seeing your vulnerabilities causing you to shut down or detach?

The Page of Swords is often misunderstood and has been described as dishonest. However, this really isn't a fair assessment. He is not a "liar," because he has no awareness of his dishonesty. He is a poser. He is unable to assess himself accurately. His ego gets in the way. The Page of Swords is not a bad person. He is in denial about some difficult feelings. He also has more maturing to do.

Maturing?! He doesn't agree! He is *never* wrong. He is always the best at what he does. He's read the most books, won the most games, and has the most achievements. He is cleverer than the other Pages. He says, "They think *I* need to mature?! They're crazy! Look at how stupid they are. I'm smarter than them anyway!" Notice the haphazard flock of birds. They are not flying in a unified, cohesive formation. The Page of Swords does not work well with others, and this ensures disharmony in organizations. It does not bode well for cooperation in relationships either.

Look closely at the Page of Swords' position in the picture. He is guarding himself. The sword is raised to swing at any incomer. It is difficult to hug this Page. You just can't seem to get close. He is in a totally defensive position. Even the biting winds of his words warn you to keep distant. The cold winds upset the birds above and lash at the trees. All this defensiveness is a mask for hurt. A feeling of vulnerability that others will discover the Page of Swords doesn't feel 100 percent confident about what he is doing. If he could open himself to taking honest feedback and admit that he doesn't know everything, he would experience a huge breakthrough.

The Page of Swords represents the part of us that resists having vulnerabilities seen. He shows up in ourselves when we lash out in defense of our pride. He also appears in the form of other individuals in our day-to-day interactions who have no self-awareness. When the Page of Swords comes in the form of another person, he will often trigger your own inner Page-of-Swords reaction. This is why he can be *so* irritating when he appears in the behaviors of people at work or of family members you are struggling with. Don't get irritated or triggered when the Page of Swords appears. Thank him! For he is revealing the resistant part of *you* that needs to be more vulnerable and open in order to improve. Pages can represent the young-at-heart of any gender.

Page of Swords Reversed

If the Page of Swords appears reversed, he reminds you to be aware of how you are communicating with those around you. Bring resolution to conflicts with others through respectful communication. The Page of Swords is a master communicator. He can be witty and mercurial, and yet he also has been known to lash out with a sarcastic tongue. Your words are very powerful, and they can immediately transform the energy of your environment. Don't engage in speaking that depresses the energy around you. Use your voice in a manner that empowers yourself and others.

Also, watch the "temperature" of your communication today. Your words are like the winds. Are your words kind and warm like a summer breeze? Or are they biting and chilly? You can choose the voice you speak with. There are enough nasty things said, drifting over the airwaves and on the winds. Don't add to the pollution. Elevate the energy with positive words.

The Page of Swords (upright or reversed) appears when it's time to find the place within that feels most defensive. This is where a fear of vulnerability is residing. Openly facing this fear and being honest with yourself will make it possible to grow. It is so easy to detach, deny, and forget your vulnerabilities. If you are a smart person like the Page of Swords, you might have rationalized your best areas for growth away. Release the need to prove you are correct today. Don't insist on running to your own defense. If the feedback you are hearing isn't valid, then you'll know it. No need to react in an unseemly manner.

If the Page of Swords reversed represents another person, maintain an appropriate amount of distance. This individual may lash out at others and refuse to take responsibility for their own issues. Don't take this behavior personally. It's about them and not you.

KNIGHT OF SWORDS

Slow down.

The Knight of Swords is an ambitious man. He is always striving to prove that he is a successful adult. No matter how much he achieves, he can't seem to be happy or rest. The only thing he knows how to do is push ahead. Once he has completed his objective, he doesn't even know how to absorb it. With his red plume and cloak, he is already rushing ahead to the next task, driving himself mercilessly to win, hoping that someone will acknowledge his value through deeds.

Are you rushing through life? Do you stop to savor successes you've already achieved, or do you race ahead toward the next task? Do you feel guilty about resting when there's so much to do? Do you cram your day with so much activity that you feel drained and depressed?

The Knight of Swords reminds us that this is no way to go through life. In fact, this is downright harmful to your health. In this card's imagery, the horse represents our physical body. The horse is uneasy, anxious, tight, and trying to outrun his rider. The horse looks back at his master with an expression that says, "Seriously, you want me to run faster?!" The Knight brandishing the sword represents the cruel taskmaster within. That nasty voice that tells us to shut up and keep going, even when we feel we are going to drop.

Western culture glorifies suffering through work. When someone in America says you are a hard worker, that's almost as good as being one of the troops! "She worked until the day she died," is another one of our highest honors. But is your tombstone really going to be inscribed with all the hours you heroically put into your job? Is that really an authentic encapsulation of what you amount to? Why don't Americans allow themselves a siesta like other countries? Is it a sin to have more vacation time than one paltry week a year?

Today, you must take responsibility for your own health and wellness by scheduling relaxation. No one is going to say, "Boy, he needs a break, let's make him take one!" Working toward an achievement is marvelous, but as with everything, it needs balance. The Oracle at Delphi had a saying that guaranteed a satisfying life: "Nothing too much."[18] That includes work, activity, play, food, drinking … everything!

Slow down today. Turn off the phone and take a relaxing walk or sit in the yard for twenty minutes. Stop being a slave to clocks, demands, emails, texts, televisions, and social media updates. You aren't living a full life if you are constantly cracking the whip across your own back. Balance work with rest today, and your body will thank you.

The Knight of Swords can also represent another person who is rushing through life. He is often so fixated on his own goals and destinations that he does not care whom he is running over to succeed. He is not a bad person, but he can be very self-absorbed. Knights can represent youngish adults of

18. Pausanias, *Description of Greece*, 4:507.

any gender. Knights are usually people who are phasing out of one way of life and into another.

Knight of Swords Reversed

If the Knight of Swords appears reversed, he calls your attention to how you are managing increasing external demands in your life. The horse on the card is a symbol for your physical body while the Knight is the taskmaster within. The Knight of Swords reversed usually appears as a warning to slow down and replenish yourself. Stress is a fact of life. However, just because there is stress, that does not mean that you should be cruel to yourself while confronting it. The main critique of the Knight of Swords is that he is so focused on accomplishing his goal that he forgets to be present. When reversed, this can indicate that he is also unknowingly hurting himself in the process. Ask yourself, "How does my body feel while I am getting these tasks done? Have I been getting enough rest, nutrition and water? Is there a way I can be kinder to myself as I get all of this done? Is there a way I can make this stressful task more fun or enjoyable?"

The Knight of Swords reversed can also represent obsessive thinking. If you are noticing that you are exhibiting tunnel vision at this time, you may need to consciously choose to place your thoughts on something else for a while. Restore your personal balance and look around you. Take the time to appreciate something beautiful. Have your lunch in the park today. Consciously let go of your tasks for a moment and give yourself a break. The Knight of Swords reversed asks you to be your own best advocate and to realize that your mind and your body are on the same team. Each part of yourself needs to be kind to the other. Take a deep breath in and exhale all the tension and the stress. Slow down and allow yourself to feel at peace with certain areas of your life still being works in progress. Give yourself a little gift today to show your appreciation to your body and mind and all that they do for you each day. The present is where beauty and magic are happening. Restore yourself now, not later.

When the Knight of Swords reversed represents another person, he can be obsessive and compulsive. He may also inadvertently cause damage to his relationships by being thoughtless or selfish. He doesn't always think before he speaks. You will often have to be the bigger person with this individual.

QUEEN OF SWORDS

Personal authority.

The Queen of Swords symbolizes bringing order to chaos through clarity and boundaries. She is also an archetype that does not apologize for her right to have a place at the table. The Queen of Swords stands up to bullies and societal pressures. She questions the legitimacy of structures and rules that do not make logical sense. She keeps an eagle eye on maintaining her strength, integrity, and personal authority.

Are you uncomfortable with setting up boundaries with others because you might look mean? Is your career path in harmony with your Authentic Self? Is it difficult for you to stand up to the pressures of what others think you should be or do?

The Queen of Swords gets a lot of bad press. This is because she is not a docile, submissive, or objectified woman. She is too powerful to be minimized by mindless societal roles and conventions. She uses her sword to cut through the hypocrisy of others' assumptions concerning how she should act and what she should be. She knows that if she bows down to the demands of what others want her to be, she is selling herself short. She places strong boundaries because this is how people and organizations become healthy and grow. She is a master of transforming the energy from victimhood to being victorious (look at her butterfly crown). She commands respect because she respects herself first. The Queen's cloak is decorated with clouds. She protects herself with her mind. The head of the sylph on her throne represents that this Queen lives in a world of ideas. However, even she will eventually have to contend with the awareness that occurs below her neck. One solitary bird can be seen flying above the Queen. She often prefers to go it alone, and yet the frown on her face shows what prolonged isolation can do to her mood.

Even our modern society still seems to have problems with women exhibiting intellectual leadership. Early on, we are taught that women should be likable and selfless rather than strong, powerful, or ambitious. Women who embody the energy of the Queen of Swords are sometimes ostracized, despised, and ridiculed for no other reason than, "I just think she's a bitch." No wonder this Queen isolates herself! However, some of the best rulers history ever produced were strong women like Queen Hatshepsut of Egypt, Queen Elizabeth I of England, and Empress Catherine the Great of Russia.

Whether you are male or female, the Queen of Swords appears to reacquaint you with your personal authority, strength, and power. You may also need to be more self-disciplined or create some much-needed boundaries. Don't worry about being *liked* as much as being honest with yourself. Speak up and solve present issues and problems. You are strong and capable.

Do not apologize for your strength, power, or Authentic Self. Own it.

The Queen of Swords can also represent a person who is direct, capable, and extremely intelligent. She may not exude the softer qualities of the other Queens. However, if she is offering you practical counsel, listen to her. Queens can be mature individuals of any gender who wield strong feminine power.

Queen of Swords Reversed

If the Queen of Swords appears reversed, she warns you to not become too isolated from others. There is a remote quality to the Queen of Swords reversed. She would rather do everything by herself. Boundaries and self-respect are important, but equally important is allowing for vulnerability and connection. The Queen of Swords reversed sees herself as a loner. Like the Page of Swords, she keeps herself isolated with a sharp tongue, and her appearance warns against speaking harshly or without tact.

Even the most powerful people do not ascend to great heights all by themselves. The Queen of Swords reversed reminds us that we need other people. Success is much easier when collaboration is happening. Use your voice to speak up for yourself, but with respectfulness. Also use your words to open more to life around you. It's time to reconnect again.

Be mindful of the dignity of every human being. Speak with your best voice today. Use your powerful words to encourage others, create healthy boundaries, and bring clarity to miscommunications. Avoid using your voice as a weapon to inject toxicity into personal relationships. Show your fearlessness with an open heart.

When the Queen of Swords reversed represents another person, she could be a loner or appear to have a chip on her shoulder. She may also bark orders or seem combative. This is usually a mask for a deep insecurity. Don't get into a war of words with this individual. Silence is golden.

KING OF SWORDS

Challenge your assumptions.

The King of Swords appears to be a stern man. In fact, for many, he is the archetype of *the* Man (the societal structures that unconsciously direct us to assume our place). The King of Swords asks us to examine how we might be limiting ourselves based on our own assumptions. The King is concerned with hierarchy, balance, and structure. Even the two birds in the distance fly with one clearly being on top.

Are you unconsciously allowing old, fixed views to color your perception of yourself or others? Do you feel like you are limited or can't get ahead because you're a woman, a minority, gay, poor, or disabled, or do you just feel like the deck is stacked against you? Do you look at others who are different than you with assumptions before you really get to know them?

All of us are raised in a world of assumptions. As children, we are unconsciously presented with attitudes of racism, sexism, and phobias that color our eventual view of the world. People fear what they don't understand. People also find it uncomfortable to question a conclusion they arrived at long ago. When the King of Swords appears, he places you in contact with your own assumptions. Every now and then, we need to challenge our assumptions in order to grow. Sometimes the assumptions that need to be released are narratives that you have unconsciously absorbed from external society about how far you can go and how much you can achieve.

The King of Swords is not an evil king. His real interest is preserving the security of "the System." He argues that established precedent is far better than change. Sometimes the King of Swords symbolizes a difficulty with changing your mind about something that seems settled. Although the King looks fixed, look closer. There are butterflies covering his throne. This represents that systems can be changed, assumptions can be transformed, and old divisions can be healed through *understanding*. The King of Swords can change his mind! Here's the biggest secret: the King of Swords is part of us. The part that needs to lose its rigidity.

What part of you feels rigid? Are you dismissing whole groups of people simply because they have a different viewpoint, politics, ethnicity, or other social identifier? What calcified attitudes in the world would you like to see changed? Are you encountering these traits in someone else around you?

In order to change fixed attitudes, you must understand them. The King of Swords represents understanding things more acutely so that you can make reasoned arguments and arrive at conclusions that are evidence-based. The King of Swords is at his best when he applies critical thinking and logical arguments. Sometimes the King of Swords appears in the form of a loved one who challenges your viewpoints and assumptions. They may say the craziest things and may be incorrect with the facts, but they do serve in making you question your own conclusions.

You will never win a full-on battle with the King of Swords. He's heavily entrenched and armored. He can be a fixed personality, or he may represent an institution or organization that is set in its ways. When the King of Swords appears, win him over with clarity, evidence, and reason. This King *can* change his mind, but only if it makes logical sense to do so. The King of Swords can represent a rigid authority figure who is slow to change. Kings can be mature people of any gender who are leaders or figures of authority.

King of Swords Reversed

If the King of Swords appears reversed, he is offering you knowledge to overcome something that is keeping you stuck. Many times, we remain entrenched in something that is not working because we lack more information about what is truly possible. The King of Swords reversed may be calling your attention to fixed attitudes or opinions that need questioning. The butterflies on his throne now appear at the base of the card. This signifies that you have begun the process of discarding outdated, self-limiting thinking.

The King of Swords reversed is challenging you to resist reverting to fixed assumptions about yourself or your possibilities without questioning them. Reach out and open yourself to perspectives that may not be aligned with your comfort zone. Walk in another's shoes for a day. Look at challenging issues with another's perspective instead of dismissing them outright. Instead of avoiding what you don't understand, dive in and learn more! Engage in reasoned, dispassionate debate. Arm yourself with knowledge. The ancient Greek philosopher Socrates once said, "The unexamined life is not worth living."[19] We must all occasionally question our beliefs, especially about other people, in order to attain wisdom. When this card appears reversed, it indicates once-fixed perspectives are shifting. New possibilities are opening. Allow yourself to be flexible enough to invite an evolution to your own perspective.

If the King of Swords reversed represents another person, he may represent someone who questions *everything*. This may be a bit annoying to be around because everything that is accepted as reality is challenged by him. He may also represent someone who believes conspiracy theories or can even come across as impractical or paranoid. The King of Swords reversed may also appear dogmatic or off-balance.

19. Plato, *The Apology*, 133.

THE SUIT OF CUPS

Your feelings and emotions.

The Cups suit represents the realm of feelings and emotions. Feelings and emotions color how you experience reality. Feelings are fuel for whatever it is you are focusing on. In a reading, Cup cards can highlight strong feelings you are harboring and what is coloring your perception from within. Cups will always show how you are *feeling*, not necessarily what is really *happening*. Each of the Court cards in the Cups suit reveals a sensitive figure.

Cup cards in a reading will also represent your most important relationships. When these cards appear, they can describe the different people in your life who illicit strong emotions in you. Sometimes Cup cards show how you are interacting with others or how others are perceiving you. Their position in a spread can often bring clarity to the emotional sphere of your life. When Cups appear, they ask you to look deeper beneath the surface to discover what feelings might be affecting your current concern.

Cup cards always ask you to examine what emotions are influencing your perspective from within. Cups represent the basic human need to relate, to connect, and to feel loved. Although Cups can signify relationships, friendships, and significant others, they can also highlight the emotions of individuals around you. Cups also describe the vibe you are giving off or that is permeating your environment. Cup cards bring information regarding your feelings to the surface so that you can understand them and channel them accordingly.

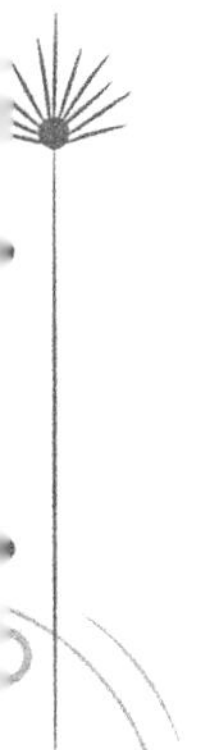

ACE OF CUPS

Renewal.

The Ace of Cups represents love, renewal, and rebirth. This card reminds you that love surrounds you from all directions. North, south, east, west, ahead of you, behind you, within, without, in what you can perceive, and in mysteries too vast to comprehend. If you are looking for inner peace, then love is what you need to reconnect with. All religions talk about this love. Love is everywhere, and yet sometimes it's so tricky to perceive. All the poets, artists, and singers try to capture it. Love permeates everything, and yet sometimes we can't see the forest for the trees.

When is the last time you gave yourself over to feeling overwhelming love? Has your cup felt like it's dry or empty? Were you taught that true love only exists after you find the right person, blinding you to love's true immensity?

A heavenly dove flies down from above, bringing a message of peace and hope. The dove has been associated with love and the realm of Spirit in countless traditions. To the ancient Greeks, the dove was a symbol of Aphrodite, the Goddess of love and beauty. For the Christians, it embodies God's messenger, the Holy Spirit. The dove represents the realm of the spiritual and the supernatural. An angelic hand offers the large cup overflowing with divine love. The water streams into a pond of lotus flowers, which are symbols for enlightenment. Love "en-lightens." This means it lightens our burdens from within. The *W* on the cup could symbolize the cardinal direction west. The west is the realm of the element of Water. It is also the direction the sun sets in. This reminds you that every sorrowful ending is always followed by a joyful new beginning.

The dove carries the equal-armed cross, a symbol of the four cardinal directions: north, south, east, and west. This reminds us that love is everywhere. It's in every culture, every country, and every place that you can imagine. The equal-armed cross links the dove to the High Priestess. The cross also creates an *X*. Every child knows that *X* marks the spot for hidden treasure. The treasure in this case is your center, your Spirit, and your unique essence. A divine cup of unconditional love is always being offered to you, even if you feel so overcome with troubles that it's hard to perceive.

All aces in the tarot symbolize new beginnings. In this case, the Ace of Cups is appearing to encourage you to renew your love for yourself and your experiences. If you find yourself unhappy with the current conditions you are experiencing, it could be because you forgot to let love be the answer. It's time to open yourself to love. You absolutely deserve it. Love, peace, and joy are your natural states. They're in your core and at your center. You can return to this center, especially during sorrows and difficulties. Love is the voice within that gives you the reassurance that everything will be fine, because *you* are forever, not this particular situation. Try addressing your current problems by releasing them to love. Transcend your tightness and resistance. Watch how easily tension resolves when you smile at your challenges and love yourself enough to know that you will prevail through transcendence. This release of tension occurs because you are no longer fighting against your true nature.

Turn to love as the solution, and watch miracles begin to happen.

Ace of Cups Reversed

If the Ace of Cups appears reversed, it reminds you that the energy you pour into what brings you joy is never wasted energy. You would think that a cup turned upside down would lead to emptiness, but this image turned on its head is still refilling the pond. The cup pours its waters toward the dove, a universal symbol for Spirit. Your energy (symbolized by the water) that is spent on the pursuits of your Spirit (the dove) replenishes you (the pond) and is never wasted.

When reversed, the *W* on the card becomes an *M*. Many languages across the globe start their word for "mother" with the letter *M*. The Mother is the ultimate archetype of nurturing. Perhaps you are being reminded to lovingly nurture yourself to replenish the source of your energy.

If you feel depleted and need to feel a burst of renewed energy, then it is time to nurture your Spirit. Pour your energy into what you love and what truly brings you joy. Stop depriving yourself of enjoying the moment by allowing how busy you are to be your excuse. Do something you enjoy today… more still, do something that feeds your Spirit. Do you need to reread that special book that reminds you of magic? Maybe it's time to immerse yourself in that favorite subject that you love to get lost in. Perhaps it's time to reconnect with nature. Allow yourself to dive into activities for no other reason than that you enjoy them. If the Ace of Cups reversed symbolizes a relationship, it indicates that you must replenish and love yourself first before you can give to another.

TWO OF CUPS

Relationships and communication.

The Two of Cups symbolizes harmonious partnerships that are meant to be. These relationships can be based on love (as is the case with the couple pictured here); however, they can also be platonic partnerships based on mutual interests or goals. The message of this card is to create harmony in your most important relationships through positive and honest communication.

Who is the "other" in your most important current relationship? Do you let this person know how much they matter to you? Do you need to get out of your own head and see another's perspective to restore harmony?

The Two of Cups pictures a loving couple. The woman is crowned with a wreath, reminding us of the World card and the completion of her old life. The man is crowned with flowers, reminding us of the Strength card. He now has the self-discipline and inner strength to open his heart to another. The couple is separated by the staff of Hermes, the Greek messenger God of communication. Topping the staff of Hermes is a giant lion's head with wings. This represents that each person in the relationship will have their own sense of pride. They are very different, and yet it is important that each feels their differences are honored, not disparaged. The lion head can quickly override the relationship if the ego is damaged by either party. A wounded ego can severely damage a once loving partnership. The only way to ensure harmony is for both parties to communicate (the staff of Hermes) in a manner that makes each feel equally important and valuable, leaving their personal dignity intact.

The Two of Cups asks you to see the other person's point of view and to communicate in a manner that gives everyone the ability to walk away with their dignity affirmed. This goes for personal relationships, business partnerships, friendships, and familial relationships. The message of the card is that no one gets to where they are all by themself. We need cooperation to survive in this world.

When the Two of Cups appears, it is time to reaffirm and reconnect with the people who make up your most important relationships. The card also ensures success through collaboration. Do some relationship maintenance. Let another know how you feel to get an issue resolved. See another's perspective. Resolve differences with honest, kind, and open communication. The Two of Cups reminds you that you can't do everything alone. It also advises you to validate the people you care about most.

People you love need to know that they matter. Don't assume that they already know. Give a thoughtful gift or send a loving message. See the divine light in their eyes and recognize how much richer they make your life. Communicate in a way that restores harmony.

Two of Cups Reversed

If the Two of Cups appears reversed, it highlights miscommunications in relationships. It also asks you to take responsibility for your part in intensifying or deescalating conflict. The large lion head on the card represents ego. Many of the miseries we experience in our relationships are rooted in pride. Sometimes this card can indicate you are experiencing the ego of another. When encountering wounded egos, it is important not to activate your own ego in response. This has the same result as throwing gasoline on an already raging fire. The Two of Cups reversed asks you to talk less and listen more. Be open and curious about what others have to say.

This card is also the harbinger of resolution to misunderstandings and miscommunications with others. The most important thing to convey is openness, love, and understanding.

Let go of your pride, your need to be right, and your need for the last word. Stop wasting energy on pettiness or conflicts. Do your part to bring light and healing to the world. There is no need to exacerbate already raging conflicts. Send love to those who've hurt you and be okay with peacefully walking away from those who are not receptive to resolution at this time. Send them love from a distance. The Two of Cups represents the old saying that you can lead the horse to water, but you can't make it drink. Raise your personal standards of what a healthy relationship constitutes for you. Accept only the best for yourself and be selective about whom you trust. Air out old issues and finally let them go. This will free you from a wounded ego. Rise above all the traps set by your ego or the ego of another. Reestablish harmony by surrendering pride.

THREE OF CUPS

Personal charisma.

The Three of Cups portrays the famous Three Graces from Greek mythology. The Graces are Goddesses of charisma. It was said that wherever they walked, flowers sprang up and joy and laughter abounded. The Graces (also called Charities) each stood for attributes you can embrace to elevate your personal energy, transforming it from depressive to jubilant. We get our word "charisma" from the three Charities. Charisma is that magical energy that makes others like you. Charisma is a gift all of us can develop. Anyone can increase their personal charisma by embracing their authenticity, lightening up, and bringing positive energy to others.

Does the energy in your environment feel bogged down? Do you feel too distracted by stress to even think about lightening up? Did you know that you can lighten up your environment by embracing your own charismatic energy?

The Three of Cups depicts the three Graces in their unique colors: red, white, and gold. The names of the Graces are Euphrosyne, Aglaea, and Thalia.

The central figure is Euphrosyne, who is wearing a red robe. Her name means "to delight, cheer, and gladden." Essentially, the Three of Cups represents joy, happiness, and celebrations. Euphrosyne shows that our environment becomes more vibrant when we embrace our humor. Anytime we make someone's day better with a smile or lift the energy with laughter, we are channeling her gift. Euphrosyne's message is to "lighten up!" Use humor to diffuse what you are afraid of. Laughing at what brings you anxiety is a useful tool for overcoming it. Red is the color of courage, vitality, and passion.

On the left is Aglaea wearing her white robe. Her name means "radiance, bright splendor, and light." Every time you share your inner radiance, you are embracing her gift. When you are embracing your inner light, you create a palpable positive force of energy around you that others will immediately perceive. Being relaxed in who you really are causes others to feel safe enough to be open with you. When you look into another's eyes and see that their inner light is also sacred and radiant, you are touching Aglaea's gift. White is the color of purity, truth, and Spirit.

Thalia is on the right wearing her golden robe. Her name means "to warm, to foster, and to bloom." Her gifts of an abundant, fruitful harvest surround the three sisters. Each time you patiently nurture something (yourself, a talent, a dream, a child), you are embodying Thalia's energy. Tending to your hopes and wishes makes life meaningful. Thalia brings success through the gentle tending of your goals. She also teaches that helping others with the things you struggle with is the quickest way to boost your own feelings of self-esteem. Gold is the color of success, wealth, and the warmth of the sun.

Everyone can elevate their personal charisma. Like any skill, the more you use it, the more natural it will become. Charisma raises energy. It also makes it much easier for you to get ahead in life. Sometimes we are taught that if we don't fight, we won't get what we want. This sets you up for a combative existence. It is so much easier to get through life if you tap into the gifts of the

Graces. People love to help likable people! Charisma elevates the energy of any room as if by magic. That is why talented people exuding tons of personal charisma get top dollar. We want them to raise our energy and bring us the same joy through music, words, and entertainment.

Today, tap into your personal charisma through humor, radiating your authentic light, and offering warmth and kindness to others. Watch your environment immediately improve with the gifts of the Graces. You'll be amazed at how much easier life will feel if you bring positivity to this situation. The Three of Cups always symbolizes joy.

Three of Cups Reversed

If the Three of Cups appears reversed, it indicates that you may be too distracted by other matters to remember the joy that is all around you. When we get preoccupied with duties, worries, preparations, and stresses, we forget that our sense of joy can be accessed at any time. It's as easy as listening to your favorite song, eating your favorite treat, delving into a great book, or accessing your creativity. Don't put off your joy for another day. Today is the day for your Spirit to sing.

The Three of Cups (upright or reversed) reminds you that you can elevate your energy no matter where you are or what is happening. Forgetting your joy is often easier than remembering it. There are many excuses to not allow yourself to feel good. There are still a million things to do, negativity in the world, and many wounds from the past. However, this card reminds you that joy is something that must be consciously chosen. Today, it's time to switch mental gears and allow joy to prevail.

Joseph Campbell used to say, "Find a place where there's joy, and the joy will burn out the pain."[20] Don't let another minute go by today in which you aren't tapping into the gifts of the Graces. Neutralize negativity by turning it into laughter. Tend to your brightest hopes, goals, and dreams. See the luminous radiance in your own reflection and twinkling in the eyes of those around you. Use your personal charisma to elevate your interactions with others. You can truly be happier whenever you make the decision to be. Don't forget your joy!

20. Osbon, *A Joseph Campbell Companion*, 152.

FOUR OF CUPS

Seeing and accepting blessings.

The Four of Cups reminds you to see all the good things being offered to you in the present. Thinking too far ahead or dwelling on things long past can rob you of *now*. The present is where life is happening! This current moment is also loaded with abundance, blessings, and positive energy. Are you open to receiving them? The Four of Cups asks you to start seeing the current gifts being offered to you.

Are you worrying about the future? Are you shutting down with a numb heart because of something that happened in the past? Is something distracting you from seeing the multitudes of miracles and blessings present in your life?

The Four of Cups shows a sulking man sitting under a tree. He is fixated on three earthbound cups. These could represent his worldly acquisitions (money, reputation, and image). He is not acknowledging a miracle right behind him! An angelic hand is reaching out of a cloud and is offering him a divine gift. The only other cards we see this angelic hand appear on are the Aces. A new beginning is being offered, and the man cannot receive it. Not only is he not open to accepting (his arms are in a crossed, closed position), he is unable to see it.

Western culture tells us to be constantly worried. Even when we aren't running around at our jobs, our minds are still running. Constantly planning. Avoiding pitfalls. Constantly pushing to be better. Endlessly striving. This is just fear in disguise. Fear of being hurt by something. Fear of being caught unaware. Fear of the past repeating itself. Fear of rejection. Fear of loss. Fear, fear, and more fear! Have you ever heard the saying that fear robs you of the joy of the present? Well, it does! And the more you engage in it, the more blind you get to the good things in life.

The man on the card isn't happy. If the golden cups represent gifts, then he already has three, and there is another on the way. He is not open to receiving because he has emotionally closed down. Look at his posture. His arms are crossed, as are his legs. Much like with the figure on the Four of Pentacles, he is blocking his heart. Some major pain from the past must have happened to him. His whole present is focused on how to prevent that hurt from happening again. As a result, he has closed access to his heart and his ability to receive. He is lost in projections that aren't there. All he needs to do is look around him. Think how ecstatic he would be if he only noticed the gift being delivered especially for him from above!

The Four of Cups urges you to accept, receive, and open yourself to the good things being offered *at this moment*. If someone tries to do something nice for you, say, "Thank you so much," not "No, no, you don't have to do that." Look around you right now. Do you see the colors surrounding you? Do you hear the sounds? Do you see light everywhere? Take a deep breath and let it all in. What is wonderful about your life *right now*?

Open yourself to all the good that is occurring. If you shift your focus to blessings, more will come.

Four of Cups Reversed

If the Four of Cups appears reversed, it requires you to snap out of the illusion that you are alone. If you've been doing everything by yourself or habitually refusing help when it's offered (or not asking for it), you may find yourself shutting down emotionally. The feeling of being completely isolated and not understood by anyone is an illusion. The truth is that you can feel connected anytime you choose. However, you must allow yourself to be more vulnerable.

When you emotionally shut down to the good things being offered, it's usually because of fear. This fear can quickly rob you of energy, joy, and new blessings trying to find their way to you. When the Four of Cups appears reversed, it asks you if you've made a habit of going it alone. It may be time to take down the walls you've built around your heart and allow others in again. Maybe it's time to invite a friend to dinner, throw a party, or accept a kindness when it's offered. The meaning of this card might be as simple as saying thank you when someone does or says something nice instead of keeping others at arm's length. Nature is based on laws of giving and receiving. If you only participate in one, imbalance will most assuredly occur. Today, don't let your fears keep you from connecting and accepting.

FIVE OF CUPS

The trance of negative thinking.

The Five of Cups symbolizes the trancelike state of focusing only on the negative, even when all is not lost. The figure on the card gloomily stares at three spilled cups. He fails to notice the two perfectly upright cups still standing behind him. Behind the two standing cups is a bridge. This bridge symbolizes that the way over your obstacle will be made clear when you focus on what is working and what is positive in your life. This card also reveals that just because everything in your life isn't *perfect*, that doesn't mean you need to feel bad about it all day, month, year, or decade!

Does your mind ever feel hypnotized with problems? Is it difficult to see all the blessings you currently have because you can't stop focusing on your losses? Does ruminating rob you of countless hours in your day?

If you've ever experienced this sort of hypnotism, you know it seems very difficult to snap out of. It usually occurs when the mind is idle. "An idle mind is the Devil's workshop," or so the saying goes. If you are traditionally a problem solver, it can be difficult to be at peace when there is no task to do. The mind immediately shuffles through its memory banks to drudge up something that you should have anxiety about. Then the mind says, "Here's a doozy! Remember this horrible time? What if it happens again?" Then the trance begins, and soon twenty minutes have gone by, leaving you feeling hopeless about yourself and your prospects.

Look at the image of the spilled cups. It appears they contained wine. However, there is another spill, pictured in the foreground, of pure water. This is a symbol for an emotional disappointment that may have occurred in the past but is having real-world implications or setbacks in the present. If the expectation is that something will fail, the likelihood of its failure exponentially becomes more likely. The Five of Cups encapsulates the effect of our emotional state on our future opportunities and prospects. When this card appears, it's time to snap out of negative, emotional rumination.

A nice strategy for shifting focus from negative thoughts is to remember the details of your favorite place. This may be a park you visit or a particularly beautiful place you traveled to. What is your happiest memory of a place? Close your eyes and remember the details. The sounds, sights, smells, and sensations of being there. When the anxiety interjects, just keep seeking the details of the place. Details are key.

I think of a river I used to visit. I remember how the sound of her rushing waves took my anxieties with them. I remember the beautiful light that sparkled over her surface like a thousand diamonds. I remember the feel of the large, cool rock I sat on. I recall the majestic blue herons that flew overhead and the deer that came to drink the clear waters at dusk. I remember feeling completely relaxed and at peace. These were my calmest days of youthful summer.

There! I snapped out of the negative trance! Now quickly, give me something constructive to focus on! Perhaps all the goals and dreams that are still possible for me. Snapping out of negative trances gives you the opportunity to do something constructive about your future.

Shift your focus to break trances when they start. The more positive details you can remember, the better you'll feel. Ruminating doesn't help anyone solve anything, so knock it off! It is such a time waster! Place your focus on something that makes you happy or restores your faith in yourself.

You still deserve to enjoy goodness in life, even when *everything* isn't perfect.

Five of Cups Reversed

If the Five of Cups appears reversed, it represents making the choice to view setbacks as hidden opportunities. In life, there will be challenges thrown your way that you didn't ask for or deserve. When we don't get what we want, we often view the situation as negative. The Five of Cups reversed symbolizes an opportunity to dig deeper than a challenge's outward appearance. Always with this card, you must shift your perspective to the cups *still standing* in order to cross the bridge.

Don't allow yourself to feel defeated. Ask yourself, "What is this challenge teaching me?" Also ask, "How is this difficulty teaching me to become a better version of myself?"

The situation that life is presenting you with is neither positive nor negative. These perceptions of "good" or "bad" luck are blocking you from the purpose of your current lesson. Choose to see how these challenges are directing you to a stronger, more empowered version of yourself. Open your eyes to the strength of character you forgot you possessed. If you continually look at life in an aggrieved manner, your personal power will continue to elude you. Growth happens in the place where challenges occur. Being surprised that life is not going according to your best-laid plans is like being shocked that the weather is not behaving as forecasted. Setbacks appear when there is a better way forward that you are not aware of yet. Don't get mad, scared, or depressed. Get powerful. Focus on what gifts remain on the pathway to success. Negativity halts momentum. The Universe is not depriving you. It is redirecting you to a better version of yourself.

SIX OF CUPS

The past.

The Six of Cups represents looking back at what made you happy in the past. Many people look at their past and fixate on the difficult moments worthy of therapy sessions. However, if you look at your past in its totality, you will realize that along with difficulties, there were times when you were joyful and optimistic about the future. The past holds important clues as to what will bring you fulfillment in the future. If you've felt happy before, you can feel happy again.

Who were you at your happiest? Has the pursuit of security taken over your life, causing you to forget your joy? Is it easier to remember the bad things that happened in the past rather than the good?

The imagery of this card depicts a little girl's happy memory. The girl is receiving a gift of flowers. Flowers and gardens are her bliss! There are so many joyful feelings that flowers conjure up for her. In the future, she wants to have a house, garden, and courtyard, just like this! The flowers are shaped like stars. This ties the imagery of this card to the Star card and represents the renewal of hope. In this case, hope is renewed by finding the eternal elements of your bliss within your memory. The little girl feels completely safe in her secure courtyard. A guard is posted in the background to ensure that she can play in the gardens without a care in the world. To emphasize her protection, a large shield is emblazoned on the walkway rail. The *X* on the shield marks the spot for where her joy can be found. Your joy can be found where you last left it, too. The little girl has more than her basic needs met. She is free to be creative, laugh, and grow in safety and security. The flowers emerging from the cups symbolize that all is thriving happily. She looks at life with the complete confidence and optimism that her future could contain moments just as happy as this one.

When your basic needs are met (food, shelter, safety, security), you can thrive. You can begin to develop self-esteem and place your attention on the goals and dreams that you wished for as a younger person. As an adult, your chief responsibility is to see that you have your basic needs in place. This ensures you can focus on what brings you fulfillment and happiness.

The problem for many adults is that they forget to return to their bliss once their basic needs have been established. Adults can never seem to make enough money to feel safe. They can never tear away from work long enough to enjoy the afternoon. People get so caught in the routine of securing basic needs that it overtakes every waking moment. Even if the needs are met, people are programmed to keep securing more. They end up identifying more with the guard illustrated on the card and forget the child within. Pretty soon they can't even remember their hopes and wishes, which leads to their abandonment.

The Six of Cups asks you to remember what brought you bliss. What brought you happiness way back when? This will remind you of who you really are and what life pursuits will bring you fulfillment in the future.

If you've gotten your basic needs for safety and security established, it is important to return to the forgotten parts of yourself. Your dreams and wishes can still come true, but first you must *remember* them. Look back at the happier times in your life for clues as to what you want in your future. If you can remember the feeling of being happy, you can most assuredly have it again.

Six of Cups Reversed

If the Six of Cups appears reversed, it calls your attention to difficult memories that are causing you to forget the hope found in the present. The past is powerful. Looking back on it can conjure feelings, some good and some bad. The important thing to remember is that each day is new. Old hurts are not guaranteed to transpire just as they did before—unless you are replaying them in your head and not letting go.

Today, do a symbolic ritual to let go of past burdens that are disrupting your focus in the present. Take out a piece of paper and write out three things from your past that you fear may happen again. Find a large firesafe container and set the list aflame. As the paper burns, watch how quickly the past can be released. Take the extinguished ashes outside and scatter them to the winds. Those ashes are just like your thoughts. You can release them. You don't want to keep those messy ashes in your house, so why tolerate them in your head? The past only repeats itself in our minds. Every day you can choose a totally new approach. New opportunities surround you, but you must be grounded *in the present* to take full advantage of them. Today is where life's magic is happening. Let go of hurt or fear from the past. Redirect your awareness to the powerful person you are now.

SEVEN OF CUPS

Dreams and illusions.

The Seven of Cups represents dreams, illusions, and wishes. It is imaginative and fantastical. However, it is not a card of realities. Some people waste years stuck on the lessons of this card. "If I win the lottery, think of everything I am going to buy!" "One day I'll get lucky when my ship comes in, and my problems will be solved." "I hope someone famous will notice my talents and I'll be successful!" Many times, this sort of thinking is an avoidance mechanism for taking responsibility for your life and its trajectory. The Seven of Cups is also a card of forgetfulness. It dazzles us with its "castles in the air," causing us to ignore the present reality.

What crutches do you use to evade reality? Does fear of failure, disappointing others, or looking like a loser keep you from making necessary life changes? Do you lack enough confidence in yourself to get the ball rolling?

The figure emerging from the central cup is shrouded. Her arms are open to all possibilities. The shroud over her head cuts her off from the external world and its distractions so that she opens herself to the creative genius within. However, this figure is not controlling things. She is open to whichever wind blows. This is not always a good recipe for getting something accomplished. There is another cup with a wreath of victory emerging from it. If you look closely, it appears that there is a skull pictured on this cup (a symbol for irreversible change). This could represent a fear of success, since achieving your goal would change all your existing structures. All the cups have different symbols emerging from them. Some are fantastical, while others are frightening. They are the bright and shiny objects that can distract you on the path toward your goal. The Seven of Cups requires you to focus, to bring your inner visions into the outer world.

It's okay to wish and hope for a better future, *if* you are doing the work. Wishing to lose weight but still consuming four thousand calories a day without moving isn't going to get you to your goal. By setting daily attainable goals for yourself, you can build and reinforce your self-esteem.

Theodore Roosevelt had a famous code he lived by: "Get action!" By initiating action (putting out the resumes, meeting with experts, taking risks, reaching out, asking questions, learning a new skill), a magical thing starts to happen: Momentum begins. Things start to fall in place. Hope is rekindled about the future. Your dreams begin to manifest. Soon the reality you are living is better than an empty fantasy. This is because you are no longer passively waiting for life to hopefully hand you your dreams. You are going out and making them a reality.

When the Seven of Cups appears, dream big! Then get to the work of manifesting it. Think about one major life goal you have. What practical steps can you take right now to achieve that goal? Be courageous and don't let old avoidance mechanisms prevail. Instead of hoping, wishing, and waiting for what you want, go out and get it!

Seven of Cups Reversed

If the Seven of Cups appears reversed, it indicates that you are awakening from a period of sleepwalking through life. Your consciousness is shifting from being on autopilot to becoming alert, empowered, and clear about what you want. What goals do you still have? What dreams have yet to become reality? If each day feels like you are mindlessly drifting to the next without a trace of vitality, then something is wrong. You may be sleepwalking through life. Get out of your head and into your body. Wake up! Exercise. Spend time outdoors. Stop avoiding what needs to be done. You still have the power to make your dream happen! However, you can't attain your goals if you are sleepwalking through life. Today, shift the energy. Write checklists. Be brave and reach out to those who are in the know.

The Seven of Cups reversed always gives you a wake-up call. You can have your cake and eat it, too! However, you must first get out of bed, find the recipe for your cake, get the ingredients, combine them with loving precision, and be patient while the cake bakes. The Seven of Cups reversed indicates that you need to be more *awake* for success to manifest.

EIGHT OF CUPS

Seeking your Authentic Self.

The Eight of Cups represents taking the journey within to the realm of your authentic feelings. Periodically, you must go deep within yourself to hear your Spirit and reclaim strengths and abilities you forgot you possessed. Although the journey inward is of great value, it rarely feels easy to initiate. It is often accompanied by a period of depression, feeling crazy, or the sense that you've hit a patch of bad luck. The Eight of Cups reminds you that you've probably made a similar journey before, just prior to a deeper revelation about yourself. Your instincts will, once again, be your best guide.

When you are quiet, do you hear the call of your Authentic Self? Do you periodically go through periods of confusion, depression, or unexplained bad luck? How has your life improved in the past as a result of listening to your heart?

The man depicted on the Eight of Cups is reminiscent of the Hermit. He is taking a journey alone, staff in hand, returning to the realm of water, caves, and grottos. He is walking toward the sea, representing the pull of his deep unconscious feelings. These feelings were not acknowledged in his daily life and were acting up in strange ways. At first he thought he was crazy, then just unlucky. Finally, he realized his authentic feelings were not being respected or acknowledged. He wasn't being true to himself. This was the cause of his unease.

The moon is eclipsing the sun and is observing the man's journey. Our Inner Self observes our choices in the same way. Thoughts about what the man should do, or *be*, to gain the acceptance of others in his daily life (the sun), are now being eclipsed by his instinctual self (the moon). At long last, he has the courage to go within and reconnect with his real feelings. His authentic feelings are now his best friends, giving him the depth and wisdom to persevere.

The moon has been associated with instincts since the dawn of humanity. It elusively pulls at our awareness, and yet it is easy to dismiss and ignore (just like our instincts). The Latin word for moon is *luna*, which we get our word "lunatic" from. If your instincts are chronically ignored, they can make you feel crazy. Like a neglected child, unheard emotions will act up if they are habitually ignored. This often manifests as periods of bad luck, sadness, imagined illnesses, or times when you feel utterly lost and powerless. Returning within will help you reclaim your Authentic Self and arm you with the ability to set everything right again. This journey can only happen alone and in the dark places. The darkness is where the potential for healing happens.

The Eight of Cups appears to remind you to let your instincts guide your path. The very fact that you are reading a tarot book demonstrates that you have the courage to listen to these unconscious feelings. The unconscious speaks in the language of pictures, myths, and symbols. Instincts do not adhere to the laws of a logical or rationalized world. Your deeper instincts can feel messy at times and very confusing if you aren't used to acknowledging them. And yet, they must be acknowledged if you are to find your way through the barriers that thwart your progress (symbolized by the craggy rocks on the card).

The Eight of Cups depicts an image of deep healing. If you listen to your instincts, they will give you the power to overcome previous blockages. You can then return to the land of the sun with profound insight, less burdened and free.

Eight of Cups Reversed

If the Eight of Cups appears reversed, it calls you back to nature... *your* nature. You may have forgotten how to decipher the message being whispered to you through the rustle of leaves. The Eight of Cups highlights the inevitable feeling of hollowness that accompanies immersion in the artificial. All that glitters may not be gold. Sometimes the lessons of this card are revealed in a person or position you may be placing on a pedestal at the expense of yourself. Admiration is one thing, but believing you are "less than" because you haven't impressed this person or that is just another way to hurt yourself.

The Eight of Cups reversed puts you into contact with the mental barriers you erect to tune out your deeper feelings. Sometimes this card can even highlight being in a state of denial. Have you been distracting yourself from the deeper call within? Plasticity will no longer cut it.

Your Authentic Self is calling you back. It cannot be found in the external world of ego, position, image, or validation from others. This card often appears when things seem to be off and may be accompanied by melancholy or even depression. When these feelings set in, it's usually a sign that some deeper part of you is not feeling heard. When your depth is neglected, it acts up, just like a child.

Take some personal time to seek quiet. Bravely turn your attention inward to any place within your heart that feels empty, insecure, or unfulfilled. Self-investment will fill this empty place, not the attainment of something "out there."

Take a deep breath into your center and breathe out all the shallows that don't really matter to your heart. Gently turn your awareness inward and ask your Spirit what it really needs right now. It is the core part of you that has been on your side, rooting for you through your whole journey. The depth within you is repelled by anything inauthentic. Be real. Take the time to acknowledge what you *really* need to feel whole. It won't be a person, position, or *thing*.

It can always be found in the deep waters of your soul.

NINE OF CUPS

Life is a banquet.

The Nine of Cups represents the fulfillment of wishes and the enjoyment of life's luxuries. It calls you back to your body and into the realm of your senses. The Nine of Cups represents satisfaction and pleasure. Life is offering you abundant opportunities to accept good things. Every day you have a choice:

to feel passion for life, or to be numb to its wonders. The table is set for you to savor your blessings. It's time for you to take your place at it.

Do you allow yourself to partake in the pleasures of life? Do you feel like there are too many things to worry about, so you couldn't possibly enjoy yourself now? Do you feel good about what your life is currently offering you? If not, it's time to start.

The jovial merchant pictured on this card has a passion for living, feasting, and tasting. Sure, he's chubby... however, when this card was drawn in 1909, being plump meant that you were eating well! The satisfied merchant knows he's lucky. He dreams big and always seems to get his wish. His red hat and stockings represent his vitality and boldness. His arms are crossed in a satisfied manner. He's been satiated by life's abundance. The successes he's acquired are symbolized by his nine golden cups. His cups are featured as trophies, symbols for past victories. These successes weren't just given to him—he went out in the world to achieve them. However, before he acquired them, each success began as a wish. For his wishes to come true, the merchant had to know that he deserved them. The merchant can sit back and truly enjoy what he has manifested. He felt good about his prospects before they ever fully materialized, and materialize they did.

You can have your wishes, too, but you must first feel good about your life and its prospects *now*.

To turn the tide of worrying, you must allow yourself present happiness. The golden cups are laid out for you, ripe for the taking. When the Nine of Cups appears, open yourself to feeling good about this moment. Feel it, taste it, smell it, luxuriate in it, and smile! Become aware of where you are and savor all that is already laid before you. If you can find enjoyment in your life now, even more will come.

This Nine of Cups always reminds me of Rosalind Russell's 1958 performance in *Auntie Mame*. Anyone in a depressed or discouraged mood about life should watch it. Auntie Mame *gets it* when she exclaims, "Life is a banquet, and most poor suckers are starving to death!"

Nine of Cups Reversed

If the Nine of Cups appears reversed, it still indicates you should enjoy the good things in life, but it warns of excess. Even beneficial things when done excessively can lead to imbalance. This card also calls your attention to other excesses in your life. Perhaps you need to monitor if you worry excessively or change a behavior that you engage in too much. The Delphic Oracle had two famous sayings above the temple: "Know thyself" and "Nothing in excess."[21] It was believed that if people followed these two tenants, they would be blessed with balanced and fulfilling lives.

Sometimes the excess in question isn't looked upon by others as a vice. For example, someone who works excessively is often admired by others, even if it isn't good for their personal health or balance. Look upon your life from high above and with the perspective of an eagle. What behavior is taking up most of your time? What other aspects of your life are you neglecting? Are you using an excess to avoid something that scares you? Take back control and choose balance. Other cards in the reading may reveal what is being done too much at this time.

21. Pausanias, *Description of Greece*, 4:507.

TEN OF CUPS

Gratitude.

The Ten of Cups represents gratitude for the magic that's weaving through your life right at this very moment. You can't see this magic if you are on autopilot, mad, stressed, or anxious. You can only perceive it if you choose to stop feeding tension, step out of your routines, and open your eyes to the miracles at play. When you open yourself to this magic, great things begin to happen in your life. This shimmering magic is darting about everywhere, but you may have to adjust your perspective to see it.

Do problems seem to suck all the oxygen out of your day? Do you know you have it good but just can't seem to see, feel, or sense it? Is there stress, anger, or tension living in your heart?

The family depicted on the Ten of Cups is like any other. They have problems to solve, work to do, kids to raise, and routines that govern their day. And yet, they are doing something that many of us don't do enough. They are soaking in the magic at play in their lives, in the present. The home that the family shares is in the distance, nestled in a thicket of trees on the hilltop. It is where they spend most of their time. In the house, love prevails, but there is also bickering, disagreements, and squabbles between the children that need to be broken up.

Being *in* the house, it is difficult for the family to actually *see* the house. So, the husband took his wife and kids out of their home and up the road. The family stepped out of routines and held each other close. When the husband and wife looked back at their home, a magical thing happened. A colorful rainbow filled the sky, illuminating each of their blessings. Rainbows are messengers of Spirit. The message is that showing gratitude for life, just as it is, attracts even more good luck and miracles. The family truly feels alive. They have such a love for each other. This love makes everything all right.

The couple raises their hands in gratitude for the abundance they have. The children are overcome as well and dance merrily in the moment. The family now has a new awareness of the magic they don't always see. They were so close to this magic that they were unable to see it.

Choose to see the magic weaving through your life. To see this magic, you might need to step out of the house and away from your routines. If you do get a glimpse of it, it might just fill your heart and make your eyes a little misty.

When the Ten of Cups appears, it's time to open your heart to those you love most. Give them a hug and tell them how important they are. Acknowledge the love that is all around you and do something to increase it.

There is magic dancing through your life. It weaves into your Spirit and connects you with everyone and everything around you. It's in the air, the water, the trees, the people you love, and every particle of light.

Whisper a word of gratitude, for magical things are happening!

Ten of Cups Reversed

If the Ten of Cups appears reversed, the rainbow is at the foundation of the card. This symbolizes the importance of color in your life. Colors have a tremendous effect on our moods and influence our unconscious thoughts. If you've been wearing one color for too long, it might be time to switch up your wardrobe. The rainbow also represents complexity and diversity, so it may be time to expose yourself to experiences that break up the status quo.

The Ten of Cups reversed suggests that you may need to bring back some magic to this moment. If you have been experiencing tunnel vision, it's time for you to stop and step out of your routine. Brighten up your environment. Buy some flowers. Rearrange the furniture to bring in a sense of newness. Declutter the piles you've been avoiding. Treat your environment to light and color. Ask yourself what in your space wants to feel more harmonious and beautiful.

If you've been indoors for too long, it might be time to step outside. Approach the world with wonder and openness to the magic at play. Look at how beautiful the sunlight is and how it causes each surface in nature to glitter with its own vibrancy. Bring in beauty and color to elevate your mood and enhance your life.

PAGE OF CUPS

Creativity.

The Page of Cups symbolizes the creative inner child. This is the part of you that can still be amazed with wonder and curiosity at the world around you. Everybody has creative energy and expresses it differently. The Page of Cups invites you to play, be inspired, and create something beautiful. The Page of Cups follows his heart. He is the sensitive poet of the tarot. He also adores impish pranks.

Do you avoid your creativity because you feel you aren't an artist? Do you remember the joy of being creative as a child? Do you ever just let loose and allow yourself to play?

If the Page of Cups were one hundred years old, he would still find time to play. He is the archetype of creativity. He is dressed in pink and blue. Pink is the color of love, harmony, kindness, and the heart. Blue is the color of communication, healing, creativity, and depth. He is a master at communicating his feelings through creativity. He lightens the hearts of others through words and deeds. His creative expression gives voice to feelings others have trouble articulating.

Like many children, he's taken his pet along with him where he isn't supposed to. In this case, it's his fish, representing depth, creative wisdom, and luck. The fish is in dialogue with him. This means the Page of Cups is a conduit for what swims deep within his creative unconscious. The water lilies on his tunic symbolize that he blossoms in the realm of feelings and emotions. He is very sensitive but is often having too much of a good time to sit about moping.

When the Page of Cups appears, your creative inner child wants some attention! If you give in, you're sure to have a lot of fun. Children trust in the magic of making stuff to express themselves. They love to draw pictures and paint Easter eggs and are so proud of turkeys made from hand tracings. They never say, "Well I'm sorry I can't paint today, because I'm not an artist." They dive right in because it's fun! It also keeps them too busy to think of scary things like sharks, bogeymen, or monsters lurking in the closet. Keeping your creative mind occupied keeps it from imagining frightening things.

When the Page of Cups appears, tune out the inner critic that all too often whispers in your ear. Do something expressive just for the joy of it. Make your house more vibrant and colorful. Do something crafty, make something, play, and spend some time teasing a big baby (especially a grown-up one).

Let your creativity be a channel for feelings that need to find expression.

If representing another individual, the Page of Cups can symbolize a younger person who is imaginative and artistic. He is sensitive, creative, kind, and idealistic. However, he may have some more maturing to do. Pages can represent the young-at-heart of any gender.

Page of Cups Reversed

If the Page of Cups appears reversed, he often accompanies a period when your creativity feels blocked. Even the greatest artists experience lulls in their creative brilliance. If you've been feeling a lack of motivation to express yourself, it's time to shift the energy. When creativity is blocked, it is often because you are thinking too much about *perfection*. Creativity is messy, especially if it's any good. Express the imperfect more and analyze less. This will get your creative juices flowing again. Once your creativity becomes unleashed, it will gain momentum.

Creativity flows when you are in tune with your depth. Neglected feelings have the potential to hijack an entire project until they are finally felt and transmuted into your work.

The Page of Cups reversed asks you to release any pressure you feel about being productive. Creativity needs to flow naturally, much like the water depicted on the card. Accept where you are and go with the flow.

The Page of Cups (upright or reversed) asks you to lighten up and remember what you enjoy about the task at hand. Open your heart and stop overthinking.

Literalism and nitpicking are creative buzzkills. Inject fun into what you are doing and watch your brilliance flow.

If the Page of Cups represents another individual, then he usually comes off as immature. Although not a negative person, he can be extremely impractical. When dealing with him, be clear, be direct, and maintain structure.

KNIGHT OF CUPS

The brave messenger of love.

The Knight of Cups is the tarot's brave messenger of love.[22] This Knight can communicate his deepest feelings without fear or embarrassment. Everywhere he rides, love begins to flow. He represents all forms of love: romantic, passionate, platonic, and familial. He can reintroduce a lonely person into a world of friends and can bring renewed passion to an intimacy-barren relationship.

22. Hollander, *Tarot for Beginners*, 205.

This is because he does not let fear, embarrassment, or shame keep him from opening his heart. He reminds those who believe they are alone that they are connected, valuable, loved, and accepted. The Knight of Cups appears when it's time to be emotionally courageous.

Do you have a hard time expressing your feelings, even to the people you are closest to? Are you too shy or too scared to open yourself up to connecting with others? When did you last feel passionate or romantic?

The Knight of Cups is so hot! He is completely confident with his feelings, and what is more attractive than confidence? He gazes electrically with deep blue eyes and effortlessly expresses what he desires openly. He wears the wings of Hermes, the messenger God, on his helm and his feet. Fish decorate his tunic. This symbolizes his ability to communicate clearly about deep unconscious feelings that can be difficult for others to put into words. He teaches that communication about feelings heals isolation and confusion. The more difficult the subject, the more healing to be gained from talking about it. However, you must be brave enough to open your heart to others.

You might wonder why you would need to be brave to express love. The answer is that vulnerability can be very scary! Even people who have been together for years can find it difficult to express affection and intimacy. This is especially true if the heart has been wounded by a deep betrayal or loss in the past. The Knight of Cups appears to tell us that retreating further from others will never heal the heart. The heart mends when it is brave and open, allowing new experiences to take the place of past hurts.

The Knight of Cups is eternally optimistic that the future will be brighter than times before. He bravely directs his horse over the river, crossing into the realm of the heart. The horse treads mindfully and carefully into this sensitive realm. The Knight knows that the heart is not as fragile as it pretends to be. It can heal amazingly. However, it must be open to do so.

The Knight of Cups urges you to bring some passion and excitement back into your life. Share, flirt, take a risk, make new friends, but, most importantly, be vulnerable! The Knight presents his cup as a gift to you, much like the divine hand on the Ace of Cups. There is no greater gift than love. The more you give this gift, the more you receive.

The Knight of Cups inspires you to be courageous enough to express love, romance, affection, and passion. Have confidence in your worth and stop being self-conscious. You don't need to be in an intimate relationship to begin healing your heart. The first step is to be brave enough to open it.

When representing another person, the Knight of Cups can symbolize a lover or an exciting love interest. He is attractive and charismatic and says the most charming things. Knights appear on horses in the tarot, so there is also an implication of coming and going. The Knight of Cups can represent a person who passionately arrives and departs from your life cyclically. He is not necessarily unsuitable, but a relationship with him may need more time to deepen into a secure partnership. Knights can represent youngish adults of any gender. Knights are usually people who are phasing out of one way of life and into another.

Knight of Cups Reversed

If the Knight of Cups appears reversed, he indicates that difficult feelings swimming around in your heart can be released once they have been put into words. It is an ideal time to communicate about whatever you've been avoiding. Instead of retreating more, the Knight dares you to be more open and share what you are experiencing with the people you trust.

Emotions like fear, shame, anxiety, and anger can begin to feel resolved the moment they are spoken. However, they must be articulated from a position of honesty and love. Once difficult feelings are articulated, they can be surrendered. Releasing emotional baggage causes the heart to immediately lighten up, making room for feelings like joy, excitement, and love. Don't fear honesty and openness. The Knight of Cups advises you to stop carrying heavy feelings around. Release any burdensome emotions or anxieties that are weighing you down by talking about them honestly and openly. This will lead to a huge breakthrough regarding your connection with others.

If the Knight of Cups reversed represents another person, he is often someone who means well but promises more than he can deliver. This can lead to hard feelings when his limitations are discovered. He is a dreamer with ample creativity; however, he may lack ambition and structure. In relationships, he represents someone who has a difficult time communicating. He may also keep his deepest desires hidden, since he may have a hard time being open about them.

QUEEN OF CUPS

Valuing feelings and emotions.

The Queen of Cups views feelings as sacred, because they reveal life to us in vibrant colors. She is nurturing, caring, and encourages her people to see the value of their own feelings and emotions. The Queen of Cups sees sensitivity as something that makes one strong, not weak. Feelings allow us to experience joy, excitement, love, bliss, and rapture. The Queen of Cups reminds us to be grateful for our feelings, even when they cause us pain. After all, feelings give life complexity, color, and dimension.

Are you uncomfortable with your feelings? Are you afraid to be open because someone or something might potentially hurt you? Do you bottle up your feelings and deny they are even there?

Cups and water in the tarot symbolize feelings and emotions. The Queen of Cups places her feelings in the most precious chalice of the entire tarot. Her cup is gilded in gold and adorned with angels. Just looking at her cup's beauty brings the Queen joy. This symbolizes that she honors feelings as something sacred. The Queen of Cups sees the worth and value of feelings because they give life color and complexity. To prove this point, she is surrounded by colorful beach stones.

If you've ever collected stones on the beach as a child, you'll remember that when they are dry, they are rather dull. However, if you place these stones in water, suddenly the stones become alive with vibrant colors and textures. The vibrancy of the stones is revealed through water. Likewise, a dull or boring life can reveal its complexity if you open yourself to *feeling* it instead of being detached from it.

So many people nowadays are afraid to feel. We are told to "not be so sensitive," as if feelings make us weak. We are told to toughen up. This is especially true for boys, who, above all others, are not allowed to be sensitive or weak (although many girls are increasingly experiencing this, too). The trouble with this is that we all *have* feelings. Denying our feelings leads to imbalance internally and with the world around us. The more emotions that are bottled up, numbed, or not experienced, the more *living* we miss out on. Many people avoid feeling because it might hurt. However, this is just fear chiming in again. Fear robs us of experiences that could potentially bring us joy.

To experience the vibrancy of life, follow the Queen's example and look for beauty. Beauty activates emotional responses that feel good. Science confirms that beauty releases pleasure from the brain and into the bloodstream. Buy some flowers or beautiful art for your home or work environment. Admire the beauty in the natural world around you. It's everywhere! Cherublike undines decorate the Queen's throne. The Queen of Cups is especially loving and protective of children and is a caring mother.

Look for what appears to be just dull beach stones in your everyday life. View these things through the lens of your feelings. Open yourself to the rapture of experiencing love and beauty. Watch life's vibrancy reveal itself to you.

The Queen of Cups does not avoid her feelings. She takes them all: the good, the bad, the hurt, the sad, the love, the joy, the grief, the hope, and the happiness. She places them in her sacred chalice and honors them. Your feelings give life dimension, complexity, richness, color, and meaning. Honor them.

When the Queen of Cups represents another person, she is a kind, nurturing, and maternal figure. You can trust her advice and her influence. She really cares for others deeply. She is also sensitive and has an eye for beauty and great style. If she is a parent, she is the best sort. Queens can be mature individuals of any gender who wield strong feminine power.

Queen of Cups Reversed

If the Queen of Cups appears reversed, she signifies that you may be passing through life without soaking it in. All your rites of passage, your achievements, and your self-improvements need to be acknowledged and felt at this time. The Queen of Cups encourages you to honor your feelings and reminds you that your feelings give your life meaning, awareness, and colorful vibrancy. Don't make life a race from one achievement to the next without processing it on an emotive level. Be present with the beauty that surrounds you and the achievements you have manifested. Acknowledge yourself, love yourself, and appreciate yourself for the work you do every day to improve your life and the lives of others.

The Queen of Cups reversed can also signify a need to release emotional burdens. Opening yourself to feelings can sometimes bring about emotional discomfort. These feelings especially need to be felt, acknowledged, honored, and then surrendered. Crying is especially good for releasing blocked emotional energy. This will ensure that difficult emotions don't become bottled up, creating problems for you unconsciously. To avoid getting stuck on painful feelings, ask yourself what the feelings may be teaching you at this stage in your life. What are you learning from being present with them? To shift your awareness from negative emotions, focus on something beautiful.

Upright or reversed, the Queen of Cups asks you to take care of your feelings. Filter out whatever is painful and release it. Choose to focus on beauty and life's magic. Stop going through life without feeling it! Feelings are very precious. Let them flow. Be at peace with them and with yourself.

If the Queen of Cups reversed represents a person, she is often overwhelmed by her great sensitivity and may need assistance dealing with her feelings. She may also be smothering or needy in personal relationships. Try to encourage her toward self-reliance and empowerment.

KING OF CUPS

Channeling feelings for positive results.

Everybody likes the King of Cups. He is kind, affable, and forgiving. He has nothing left to prove to the world, which makes him unpretentious. This is because he is completely at peace with his feelings about the past. The King of Cups has experienced both stormy seas and still waters that run deep. Water and cups represent feelings in the tarot, and the King of Cups is perfectly at home in the realm of his emotions. A fish talisman guards his heart, showing that the King truly wears his heart on his sleeve. The lotus staff symbolizes that the King of Cups works to achieve emotional enlightenment. He tells us, "You are always going to have feelings; why not channel their power into something constructive?"

Where are your emotions being channeled now? Were you taught to repress your feelings and emotions? Are negative past emotions leaving you feeling sad, scared, unmotivated, or depressed?

The King of Cups knows that emotions can buoy or sink us. Feelings can be helpful or destructive, just like the ocean. Emotions aren't good or bad—they are energy. The mind filters where feelings flow. Once unleashed, emotions can create a powerful current that manifests results, either positive or negative. Therefore, you want to keep your feelings flowing amid currents of joy and happiness to serve as fuel for what you are trying to manifest.

Two symbols appear in the background of the King's card: the whale and the ship. Whales are the recordkeepers of the ocean.[23] They are the ancient giants that remember all the way back to a time when they used to live on land. The whale symbolizes the ability to access old memories from the depths. Whales breathe air, giving them the ability to bring old memories and feelings to the surface for understanding and healing. By making peace with the past, you don't have to work so hard to resist it.

The floating ship represents the power of the mind to invent solutions to harness the water (feelings). The seas and oceans used to be large barriers before humans could build ships. After people started inventing boats, the waters became superhighways. Ideas were exchanged and trade increased. The waters were channeled into a positive result.

The King's throne remains stable above the waves. He is not ruled by his feelings but governs them. He stays in contact with his deep emotions and memories (the whale), but he is not overcome and submerged by them (the ship). He can focus on a goal and then harness the powers of his emotions to achieve it.

When the King of Cups appears, you can choose whether to sink or swim in the realm of your emotions. Heed the King's advice and make peace with the

23. Sams and Carson, *Medicine Cards*, 201.

past. Forgive yourself for whatever was keeping you stuck. Forgive others who have hurt you, or *they* will continue to rule the direction of your feelings.

The King of Cups can also signify a kindhearted man you can trust. He is an ideal relationship partner and is protective of those he loves. He can also symbolize a trustworthy friend or ally who can assist you. Kings can be mature people of any gender who are leaders or figures of authority.

King of Cups Reversed

If the King of Cups appears reversed, he advises you to stay calm despite stormy seas. As you can see, the King is surrounded by waters making great waves. Water signifies feelings in the tarot, and reversed Cup cards can indicate a degree of emotional turmoil. The King of Cups is seated on a firm stone platform, unaffected by the swirling waves around him. This indicates that the King can remain centered amid situations that elicit strong emotional reactions.

The King of Cups is also associated with the astrological sign of Cancer, the sign of house and home. If you wish to reclaim stability amid stormy waters, get your own house in order (literally and figuratively). Throw out things you don't need anymore. Remove clutter. The more you clean out your personal environment, the less heavy and stressed you will feel internally. You may also see external conditions improve. Your environment has the power to unconsciously affect your mood and self-esteem. If you have a stable base of operations from where you feel centered, you can handle any waves headed your way.

If the King of Cups reversed represents a person, he may be someone who has a hard time letting things go, both emotionally and physically. He could also represent someone who needs help with depression or the past. Upright or reversed, the King of Cups is rarely unkind. When reversed, the King of Cups needs to feel secure before he can progress.

THE SUIT OF PENTACLES

Your sense of worth and practical concerns.

The Pentacles suit represents the external world and the opportunities found there. On the most fundamental level, Pentacle cards reveal your financial concerns and prospects for monetary success. Pentacles (or Coins) are symbols for the element of Earth. In tarot, the Earth element governs money matters as well as your sense of worth and worthiness. Pentacle cards can easily reveal if you truly feel worthy of receiving what you value. Each of the Court cards in the Pentacles suit reveals an earthy figure.

Pentacles will always illuminate what is happening in the real world. They reveal if your plans are practical or if they are unrealistic. Pentacles also signify structure and stability. If you are wondering if external success is likely to manifest, take note of which Pentacle cards appear. Also, pay attention to Pentacle cards that appear at the foundation section of a tarot spread. They will reveal your current state of security.

The element of Earth encompasses far more than superficial markers of success. It rules stability, character, legacies, logistics, health, and prosperity. Pentacles will highlight your skill set and what you value. Pentacles will also reveal where more patience is needed. They encourage investment in bank accounts, property, people, projects, and businesses. When many Pentacle cards appear, they encourage you to be methodical and practical with the situation at hand. Other cards that appear amid clusters of Pentacle cards can reveal what may bring you prosperity or security.

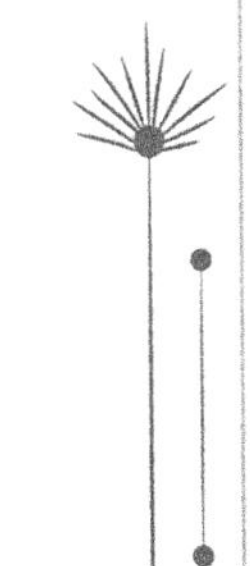

ACE OF PENTACLES

Prosperous beginnings.

The Ace of Pentacles represents prosperous new beginnings. It symbolizes positive financial thinking and fresh prospects for success. A new opportunity is being presented. It is illuminating your pathway toward a wealthier state of mind. Prosperous thinking begins with knowing your self-worth and expressing gratitude for your existing blessings. Positive thoughts about your possibilities entice even more abundant opportunities to seek you out, like bees to honey. When the Ace of Pentacles appears, a gateway of prosperous opportunities is opening.

What is your attitude about your financial life? Do you feel open to receiving prosperity? Are you actively seeking out new opportunities to improve your financial life?

The imagery of this card shows a divine hand holding a shining, golden coin. This symbolizes that Spirit is blessing us with abundance and opportunity every moment of every day... we just might not be seeing it. Humans are impatient creatures prone to lethargy. We want it now! We often say to ourselves, "Why am I not getting my just reward? I'm spiritual! I thought I could just sit back and let opportunity find me; isn't that how it works?" The Ace of Pentacles presents us with new opportunities but also requires us to do the work.

The Ace of Pentacles depicts a garden. Gardens take time, patience, and work to grow. If approached as a labor of love, the garden will flourish. This illustrates that while you can change your mind to think in wealth consciousness in an instant, it doesn't mean that money will suddenly rain down from the sky. You must tend your state of mind just as you would tend a garden. This includes weeding out negative thoughts and habits while having patience with your unique growing process. You would never get frustrated with a flower for not blooming two days after the seeds were planted. Why would you then expect your life to display a finished product immediately?

The garden also features a gateway. This represents doors of success that are currently opening to you. In the distance beyond the gate are mountains. The mountains represent stability, reputation, and overcoming obstacles. It may be time to increase your public profile and be seen. In feng shui, it is believed that a picture of a mountain hung on your "fame wall" can increase personal renown. The fame wall is the wall that faces the door you habitually enter your home through. Are you courageously ascending the heights toward success?

The gateway also symbolizes that you must occasionally leave the comfort of the garden to improve it. This means going out into the external world and seeking out the elements that will help it flourish. Pursue opportunity and you will create it. Fortune consistently favors the bold.

The Ace of Pentacles asks you to tend your thoughts. New opportunities are presenting themselves to improve your life, but you must take full advantage of them. If you are willing to do the work, abundance and success will follow. Be grateful for the riches you already possess, and more will be on the way. Open your eyes to new opportunities!

Ace of Pentacles Reversed

If the Ace of Pentacles appears reversed, it indicates that procrastination may be *the* major obstacle to seeing your dream become a solid reality. Upright or reversed, the Ace of Pentacles exemplifies the Earth element. The element of Earth rules all that is solid, tangible, and real. When goals are acted upon (and not just thought about), success follows. The Ace of Pentacles reversed highlights a hesitancy to get the ball rolling. Many times, just getting started is the most challenging obstacle to seeing your dream manifest. Don't let anxiety and resistance psych you out before you've even begun. If you act, you will undoubtedly win. If you avoid initiating the start of your project, you will block your own ability to succeed.

The Ace of Pentacles reversed encourages you to *try*. So many successful ideas are abandoned before they have a chance to take root because of fear and anxiety. Don't talk yourself out of success. What do you have to lose (aside from your fear of being limited) if you bravely attempt your dream? Today, accept your worthiness. You deserve abundant new beginnings, prosperity, and a fulfilling life. Any thoughts to the contrary need to be weeded out and released. These thoughts are truly blocking your success. You can accomplish great things, but first you must begin!

TWO OF PENTACLES

Flexibility.

The Two of Pentacles represents juggling unexpected events. These experiences aren't bad or good—they are merely unpredictable. The infinity symbol binding the two coins represents the eternal truth that life does not always go according to plan. The juggler on the card survives the undulations of fortune because he remains flexible and adaptable. This is symbolized by the boats that remain afloat amid the tumultuous waters.

How do you respond when things don't go according to plan? Do you get angry or become resistant? Are you able to retain your good humor?

The juggler depicted on the Two of Pentacles is an entertainer. He takes life's lemons and makes lemonade. He transforms the troubles life sends him into entertaining, teachable moments to uplift himself and others. The Two of Pentacles reminds us not to fight the waves life hurls at us, but rather to float above them. Know that in life, there are always going to be waves. Don't take them personally! Instead of asking yourself, "Why is this happening to me," tell yourself, "Thank you for this valuable lesson to remain flexible." In nature, life that cannot adapt becomes extinct.

The symbolism of the Two of Pentacles links it with two Major Arcana cards: the Magician (another juggler with an infinity symbol) and the Wheel of Fortune (the unpredictable ups and downs of life). In early French decks, the Magician was even called *Bateleur* (Juggler).[24] Like the Magician, the juggler depicted here is in control of his *response* to the unpredictable motions of the Wheel of Fortune. His tall, funny-looking hat symbolizes that he is *stretching* his mind to transcend his struggles through humor and wisdom. Instead of thinking negatively and feeling victimized by life, the juggler views events lightheartedly. His hat also symbolizes that he is stretching his mind to align with a higher perspective.

The Two of Pentacles encourages you to ride the waves instead of fighting them. Let unexpected eventualities roll off your back. Learn to laugh at them and use them to stretch your own mind. You can juggle anything life sends your way with transcendent grace and ease. The Two of Pentacles can also indicate a juggling of finances. Transferring energy or assets flexibly will restore harmony.

Two of Pentacles Reversed

If the Two of Pentacles appears reversed, it represents potential emotional turmoil that should be approached practically. Holding fixed expectations of how life *should be* is a swift route toward unnecessary suffering. The Two of Pentacles symbolizes unexpected events, and when reversed, the juggler loses his sense of humor, becoming rigid. Unforeseen responsibilities, deadlines, time restrictions, unexpected bills—the Two of Pentacles reversed highlights multiple life events

24. Pollack, *Tarot Wisdom*, 28.

that chaotically converge. The key to making this card work for you is to follow the example of the upright juggler and remain flexible and good-humored. Remember not to fight against the waves pictured on the card, but to sail over them. You must accept your present challenges without reacting explosively.

It may feel like you are being overwhelmed, but this is an illusion. Water in the tarot symbolizes feelings. When the Two of Pentacles appears reversed, it asks you to rise above the tumultuous illusion that your ship is sinking. Once you transcend your emotional reaction to the situation, you can get organized. Laugh at the all the craziness swirling around you instead of personalizing it. Turn it into a sarcastic joke. Use humor to buoy your ship above the waves. Before you know it, you will return to safe harbor.

THREE OF PENTACLES

The learning process.

The Three of Pentacles depicts a young man learning a trade at a monastery. This card symbolizes the refinement of skills or talents. The Three of Pentacles exemplifies work that is worthwhile and meaningful. In order to excel at it, you must be patient with the learning process. This means being open to making mistakes and not giving up when setbacks happen.

What skills are you currently learning? Are you expecting yourself to be perfect? Do you constantly compare your skills to those of others and feel that your abilities aren't good enough?

Although the Three of Pentacles symbolizes "perfecting" a skill, it does not require us to *be* perfect. Quite the opposite—this card asks you to look at the big picture. Look at how far you've already come with what you are learning. Look at what you can still achieve! Improvement can only happen if you remain teachable. No matter how good you are at your talent or skill set, you can always get better.

In the learning process, mistakes will be your best teachers. Mastering anything is all about trial and error. You will make mistakes. The more mistakes you make, the better you will get. You may occasionally feel like you look stupid, but don't give up. If you keep refining your skills, you will achieve your goal.

The learning process is rarely a straight beeline toward a goal. It is a winding path of hills and valleys. Sometimes the path loops around and makes us feel as if we are going backward and learning nothing at all. This is an illusion. Like a spiral, the path winds around and back, and yet always upward. Sometimes success isn't achieved right away. It's as if the Universe wants us to learn something important about where we are right now instead of rushing us to the next thing. Are you impatient to get this phase of your life over with? Slow down! You are probably missing something important. Other cards may reveal what that *something* is. Sometimes, the thing we are learning isn't academic, but rather an important life lesson. The Three of Pentacles always highlights an area for self-improvement and refinement.

The Three of Pentacles can also foretell beginning an area of study or the acquisition of important knowledge that will have long-term implications for your future. Be patient with the learning process. Recall the passion you once felt for the skills you are honing.

The Three of Pentacles can also represent the manifestation of plans. On the image, one of the monks is handing the workman a set of plans for the architecture he is chiseling. If you look closely at the plans, they reveal the exact scene the workman is creating. This card can symbolize planning, perfecting, and enacting ideas that are destined for realization. Aside from themes of learning and teaching, the Three of Pentacles represents collaborative efforts that will prove successful if you cooperate with others.

Three of Pentacles Reversed

If the Three of Pentacles appears reversed, it asks you to identify what life lesson you seem to be relearning. This repetition will highlight one of the important things you agreed to work on while you're on this planet. Instead of getting frustrated or just wanting to get the lesson over with, it must sink in before you can progress.

Perhaps you are struggling with learning to finally accept yourself and where you're at. Perhaps you are learning patience. Maybe the frustration surrounding the skill, craft, or job you are perfecting is mirroring the self-improvement going on within. Accepting yourself without having achieved perfection is a tough lesson for many. Remember, the process of perfecting yourself never results in *being* perfect. If you are trying to improve yourself every day, that is enough to feel proud of.

We are all here to learn. Everybody is engaged in at least one learning process or another. Learning keeps us mentally engaged with life and enables us to evolve and grow. Learning involves setbacks, mistakes, disappointments, surprises, successes, and failures.

The Three of Pentacles reversed can illuminate the hard lessons where the greatest evolution for your soul is occurring. Never give up. Choose to view your life lessons with compassion. You may not always see it, but you are getting better, wiser, and stronger every day.

FOUR OF PENTACLES

The search for security.

The Four of Pentacles represents material security and stability, which is very different from being secure *in yourself.* Although this a wonderful card financially speaking, it warns against the pursuit of security solely through the acquisition of external *things*. The Four of Pentacles reminds you to balance your expectations of worldly success with the needs of your Authentic Self.

Do you feel safe and secure? Are you erecting barriers between your Authentic Self and others? Do you sometimes feel that no matter how much you achieve or acquire, it still doesn't feel like enough?

The miserly man depicted on this card had a difficult early life. He knows well what it was like to go hungry. He was the eldest child in a poor family. Dealing with extreme poverty in his childhood created a lot of emotional turmoil accompanied by feelings of being *less than*. One way for the man to medicate this sense of inequity was to make a lot of money. He decided to be the best at everything he did. He thought that if he gained enough money and status, he would finally prove to the world that *he* was worthy. The man moved to a big city buzzing with opportunity and flashy personalities. He did everything to gain the people's acceptance and soon became the wealthiest man of them all. And yet, no matter how much money he earned or how much approval he gained, he still felt empty and insecure.

Here we see the miser clutching his four coins. They are symbols for status, money, power, and achievement. These are not bad attributes to have so long as they are held by one who is already secure in himself. As tightly as the miser holds these attributes, they never seem to bring him an authentic sense of security. Just look at his face. There is still suffering happening there. Internally, he remains a scared, neglected boy. Now, he's in turn neglected the needs of his Inner Self. His four Pentacles have become barriers. The one on his head makes him forget his connection to Spirit. The one clutched to his heart blocks him from receiving love and feeling his feelings. The two Pentacles under his feet cut him off from being grounded in nature. *His* nature.

There are many towers depicted on this card, linking it with the Tower of the Major Arcana. The towers symbolize states of denial that can separate you from reality. One of the biggest lies people tell themselves is that they don't matter unless they are validated by others. If you've been suffering, then you must stop looking to your internal miser to bring you security. It may be time to stop grasping for veneers and confront your heart's truth.

The pursuit of position and wealth is not inherently a bad thing. By all means, be a great financial success! The problem lies in distancing yourself from the truth of your humanity to gain status. Your humanity can be described as the part of you that feels love and compassion for yourself and others. It is the quiet, supportive voice of your Spirit. Many people in our culture use their work or worldly position to seek validation. And yet pharmaceutical, insurance, and social media companies are getting rich because these same people are depressed and miserable, seeking an authentic feeling in all that is artificial. Seeking security in someone or something outside of yourself will always lead to a sense of not quite measuring up.

Listen to the needs of your true nature. True security can only be found within.

On a purely financial level, the Four of Pentacles can symbolize good financial prospects and material security with a caution to be conservative with your money at this time. If you don't know which financial action to take, save your money for another day.

Four of Pentacles Reversed

The Four of Pentacles reversed appears when you are courageously releasing avoidance behaviors that keep you from connecting with your true feelings. These behaviors could include excessive eating, drinking, working, or shopping, obsessively checking your phone, or binge-watching television. The Four of Pentacles reversed symbolizes the removal of barriers that prevent you from connecting with your feelings and with others.

The Four of Pentacles reversed can also represent giving and sharing. You may need to be more generous with your time, resources, or abilities to assist someone looking to you for help. The man on the card is suffering because he is not open to sharing. The Four of Pentacles reversed advises you to be generous while sharing your best qualities with others. This card could also indicate that you need to share your true feelings instead of bottling them up. The walls are coming down, and it is time for reconnecting—not just with your Inner Self, but with loved ones as well. Being openhearted and vulnerable will lead to healing. Have the courage to reject anything plastic or artificial and feel your real feelings.

The Four of Pentacles reversed represents transcending numbing distractions. Although it may feel like confronting your feelings will be uncomfortable, this card shows that the prolonged avoidance of them is what leads to more suffering. Give yourself the gift of quiet. Light some candles and some incense. Give yourself a reading. Take a contemplative walk in nature. Start a dialogue with your heart. Ask your heart how it's been feeling these days.

Being open and honest will lead to a tremendous breakthrough.

FIVE OF PENTACLES

Poverty consciousness.

The Five of Pentacles represents poverty and neediness. Poverty is not just a financial condition one suffers; it is a pervasive state of mind. "How am I going to pay for this?" "If I don't give him more money for the hundredth time, will it be my fault if something bad happens?" "I wish I could get lucky and finally win the lottery." "I'm just not good with money." "When can I get out of this debt?" "Why am I so worthless?" "Why don't they appreciate me?"

These are all examples of poverty consciousness. Even rich people can get stuck in poverty consciousness. This is because poverty isn't just about money. It's also about self-esteem.

Do you ever feel that success is granted to everybody else but continues to elude you? Are you adequately compensated for the work you do? Do you feel confident enough to put up boundaries with others? Do you value yourself and the services you provide? Do you need to get a new job?

The people depicted on the Five of Pentacles have been overrun by hard times. They are sick and injured. Behind them is a cathedral, glowing with light and emitting warmth. The poor folks on the card don't even think to enter. They are rejected by society and consider themselves untouchables. They believe they have no place within and stay outside in the snow. The only other figure who walks over a snowy landscape in this deck is the Hermit. The people on the Five of Pentacles have numbed their feelings with ice. However, they lack the warmth of the starry lantern of the Hermit, leaving them simply feeling *alone*. Without the guiding voice of their inner Wise One, the poor people on the card truly don't consider themselves worthy of belonging inside. They have allowed poverty consciousness to overthrow their sense of value. Once this corrosive belief is accepted, it's challenging to cast out.

In ancient Greece, the Goddess of poverty was called Penia. This Goddess would wander from house to house, much like the vagabonds on the card. Penia would bang on the doors of everyone until someone without boundaries let her in. Once Penia was in the house, it was difficult to get her to leave. She would constantly make the occupants feel obligated, worthless, and guilty. Penia stayed indefinitely, draining the resources of her hosts until they took back their home by casting her out. In this case, the home is a symbol for one's heart.

Giving to others and being of service must be done with boundaries. The old saying "give a man a fish, feed him for a day; teach a man to fish, and you feed him for a lifetime" encapsulates this truth.

There is one force on the planet that can eradicate poverty consciousness: *self-esteem*. When you feel smart, capable, competent, and confident, you believe in your worthiness. When you feel valuable, poverty consciousness cannot gain a foothold. Unscrupulous individuals can't use people who are strong in their sense of self-worth. Users and manipulators are like predators. They go for the weakest one when hunting for their prey. The Five of Pentacles alerts you to any person or situation that seeks to make you feel "less than." It's time to create strong boundaries. If you are experiencing poverty consciousness, you need to examine the vitality of your self-esteem. To improve your self-esteem, work on yourself. Exercise, meditate, or place yourself among people who make you feel good.

Know your worth and value. Stop giving yourself away if you are running on empty. Put up boundaries with needy individuals and tell them, "No!" Speak up for yourself. Help others only if they are helping themselves. Go for your best opportunities.

Five of Pentacles Reversed

If the Five of Pentacles appears reversed, it asks you to identify any areas of your life that you are pouring energy into without seeing any improvement. This can come in the form of giving your energy to "psychic vampires," wasting your time on people who don't respect it or pouring your money into a situation or person who continues to deplete you. At the root of these experiences are questions of worth and, more importantly, what sort of life you feel you are worthy of. Stop spending energy, time, and money on people or situations that leave you feeling exhausted and empty. Ask yourself, "What area of my life is the biggest energy waster?"

The Five of Pentacles reversed also asks you to monitor the quality of your thoughts. You don't have to hold on to thoughts just because you have them. Some thoughts are garbage and need to be thrown away. Upright or reversed, the Five of Pentacles asks you to reject any thoughts that undermine your sense of value. Affirm only those thoughts that make you feel good about yourself.

The Five of Pentacles reversed reminds you to stop depleting yourself with experiences that make you feel empty. You can choose to throw out any thought, influence, or experience that does not make you feel good about who you are, how far you've come, and where you are going. Become aware of the love, blessings, and abundance that surround you. You are coming out of the bitter snow and into the warmth of the hearth. Remember that you are worthy of each blessing you have and all those that are still on the way.

It's time to raise your standards for what you believe you can receive.

SIX OF PENTACLES

Entertaining angels unaware.

The Six of Pentacles represents compassion, generosity, and hospitality. It encapsulates acts of kindness and the concept of good Karma. This card reminds you that the *true quality* of a person is not measured by how much they suck up to the influential people of society. Instead, it is measured by how they treat people they stand to gain nothing from. When you show kindness and generosity to those you would probably gain "nothing" from, you may find that you walk away with a gift far greater. Sometimes the one who most needs to accept the kindness being offered is you!

Are you forgetting to see the divine spark in the eyes of those around you? Do you have difficulty accepting help when it's offered? Does making eye contact frighten you, causing you to avoid connecting with others?

The rich merchant on this card has worked hard to escape the crushing poverty of his youth. However, he will always remember what it was like. He had to deal with a lot of other poor people in survival mode. The merchant knows that he could have ended up just like the people society ignores. If he'd been born without certain privileges, had not had mentors, had gotten sick, had a disability, had made a wrong decision somewhere in the past—well then, he might be begging for scraps, too. By valuing the beggars pictured here (so like the figures on the Five of Pentacles), the merchant affirms their worth as human beings. This act validates the dignity of people who may feel they are not welcome.

The merchant holds the scales. This shows he sees *both sides*. He also remembers that many poor people showed him loyalty and kindness in his youth. These folks embodied qualities far more valuable than what can be found among the upper echelons. He learned the dignity of hard work and how to keep fighting to overcome obstacles. Therefore, he sees value in people society might overlook. You see the merchant here, willingly handing out four coins to a beggar in need. Four is a number associated with creating new, solid foundations. The merchant hands the coins to a beggar in a gesture of blessing that mirrors the Hierophant. This symbolizes there is a higher, spiritual purpose to this act that transcends mere generosity.

The merchant also knows another magical truth from his youth: that angels disguise themselves as social outcasts all the time, waiting to bless those who stop and notice the light in their eyes.

There are many myths, fairy tales, and religious stories that stretch far back into human history and share the same theme. A test is presented to someone who is privileged in some way. A God, a fairy, or an angel appears before the fortunate individual, disguised as a beggar. If the individual treats the beggar kindly, the divine being offers some sort of magical assistance (such as the Goddess Hera disguised as a crone before helping Jason retrieve the Golden Fleece). If, however, the privileged person treats the beggar as worthless, something terrible always happens. The uncaring person undergoes a horrible transformation. Their outsides begin to reflect the ugliness they harbor within. Remember the fairy's curse in *Beauty and the Beast*?

Giving strangers a warm welcome, offering food, and showing respect was one of the most sacred customs in ancient Greece. It was a custom decreed by their king of the Gods, Zeus. The Greeks believed that Gods and Goddesses appeared before men as "lowly people" all the time, testing their humanity. If the Gods were treated well, they could miraculously change one's fortunes. Some Christian stories also describe angels doing the exact same thing.

Today, you too could be interacting with an angel unaware. Don't ignore the light within the eyes of those around you. Also, don't assume you know another's "societal worth" by their outward appearance. Spiritual beings love to disguise themselves as what society deems as outcasts or "crazy people." I believe angels or Gods can take over their bodies (I've seen it myself). It's probably easier for angels to take over the minds of eccentric people. People without an open mind seem to have a "closed" sign up for the angels.

What will you do today to ensure your own good Karma? Perhaps you already have been doing this work. If so, your rewards are currently finding their way to you.

What goes around comes around.

The Six of Pentacles can often signify that another person may be playing the part of an angel for you. Offerings of assistance, opportunities, and support may appear from a benefactor who wishes to invest in you. Allow yourself to receive when these magical helpers appear. Being able to receive is an indication that *you* feel worthy.

Six of Pentacles Reversed

If the Six of Pentacles appears reversed, it can represent a lack of confidence in *your* abilities as a result of placing others on a pedestal. Thinking that you can't achieve your goals without the blessing of someone you are placing on a pedestal is a form of devaluing yourself. When you look to others to take control and hand them the power over your dreams, you surrender control over your own destiny.

Sometimes this card appears when we think we *need* someone we perceive to be better than ourselves because they hold a higher social position or are further along with something we wish we could excel at. Although you may not realize it, this is an unconscious form of devaluing yourself, and it can lead to an erosion of self-confidence. Upright or reversed, the Six of Pentacles represents assistance offered from others; however when it is reversed, it warns of excessively looking to others for help before looking within yourself.

The Six of Pentacles reversed asks if you are truly valuing your skills, your creativity, and yourself. If you feel you aren't succeeding, it probably isn't because you don't know the right people or have the right connections. You may have forgotten to take a good long look in the mirror and see the light of worthiness within your own eyes.

The Six of Pentacles is always a card of assistance. When it appears reversed, it asks if you are honoring the light assisting you from within. This card reminds you that you are qualified, competent, and deserving. All the elements for your eventual success are already found within you. You may just need to accept it. What we admire most in others we already possess and are developing within ourselves (see Page of Wands). Gladly accept help when it's offered, but don't become dependent on it.

SEVEN OF PENTACLES

Acknowledge your progress.

The Seven of Pentacles represents acknowledging and appreciating your progress. It symbolizes the need to periodically evaluate your accomplishments, what you have improved, and what goals you're still working toward. The road may not have been easy, and the work may not be over, but your foundations are firmly rooted. This card reminds you to stop ignoring or minimizing your successes!

What positive results have you manifested in your life? Have you ever written down your achievements to review how much you've done? Do you ever stop to look around and appreciate all that you've manifested?'

The farmer depicted on the card is taking a break from working in the fields. His crop isn't quite ready for harvest, but he surveys the work that he did with a sense of pride. He did this himself, and he sees the results he created. He leans on his garden tool, much as the Hermit leans on his staff of wisdom. The field has been the farmer's sanctuary of self-awareness and exploration. He sees the fruits of his labors, not just a finished job. These accomplishments are tangible proof of what he's manifested. The farmer allows himself to stop being productive long enough to truly appreciate his progress. He is humble, yet he possesses the healthy sense of self-esteem that only hard work can engender.

Are you able to recognize the progress you've made in your life? Begin by writing five life accomplishments you've fought hard to achieve. Recall five things that you could have given up on if you had taken the easy way out. These five things proved you *can* succeed! What accomplishments illustrate that you can persevere? What achievements are you most proud of? Take your time and think... Got your list?

Now look at the items on the list as if you were a stranger seeing them for the first time. Remember the phase in your life before you achieved them. Do you remember what life looked like then? What fears did you challenge to get to this point? What was going through your head at that time? Take pride in each item on your list. Thank your body for not quitting and your mind for not breaking. Thank your heart for mending itself through the painful times. Thank your Spirit for raising you up and over the obstacles. This is what you manifested, and your Inner Self needs to be thanked for it. To continue making progress, you must clearly see (and appreciate) what you've already manifested.

You can achieve any positive result you want for your future. Just look at your list; you've done it before!

The Seven of Pentacles always implies that there has been a great deal already accomplished, but that there is still more work to do. You have gotten over the hump. The tough work of tilling the soil and planting the seeds of your success has taken root. Now you just need to be consistent and gently tend your garden until harvest time. Keep working at it, and you will succeed!

Seven of Pentacles Reversed

If the Seven of Pentacles appears reversed, it represents mistaking negative thinking for *being realistic*. Too often we accept a negative thought as true while being resistant to positive thinking. In truth, this means that we've trained ourselves to believe that setbacks and hardships are more likely than limitless opportunity. Believing the worst about your prospects will *not* protect you from future disappointments. In fact, it guarantees disappointment before you've even given your best effort. Just because something is negative, does not mean it is more likely or real. Life does not have to be approached with an attitude of toil and struggle.

The Seven of Pentacles reversed can also represent feeling discouraged by too many details. Try to work in broad strokes to get yourself started. Like an artist refining a rough sketch, you can always circle back and fill in the details later. Formulate a broad plan of action. The Seven of Pentacles (upright or reversed) is a card that rewards effort. The greatest work that needs to be done now is training your mind into thinking positively. Success can be just as realistic as failure if you believe it is possible.

EIGHT OF PENTACLES

Meaningful work.

The Eight of Pentacles represents immersing yourself in work that gives your life meaning. It suggests giving 110 percent to the tasks in front of you. This card reminds you to value the skills you are mastering and acknowledge how they improve the lives of others. Giving your best effort ensures that you can go out into the world with your head held high, confident in your abilities and your value.

Do you truly appreciate the work you do? What skills are you honing each day to improve your life? Is it time to stretch yourself past your comfort zones toward fulfilling work?

The craftsman on the card busily inscribes his Pentacles (symbols for manifestation) with a hammer and chisel. Hammers represent focused power and accuracy. They channel energy toward their target. We've all heard the phrase, "Hitting the nail on the head." The craftsman loves his work. It provides a means of focusing his powerful creative energy. He wears a blacksmith's apron, giving him the power to bend even the strongest materials toward his vision. A pathway connects his workshop to the little village in the distance. This symbolizes that his work connects him with others. To the townspeople, he is not just "the craftsman." He is also the master of eight apprentices and the beloved teacher at the monastery, gaining the town's affection for his compassion and kindness. The craftsman is also very funny, bringing laughter to the villagers with his dry wit and humor. The craftsman doesn't just do work for the village for financial gain. Each day, he uses his work as a vehicle to improve his community, connect with others, and better himself.

Being fully engaged in the work that you do is very empowering. It transforms your energy from being reactive to being proactive. Your job is not merely a means of making money. The skills you are mastering connect you with society, which provides you with a platform to improve it. This allows you to put your own unique stamp on the world and to change the energy of your environment. How are you improving your world with the work you do? Are you making it a better place?

Today, enthusiastically take up the tasks in front of you, giving them 110 percent. Value the work that you do, and others will, too. Work isn't just *labor*. It is your contribution for the betterment of all. If your current work feels limiting, then it's time to find something that utilizes your best attributes and talents. Instead of resenting the job at hand, change the energy. This may require you to place yourself in a new position that brings more learning or fulfillment. You are in control of how you employ your skill set and where you focus your energy.

Don't just *endure* work. It's more than a job; it's your platform for making the world a better place. The Eight of Pentacles foretells hard work ahead, but with great success as a result.

Eight of Pentacles Reversed

If the Eight of Pentacles appears reversed, it urges you to be mindful of the energy you are infusing your work with. If you feel that you are grinding every day on the same joyless hamster wheel, then it's time for a change. If you find yourself complaining about the tasks ahead, you are injecting your life with the expectation of strife and conflict. What you energetically put out into the world is exactly what you will receive. It's difficult to feel love for what you do when you are stressed. The work you choose to do in this life should fill you with a sense of purpose and joy. If it isn't meaningful to you, then perhaps it's time to affirm your self-esteem and redirect your energy into something that brings you bliss. You don't necessarily have to quit your current day job, but you may need to secure a window of time each day and pour your energy into another pursuit that really gives you purpose. Perhaps it's time to hatch new plans about the future.

The Eight of Pentacles reversed also asks if you have been depleting your energy on a pursuit that isn't showing signs of progress. Western culture continually sends us the message that hard work and achievements will cure all your suffering. This is not always the case. This card can represent an overdrive of productivity. Are you excessively stressing?

The Eight of Pentacles reversed always asks your heart, "Am I enjoying this?" No matter if the answer is yes or no, there is always an opportunity to make the task before you more meaningful. How can you infuse your work with more joy?

Finally, the Eight of Pentacles reversed can indicate that you may be neglecting important self-work that must be done. Make sure you are giving yourself just as much care and attention as you give to your job, loved ones, or family.

NINE OF PENTACLES

The wealth card.

The Nine of Pentacles represents wealth and security. It also symbolizes luxuriating in your accumulated successes. Every financial guru teaches that gratitude leads to more wealth. The Nine of Pentacles teaches that wealth follows your focus, which must be trained. Being truly prosperous is more a state of mind than a dollar amount. If you want to experience even more wealth, you will have to slow down, acknowledge your success, and be mindful of where you place your focus.

Do you take the time to slow down and savor your successes? Are you truly opening yourself to prosperity? Does your environment feel like it exudes "wealth energy"? (If not, it might be time to get a book about feng shui from the library.)

The wealthy woman on this card admires her abundant garden. It shines with the golden light of success. Her palace sits aloft the hills in the distance. She is training her pet falcon. She wears a glove over her left hand to protect herself from the falcon's sharp talons. The left hand is associated with receptivity. The woman is protective and selective about what she is allowing herself to receive. Falcons are famous for their acute vision and powers of focus. The woman has placed a training hood over her falcon. This symbolizes that she has learned how to train her own focus. She knows that whatever she places her attention on, she receives. The falcon is not racing ahead for a hunt or frantically looking for his next prey. He is instead enjoying the affection of his mistress. He is also listening carefully to her encouraging words.

The woman has another pet with her in the garden; this one is rather difficult to see but also teaches a very important lesson. Look closely. Can you spot it?

Far down in the left-hand corner of the image is a snail. Snails are slooooowwwwww. They take their time to reach their destination. In fact, destinations aren't really important to them, because snails are always home. The woman keeps the snail in her garden. Snails are very sensitive to their environments. This reminds her that, in order to ensure that even more wealth flows, she needs to slow down and clear her environment of burdensome energy. The wealthy woman makes sure her garden is only filled with imagery that conjures up a sense of abundance. This keeps her little companions healthy, ensuring wealth is continuously attracted to her.

When the Nine of Pentacles appears, it heralds a time to open yourself to wealth. Take control of where you place your focus. Enhance your environment so that it evokes feelings of wealth, success, and prosperity. Perhaps you need more greenery in your home. Maybe your house needs to be cleared of clutter. Like the snail, you are very sensitive to your environment. See to it that your home gives you a positive sensory experience in each room. Light some candles and accent your place with some richly colored pillows. Place some abundant plants by the windows or get a money tree. Ensure that your home smells good and pleases all the senses. I find the scent of cinnamon always makes me feel prosperous. When you look around, you should see an abundant environment that reflects feelings of success.

Slow down and create an environment that emanates prosperity. Abundance will follow. The Nine of Pentacles always promises prosperity, success, and comfort.

Nine of Pentacles Reversed

If the Nine of Pentacles appears reversed, it asks if you are tolerating anything in your life that is beneath your personal standards of excellence. Often when you are immersed in a messy relationship, environment, or situation, you can slowly become blind or numb to it. After a while, you forget to even notice anything that is out of balance. This becomes the new normal.

Living with garbage can unconsciously make you feel like garbage. Take an honest assessment of your personal environment. Look within your heart for any garbage that needs to be taken out. Do your environment and state of mind meet with your best standards of excellence? Are you happy with the way things are? Is there some work you need to do on yourself or your personal space to improve?

Much like the beautiful garden on the card, your environment needs to exemplify stately beauty. This includes your state of mind. Know that you deserve the best and refuse to accept anything that undermines your sense of self-worth. Speak up and take control of your personal garden today. Take the hood off the falcon and train your focus on improving anything that does not meet your standards. You deserve the best!

TEN OF PENTACLES

Legacy.

The Ten of Pentacles symbolizes the legacy that you will eventually leave. It represents investment in the things that really last. This card also highlights the value of family and tradition. When the Ten of Pentacles appears, it asks if you are truly leaving the world a better place than you found it. Cultivating your personal legacy can include caring for future generations, cultivating a talent that positively impacts the world, or exemplifying what is best in you.

What legacy do you want to leave? Where does the best part of yourself shine through? How can you ensure that your light continues to shine long after you are gone?

The old man on this card reflects on a life well lived. The roots of wealth are firmly established for the future generations surrounding him. He didn't grow up in a wealthy home. He sacrificed and scraped throughout his youth so that he could leave something better for his children and grandchildren. He is not only leaving his family a house or money. He is leaving them with his *example*. He is sharing himself and his wisdom with future generations. The love he has for his family is the greatest legacy he will leave. The family is prosperous and has more than it needs. His children have been raised right and will pass on all the love and learning they received to their children. The two dogs symbolize loyalty and devotion. Hidden above the old man's head is a coat of arms depicting the scales (see also Justice and the Six of Pentacles). Perhaps the man is an older version of the merchant on the Six of Pentacles. Regardless, the old man deserves the secure life he is surrounded by. The scales symbolize honesty, justice, and the cultivation of good Karma.

The Ten of Pentacles asks you to look at your progress toward your larger goals. The legacy you are establishing will remain long after you have gone. Your personal legacy could be a book, a business, an art form, a property, or your *example*. Perhaps your life's work is merely to be your best self and to spread kindness and love in a world that really needs it right now.

The Ten of Pentacles also asks you to place your focus on your family or community. Reconnect with loved ones. The love you share with others will always be your greatest legacy. Release pettiness and squabbles. Forgive past slights. Every human being has a mixture of good and bad. Nobody has a *perfect* family.

The Ten of Pentacles assures you that what you invest your energy in now will create results well into the future. When this card appears, your life is becoming more secure. There is no need to fear the future when the Ten of Pentacles appears. Keep an eye on the long game and be patient. Reinforce stable foundations for future success.

Ten of Pentacles Reversed

If the Ten of Pentacles appears reversed, then it is time to acknowledge your ancestors in some way. This will ensure that the legacy they worked so hard to leave survives. Sometimes this card asks you to confront generational problems that continue to emerge in your family line. What qualities did you learn from loved ones who have passed on? Perhaps it's time to learn more about your grandparents and great-grandparents or your genealogy. What adversity did your ancestors overcome in their time? What can you learn from their example? Did you have a special relationship with someone who has now passed on?

The greatest tribute you can give to those who have passed on is to champion their best qualities and pass them down to the present generation. This will ensure the legacy they worked a lifetime to establish will live on. You share not only genetics with your ancestors, but also a soul connection and traditions. Bring your ancestors' best qualities into the present generation. Allow their determination to inspire you to overcome present challenges. If they could overcome adversity, then you can, too! History is a poignant teacher. By learning from the past, we can ensure we aren't doomed to relive its darkest hours. Take what you have learned from those who have gone before and utilize this wisdom to be your best. One hundred years from now, you will be the ancestor. What do you want those future generations to remember about you?

PAGE OF PENTACLES

Passion for learning.

The Page of Pentacles represents the passion you feel for what really interests you. This can be a goal, a talent, a creative pursuit, or a career you love. To get better at anything, you must work at it. When your interests become work, it can be easy to forget why you used to love it. The job to do (and the anxiety to do it well) can soon take the place of the passion. The process of getting better at anything is strewn with mistakes. Errors are your best teachers. If you don't remind yourself what you love about the work you do, your morale can quickly sink. Throw in comparing yourself to others who do it "better," and you've got a perfect recipe for anxiety, apathy, or avoidance. In order to reclaim your passion, get back to the basics. It's time to remind yourself what initially made you passionate about this pursuit in the first place!

Why did you choose to go into the work you do? What stoked your enthusiasm when you were just getting started? Has perfecting your talents become something that gives you more anxiety than joy? How has an area of study enriched your life?

The Page holds up his pentacle with reverence. It is a symbol of his passion for learning, perfecting, and understanding. He lives in a fertile valley in the shade of trees and mountains. However, every image on this card is in its beginning stage. The cluster of trees is not yet a forest. The lone mountain in the distance is not yet a range. The small cultivated garden is hardly an expansive field of crops ready for harvest. These all symbolize the *idea* of something yet to come. Although the Page of Pentacles is a child of the Earth element, he always seems to have his head in the clouds. This kid is going places! His red hat symbolizes the passion he has for the creative ideas he is just getting started with. He is not just a dreamer, but also a doer. His green tunic represents the abundance that will result from making his ideas tangible successes in the external world.

Sometimes anxiety about doing well or being perfect causes avoidance of the very things that used to bring joy. The Page of Pentacles asks you to remember what ideas imbue you with a sense of passion and excitement. Did your passion make you feel good, or did it help someone? Is it something that highlights your unique brilliance?

The Page of Pentacles symbolizes honing your skills and ideas. He represents the excitement that accompanies the transformation of ideas into solid reality. This can be done through school, training, or personal study. In the case of new goals, this card holds the promise for their realization.

For success to take root, the love for your idea must supersede your anxiety about it.

When the Page of Pentacles represents a person, he symbolizes a precocious younger individual (perhaps a student) who is still undergoing a learning process. His ideas are usually brilliant, and he shows a great potential for future success. The Page of Pentacles is especially talented in the realm of teaching, learning, or perfecting. Pages can represent the young-at-heart of any gender.

Page of Pentacles Reversed

If the Page of Pentacles appears reversed, he asks if you are losing your passion for what used to interest you. If you feel blasé about your goals, it's time to remember why you love the work you do. This could be a pivotal moment when the direction of your energy needs to change. The Page of Pentacles reversed can symbolize feeling burnt-out with a skill, subject, or routine. Check in with yourself and ascertain if excitement for your passions feels blocked. This card can often appear for people who turn hobbies or interests into their careers. If purposeful work is not periodically injected with joy and excitement, it can soon feel like a daily grind.

The Page of Pentacles reversed reminds you to marry enthusiasm with your pursuits. Perhaps you need to take a break from work and create something just for the love of it. The Page of Pentacles loves to stimulate the mind. Allow yourself to participate in something that reignites your interests. Seek out fascinating people and exchange ideas.

Often, the Page of Pentacles reversed represents relearning a life lesson that we thought we completed. This may be a time when you are circling back over your life and reinforcing the fundamentals of who you are. This will strengthen who you are becoming.

If the Page of Pentacles reversed represents a person, he symbolizes someone who is too hard on themself. He is a perfectionist and is often nitpicking his appearance, abilities, or talents. Although others may see him as "together," he rarely sees this himself. The Page of Pentacles reversed needs to understand that he is worthy, even if he is still a work in progress.

KNIGHT OF PENTACLES

Managing expectations.

The Knight of Pentacles represents a need for patience and perspective when our current life does not measure up to our expectations. It is a card that teaches us how to use setbacks as opportunities for resilience. Only hindsight will reveal just why something we hoped for or expected didn't quite pan out the way we thought it should have. Life has a way of steering us to even better blessings than the ones we expected.

Has something not panned out the way you hoped it would? Do you feel bad about the present because you don't have something that you think others have? Are you able to see that the game isn't over yet and that there are still marvelous things in store for you?

The Knight of Pentacles rides in the fields, dreaming of the future. He is utterly disappointed with the present. The fields he surveys are brown and don't seem to be growing anything. How many more years does he have to keep pacing the same fields before they grow?! It can be so frustrating! In order to become a king, this Knight needs to demonstrate that he can make a field grow. Here's the rub: the field will never grow until he learns to be at peace with himself and his present lesson of patience and self-acceptance.

It is interesting to note that of all the Knights in the Rider-Waite-Smith tarot, the Knight of Pentacles is the only Knight who is seated on a horse that is not moving forward. This indicates that events are at a standstill. Although the Knight is eager to progress, he must learn something important that can only be found where he is now, in the present. His helm and the horse's bridle are decorated with oak leaves. Oak is the tree of wisdom, and wisdom can only be gained by experiencing both successes and failures. It is in the present where wise breakthroughs are happening for this Knight, even if he is unable to recognize them.

The Universe has a way of providing teachable moments. The lessons appear in the form of recurring setbacks that repeat themselves over and over until you absorb what you need to change about your mindset. At first glance, it might just seem like you are getting thwarted again. That's when you need to ask, "How can I use this as an opportunity for resilience?" Perhaps the recurring situations you face are teaching you patience and self-acceptance. Perhaps they are teaching you about boundaries or not needing others to validate you. Perhaps you just need to learn to be at peace with where you are in the present. When the Knight of Pentacles appears, you are exactly where you need to be, even if it doesn't feel like it. Be now.

Today, the challenge is to look at setbacks and see them as opportunities for growth. Look back at how past disappointments made you stronger and led you to even better blessings than what you thought you wanted.

Be patient and resilient.

The Knight of Pentacles can also represent a person with great potential who is still growing into their shoes. He may also symbolize someone who is frustrated with their current lot. This card is ripe with potential, and success is assured for this individual in time. Knights can represent youngish adults of any gender. Knights are usually people who are phasing out of one way of life and into another.

Knight of Pentacles Reversed

If the Knight of Pentacles appears reversed, he represents managing negative expectations. This card often appears when we are bracing ourselves for something that we assume is going to be bad. It asks you to turn your expectations on their head. How could the situation you are dreading turn into an unexpected blessing? By confronting this situation, what are you gaining? Sometimes this card indicates that you just need to be more practical and not buy into assumptions without evidence to back them up. The field in the background of this card may look brown, but there is magic happening beneath the surface. Germinating seeds will manifest into autumn's harvest. Although the Knight may be impatient, he must accept patience before he succeeds. Patience brings your awareness to the present. *This* moment is where your power truly resides.

Today, accept that not everything you want or desire is going to happen right away. Perhaps you need to make peace with the idea that your goal won't manifest in quite the way you planned. Sometimes things we don't get in life are blessings in disguise. Don't judge your current progress by how it appears in the barren fields of winter. Even in winter, new life is stirring beneath the surface. Progress may feel slowed, but this is an illusion. With patience and hindsight, you will see why this situation took the turns it did.

When the Knight of Pentacles reversed represents another person, he is often impractical and chronically seems to get stuck. He may represent a slow learner who tends to repeat a similar lesson over and over. You may want to avoid financial dealings with this individual.

QUEEN OF PENTACLES

Everything is growing in its perfect time.

The Queen of Pentacles represents success gained after patient effort. Everything growing in her garden was guided by her skilled hands. In the image, the Queen is calmly sitting, admiring her coin. Even though not everything in her garden is in full bloom yet, she finds contentment in the moment. She's present.

Are you content with your life just as it is right now? Do you fret about achieving tangible success? Does your fear and anxiety rob you of enjoying your life right now?

The Queen of Pentacles is seated on a sturdy throne decorated with the emblem of Capricorn, the astrological goat. The sign of Capricorn is ruled by Saturn, also known as Father Time. The Queen of Pentacles knows how to use time and patience to achieve her ultimate success. She also has a great sense of timing. She wisely keeps an eye on the long game.

In the foreground of the card (bottom right-hand corner) is the Queen's pet rabbit. Rabbits can symbolize nervous energy. This reminds us that we must still act toward our dreams even when we are afraid. Rabbits can also symbolize fertility (hence the Easter Bunny and the budding of spring). Rabbits were believed to bring good luck and swift fortune. The rabbit can symbolize the Queen's nervous energy, and yet the Queen of Pentacles doesn't drive the rabbit out of her garden. The Queen knows that nervous energy can be useful when properly channeled to get something done. Just now, however, the Queen is ignoring the fears of her rabbit and is instead focusing on the coin in her lap. This symbolizes that the Queen is not letting her anxieties distract her from what she is trying to manifest.

Even the Queen of Pentacles gets nervous, but you would never guess it by looking at her calm and stately appearance. Allow your anxiety to chatter in the background without losing focus on what you are trying to manifest. Don't make war with your anxiety. It can be a tremendous asset when there is a deadline to meet or an opportunity that needs to be acted upon swiftly. The key is not to make the rabbit (anxiety) the center of your focus. Be like the Queen of Pentacles and keep your eyes on the prize, symbolized by the coin.

The Queen of Pentacles also reminds you to ground yourself in the pleasures of the physical world. Acknowledge the warmth of your home, the flavors of the food you are eating, the green spirits calling from the trees, and the smell of the raindrops misting outside. Experience life's beauty with your senses. Be like the Queen of Pentacles and enjoy what you have while still holding space for what is currently manifesting. The Queen of Pentacles assures you that your efforts are ripening and blooming in their perfect timing. She is confident that you will know when the time is right to act. For now, relax in your garden. Be content. The Queen of Pentacles promises financial success and security despite your greatest worries.

If the Queen of Pentacles represents a person, she is an earthy woman who is secure financially, understands money, and can open doorways for you. She is dependable, faithful, and realistic about life. She can also advise you in long-term investments and financial planning. Queens can be mature individuals of any gender who wield strong feminine power.

Queen of Pentacles Reversed

The Queen's jittery rabbit now appears on the top of the card. The rabbit calls your attention to unsubstantiated anxiety about the future, which may be clouding your perspective of reality. The rabbit is a worrier. He frets about being late, danger, pitfalls, traps, and potential enemies. All the while he is unable to feel at peace in the present moment. The rabbit mistakenly thinks that if he braces for all potential fears, he will be ready for them when they arrive. In actuality, the constant worry leads to unnecessary suffering and tension.

The Queen's garden is growing in perfect timing but requires a peaceful environment (mentally and physically). Excessive anxiety wastes personal power and quickly depletes energy. Today, emulate the wise and patient upright Queen. Find your center. Send calm, loving energy to the nervous rabbit within. *The blossoms will still open, whether you worry about them or not.*

If the Queen of Pentacles reversed represents another person, she may represent someone who periodically struggles with anxiety. Soothing places in nature can have an amazing effect on them. Upright or reversed, the Queen of Pentacles is prone to overwork. She also prefers stability, consistency, and predictability. Try to use facts to assuage some of her fears. This will give her a reassuring sense of solidity.

KING OF PENTACLES

Success.

The King of Pentacles represents the golden path to worldly success. He possesses the internal and external markers of wealth and bearing. The bulls on his throne are symbols for the astrological sign of Taurus. They represent stubborn tenacity and a commitment to reaching your goals. The King is surrounded by abundant possessions and lives in a shining castle. The King of Pentacles is looked upon by others as wealthy. However, his wealth stems from knowing that success grows from patience, preparation, and willingness.

Are you feeling nervous about your financial future? Is there something you want to achieve, but you don't even know where to begin? Would you say your thoughts about wealth in your life are positive or negative at this time?

The King of Pentacles is among the favorite children of his mother, the Empress. He alone has been entrusted with her golden scepter, which makes all things grow. The reason the Empress trusts the King of Pentacles is because he has proven himself to be patient and prepared, and he approaches his tasks with loving willingness. He also wears the armor of his father, the Emperor, and has built a stone wall around his abundant vineyard to protect his domain. The King of Pentacles has balanced both the masculine and the feminine principles within himself.

The King's robes are covered with grapes. Grapes are notoriously fickle and need a lot of patience to cultivate. This is especially true when transforming the grapes into pleasure-bringing wine. The King of Pentacles has the perfect temperament for nurturing these magical berries. He is out in the vineyards long before the growing season, tending the soil and preparing the vines for the coming harvests. His patience and skill have made him wealthy, as everyone wants to taste his magical brew. The King understands that to truly get success from life's pursuits, you must enjoy them. You must appreciate your responsibilities, taking them up with gratitude for the security they will provide. All the King's labors are undertaken with love for what he is doing. This ensures that as the grapes grow, they are infused with sweetness, not bitterness.

To achieve the success of the King of Pentacles, you will need several things. First, you need patience. Not every day is sunny. Be reminded that the rainy days contribute life-giving water. Anything of worth requires time to develop. This includes your goals, skills, and gifts. The grapes on the vine cannot be hurried and must be tended kindly and consistently.

Second, you need to prepare for the future. Establish your goals. Write them down. Break them up into achievable bits. This can bolster your sense of accomplishment.

Last, you need to approach what you are doing with love. Infuse your responsibilities with a willing and grateful heart. This will bring much better results than if your tasks are approached with resentment, fear, or worry. This attitude will also guarantee that the grapes you cultivate are sweet grapes and not grapes of wrath.

The King of Pentacles signifies health, wealth, money, stability, success, and joy.

When the King of Pentacles represents a person, he is financially stable and secure. He also has a great mind for business, entrepreneurship, and finance. This King prefers stability and low-risk investments. He can also represent a stable family man who always plans for future security. Kings can be mature people of any gender who are leaders or figures of authority.

King of Pentacles Reversed

If the King of Pentacles appears reversed, he signals that it is time to get organized in your thinking. Future goals can quickly become overwhelming if you try to tackle every single detail from the start. The King of Pentacles advises you to break up your major goals into smaller achievable tasks. Be patient with yourself and with the process.

What is the most pressing issue that needs to be addressed in order to begin the journey toward your goal? What seems to be habitually holding up progress? Are you avoiding something out of fear? What do you need to learn more about to take your next steps?

Take your major goal and break it up into a manageable sequence of steps. Organize your tasks into a schedule and take action. The King of Pentacles is a master organizer. He patiently and lovingly tends his vineyard over time, ensuring the sweetest grapes. The best grapes cannot be hurried. The King's example can help you remove the mental clutter blocking your progress. He exemplifies the notion that Rome was not built in a day. However, the King of Pentacles (upright or reversed) reassures you that Rome was eventually built!

If the King of Pentacles reversed represents another person, he could be someone in a position of leadership who is overwhelmed by his duties. He might appear unqualified or may need to receive more training. He can also represent someone who wants to take financial shortcuts.

THE SUIT OF WANDS

Your growth, inspiration, and ambition.

The Wands suit represents inspiration, aspiration, and transformation. This suit reveals your ambition and motivates you toward achievements. When you look at the cards of this suit, you can see budding leaves sprouting from the staves. Wands represent growth. Each of the Court cards in the Wands suit reveals a charismatic figure. They each have a strong belief in their abilities.

Wands are potent symbols for the element of Fire. Fire transforms everything it touches. It burns away the old and can melt even the hardest metal into a new form. Without Fire, there would be no civilization or technological advances. Wands in a reading are immensely transformative. When Wands cluster around other cards in a reading, they reveal which area of your life is growing or transforming. The Wands suit can also light a proverbial fire under your behind to get you to grow!

When a multitude of Wand cards appears, expect events to speed up. Wands signify swift movement, energy, passion, and excitement. They can also reveal if there is more improvement to be done. This suit often represents youth and newness.

Wand cards can also signify *talent.* They reveal how to use your personal abilities to strive for a better life. Look at the other cards that appear around Wand cards to give you a clue as to where your greatest talents and potential can be expressed.

Finally, Wands are confident! They rekindle your courage and remind you to have faith in yourself.

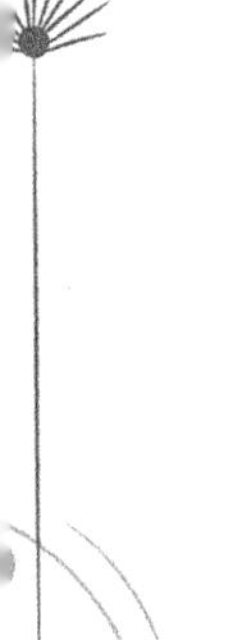

ACE OF WANDS

Magical inspiration.

The Ace of Wands represents breakthroughs, inspiration, and new ideas. It heralds a brilliant epiphany that can transform your reality. Like the many leaves sprouting from the wand, you are experiencing an exciting period of mental growth. You are branching out into new realms of possibilities. The Ace of Wands motivates fresh concepts that can carry you over old obstacles.

Do you have a lot of great ideas but lack the confidence to act on them? Do you hesitate on acting toward your dreams because you fear failure? Have you hit the same old brick wall, feeling that it is preventing you from making a huge breakthrough?

A divine hand emerges from a cloud, offering you a magic wand. This wand can provide you with the ability to make all your dreams come true. If you were to fully grasp this wand, you would be flooded with bright ideas that bring solutions to old problems. Wands are symbols of brilliant inspiration seemingly channeled from above.

An old ruined castle sits aloft a hill in the distance. This symbolizes that old barriers of outdated thinking are now crumbling. Former creative blocks are being transcended. New ideas will carry you over previously impenetrable walls.

Wands have a long history of helping characters in the fairy tales overcome seemingly impossible odds. The Fairy Godmother used her magic wand to send Cinderella to the ball in a pumpkin after all hope seemed lost. But even magic seems to have a catch. The wand's magical effects always seem to have a time limit. With Cinderella, it was the stroke of midnight. This symbolizes that you must act fast when divine inspiration strikes you. If you don't take full advantage of your creative ideas, your carriage will revert to a pumpkin, and your beautiful horses will once again become mice. However, if you do act on the magic being offered (just as Cinderella did), you can go to the ball, make an impression, and transform a magical dream into a wonderful reality.

Cinderella didn't think to herself, "Well, I am actually just a cleaning lady, so even with all these magical opportunities, I won't allow the prince to see me. What would he even think of me? Magic doesn't exist anyway, so why try?" No! Cinderella took that fairy's magic and ran with it! Be confident in yourself! You are also worthy of any success you can dream of.

Leaves fall from the Ace of Wands. This is a symbol for spring eventually turning to autumn. This reflects the truth that your opportunity won't last forever. The magic of your mind is only as good as your ability to *act without hesitation* when struck by divine inspiration. Go for it!

Ace of Wands Reversed

If the Ace of Wands appears reversed, it reminds you to stop wishing and start doing. Today, don't let your brilliant ideas slip away! Write them down and come up with a plan for practical manifestation. All solutions are available to you. Old barriers are crumbling, revealing glimpses of magical future possibilities. Why not take the action required to have your dream?! You can do it, but only if you are willing. Once your rough ideas are written down, refine them. Flesh out the details of how to make your goals realities. Seek out the correct information. Consult with those who are in the know. Research your goal on the internet. Take a risk! The Ace of Wands reversed can bring about the feeling of not knowing where to begin. Do not let this feeling paralyze you. Begin somewhere, wherever you are. Don't worry about doing it correctly; just take the first step toward your goal. If you begin, momentum will kick in and take you to the next step.

You are being offered a magic wand to wave, and this can change everything! It comes in the form of inspired ideas that have already been churning around inside your head. Write these ideas down, and then act on them. Just like the wand's magic, brilliant ideas are fleeting. They are just "fairy stories" you tell yourself, until you make them happen. There is magic working within your mind. Channel it!

TWO OF WANDS

"I'll finally be happy when . . ."

The Two of Wands represents the sense that there is something missing, and that if you were to get that *thing,* then you would be happy. This restlessness can be useful to help you set goals and make improvements to your life. However, the Two of Wands warns that achievements and acquisitions will not be what finally *makes* you happy. Getting what you desire can feel good for a time, but if you gain an achievement without authentic awareness of your true value, the achievement will soon feel hollow. This restless search for happiness through achievements, money, relationships, or status symbols can get you nowhere fast!

Do you ever think, "I'll be happy when I finally have *X*?" Do you feel restless or anxious that you haven't lived up to your *true* purpose yet? Do you somehow believe that the right salary, the right position, the right weight, or even the right person has the power to finally make you happy?

The lord of a manor looks out over the great expanse of his estate. He always felt restless as a child, feeling there was something missing. He believed that he could find joy if he just got to the right place in life. He was very poor growing up, and his family struggled for money. He saw how poverty made those around him suffer, so he thought, "If I made a lot of money one day, then I'd finally be happy." He learned how to sail and traded goods from all over the world. Soon the young man became very wealthy.

But money didn't quite satisfy this man or give him the joy he thought it would. He must be crazy! He always wanted wealth, and yet this didn't seem to be enough. He looked at the nobility around him. They all acted happy with themselves. What did they all have that he didn't? They lived in castles, of course! So, he thought, "I think I'll finally be happy if I live in a fine castle, with battlements and a beautiful view of the sea."

So, the man purchased the grandest estate in the land, with a beautiful view of the ocean. The castle is emblazoned with the same roses and lilies that appear on the Magician card. The lord's focus manifested all his rich holdings. This made him feel good finally… for a couple days. Then that old restless feeling came back. We catch a glimpse of him now in the picture. You can see him holding a globe, looking out restlessly beyond the sea. He's thinking, "I'd be happy if I finally owned the whole world with all its treasures."

How much are you willing to bet that even the *whole world* wouldn't make him happy?

The lesson of the Two of Wands is that the acquisition of things and the achievement of goals is not enough to bring happiness to an already unfulfilled heart. Money can make it easier to enjoy your life, but it will not actually provide joy. Your bliss must come from deep within.

The truth is that accomplishments, other people, how you look, and money can't *make* you happy if you aren't already happy with yourself as you are now.

If you can find self-love and joy at this moment, without achieving another goal in life, then you have freed yourself from the restless search.

Today, stop thinking, "If I lose five pounds, I'll finally be happy... If I find the right person, I'll be happy... If I get the right job, I'll be happy... If I become a doctor, I'll be happy... If enough people like my post, I'll be happy... If I just looked a certain way, I'd be happy..." It's not true! Wherever you go, there you are. The Two of Wands asks you to stop searching and reconnect with your inner bliss right now. You don't have to wait. It's here today, but only if you stop looking in all the places where it isn't.

Two of Wands Reversed

If the Two of Wands appears reversed, it represents obsessive planning and thinking about future events that you don't have control over. This card tells you that you may be getting ahead of yourself. Are you lost in a trance of a future, full of grandiosity or calamities, that hasn't manifested yet? The man on the card is lost in his machinations for the future as well. The lord of the manor on the card is not present. When reversed, this card indicates that you may have to stop hoping, planning, wishing, dreading, or obsessing about a future that is not here yet. Worrying about events that have not yet transpired can rob you of peace in the moment.

Give worrying about the future a rest. In truth, the future that you are spending so much energy on planning to the minutest detail will probably not entirely resemble your plan anyway. Like the lord of the manor on the card, you are surrounded by life's blessings right now; you just might be forgetting to experience them. Planning for the future is healthy, but obsessing about it is not. Nothing seems to ever go *exactly* as planned in life. Nature has a way of breaking the obsessive constrictions we try to impose. Sometimes the Two of Wands reversed represents perfectionism at its worst. Stop improving and start *being*.

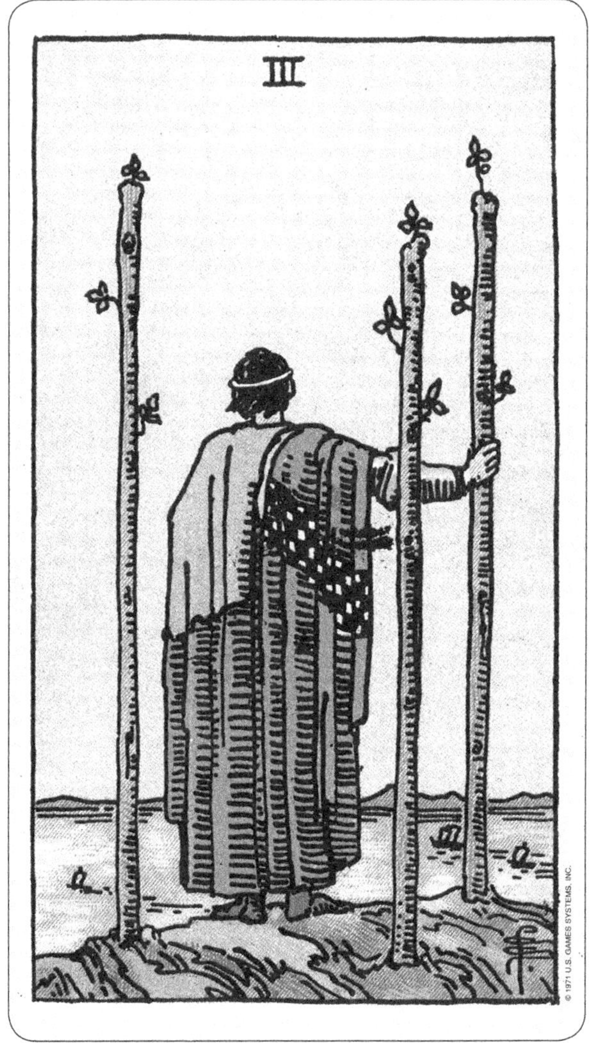

THREE OF WANDS

Life is still wide open and waiting.

The Three of Wands reveals that your life is like a large blank canvas. It is waiting for you to create a masterpiece that depicts your heart's desire. Despite your fears, nothing has been irreparably screwed up yet. There is still time! This card heralds the opportunity to take the courageous journey toward your *bliss.* The only caveat is that you must stop to identify what bliss means for you. This must occur before you can move on to new horizons. If you can name your bliss, you are on your way to claiming it!

Are you clear about what you *truly* want out of life? If someone were to ask you what you want from life, would you respond, "To be happy," without even knowing what that looks like for you? Do you believe you've messed up your life, thinking you can't get it back on track?

Let me tell you something. That's just another lie from fear. It's not true.

The man on the Three of Wands is considering his future. He's richly dressed, implying that he's an important person in his small corner of the world. Yet he feels unfulfilled. The man is not looking at you; he's thinking about life. His life.

At first glance, it appears that he is overlooking a vast desert. A sandy wasteland with little promise. What kind of future is that?! But always with the tarot, you must look a little closer. You will see that these are not barren sands, but the orange, glowing waters of sunrise or sunset. Ships are crossing to and from their ports of safety. Sunrise and sunset are the magical times of in-between. Magical transformations always happen at these times (see the Two of Swords). The man's heart is yearning to embark, to leave his small island home. Somehow, unconsciously, this has always been his dream. He wasn't sure what he was missing, but now he knows. He took the time to stop, think, and get clear about what he *really* wants out of life. Now that he is clear on his objective, he can open himself to the wonders of the world. He's going to go for it!

The Three of Wands asks you to stop, review, and think about where you want to go. Is there something you still want to have, achieve, or be? Well, you can still have it! The world is wide open and waiting. You may just have to leave your own "small island," which is a symbol for your comfort zone. If you act on what you truly want for yourself, you won't ever regret it. Taking the initiative in the face of fear enhances your courage, which in turn becomes self-esteem. Who doesn't want to feel more confident about themself?

You can still have your goal, but you must be clear on what your goal is. When it becomes fixed in your mind, it will serve as your treasure map, guiding you to unbelievable riches.

With your bliss in mind, ask yourself, "Am I doing at least one thing today that contributes to achieving this life for myself?" If the answer is no, don't beat yourself up. Get up and change it. Make it priority number one tomorrow.

Wanting to "be happy" isn't clear enough. What does "happy" really mean for you? Above the temple leading to the Oracle of Delphi were the words "Know thyself."[25] If you really do take the time to know yourself, then all you desire can finally manifest. Knowing yourself includes knowing your bliss. The Three of Wands also depicts ships in the waters, symbolizing trade and communication. Reach out to others to create new pathways toward mutual success. Cooperation, learning, and leaving your small pond will help you achieve your goal.

Three of Wands Reversed

If the Three of Wands appears reversed, it advises you that "new" does not necessarily translate to "better." Both the Two and Three of Wands are cards of yearning for new successes, new places, and new opportunities. The Three of Wands reversed represents finding happiness in your own backyard. Beware of mentally existing too far ahead, scheming, pining, or striving. Your attention is needed right here, right now. Surrounding cards may reveal what needs more of your focus presently. What do you love about your life currently? Breathe in the truth of your unlimited potential at this moment. Lovingly bless yourself with the unconditional acceptance that glows from your heart's center.

Sometimes the Three of Wands reversed symbolizes feeling lost. There are so many future options or opportunities that you may feel overwhelmed. This is a good problem to have! Seek out a trusted advisor to help you weigh the pros and cons of each potential future. Maybe you will find that you already have what you want. Return your attention to the real world in front of you. You must ground and center before proceeding.

---

25. Pausanias, *Description of Greece*, 4:507.

FOUR OF WANDS

Celebrate.

The imagery of the Four of Wands is straightforward. It shows a party or celebration happening. The figures on the card are dancing, full of mirth. The Four of Wands is all about connecting with others for no other reason than to have laughter, humor, and fun. The Four of Wands also reminds you to celebrate your rites of passage. It's important to mark even small achievements and accomplishments with a special occasion. This will ensure that you experience the joy of what you are manifesting.

When is the last time you let your hair down and had some fun? Have you been too serious lately? Do you think you can't enjoy yourself because there are twenty million unfinished things to do?

The Four of Wands reminds us that having occasional fun isn't something to feel guilty about. It's vital to remain a balanced human being! Sometimes there is just no substitute for laughing and dining outdoors on a balmy June evening with someone whose company you enjoy. Nothing beats a hot cup of cocoa, a snuggly chair, and a good book when it's cold outside. There will always be a long list of unfinished things to do. Whether you take a break or not, they'll still be waiting for you. So why not return to your tasks in a good mood? Celebrate an accomplishment you've made or a goal you've reached. Treat yourself. Celebrate that you went to the gym today. Give yourself an elegant dinner for making it through a difficult workday. You could even just celebrate because you're alive! Life isn't just about flitting from one busy task to another. It's also about occasionally stopping yourself and finding charm in the moment. Just look outside and see how prettily the light dances off the leaves.

The Four of Wands doesn't necessarily mean you have to go out and party. It's a little less intense than that. Sometimes it just reminds us to connect with people who matter to us. Send some lighthearted messages. Write a sweet card. Remind yourself of the exceptional people in your life and show them how grateful you are that they exist. Brighten their day if things have been getting too heavy for them. Tell a funny story. The best people in our lives make our journey through the hills and valleys so much more pleasant. This card also advises you to have more fun socially.

The figures on the Four of Wands are all holding bouquets, a symbol for beautiful gifts received. The message of this card is clear: "Have some fun and enjoy life's gifts!"

Four of Wands Reversed

If the Four of Wands appears reversed, it represents changing social structures. You may have outgrown old friendships, relationships, or social scenes. You may also begin to attract new individuals. Outgrowing relationships is part of life. Sometimes you may find yourself progressing while someone you care about becomes stuck. None of us grow at the exact same rate. Finding that your social needs have evolved is nothing to feel guilty about. Some friendships last a lifetime, while others fade.

The Four of Wands reversed could also be warning you of the company you are currently keeping. Are your acquaintances making you feel energized or drained after your encounters? This card highlights the social groups or organizations that affect your energy level. Surround yourself with people who make you feel positive, lively, and empowered. You don't have to feel obligated toward energy vampires! Know where others end and where you begin. You may need some time away from social circles to recharge.

When the Four of Wands appears reversed, the turret on the castle forms an arrow that is pointing downward. It is time to get back in touch with the earth and with a sense of reestablished stability. It may also be time to build a new foundation, especially concerning the company you keep. Try to detach from drama.

FIVE OF WANDS

The immaturity of the comparison game.

The Five of Wands traditionally represents competition, ambition, and struggle. It symbolizes the inner tension we feel when we are caught up in our egos, constantly comparing our "status" in relation to others. Early on, kids are taught, "You must be the winner!" Life is a series of competitions: best at music, best at Monopoly, best at softball, best at spelling. You must win at each thing you try, otherwise you must be a loser, a nothing, or a failure at life. This sort of all-or-nothing thinking sets up impossible standards that can never be attained. As kids grow into adulthood, they carry this toxic baggage, feeling that there is something wrong with them. No wonder so many adults struggle with self-esteem!

Do you constantly compare your status with that of others? Do you feel that you must be perfect at everything? Have you ever stopped to think how adolescent that is?

The adolescents on the card are competing.[26] Each is trying to prove that he has the biggest stick. Each of the competitors thinks there can only be one winner. The central figure is wearing a hat, symbolizing his belief in his superiority. The competitors think to themselves, "Either I win this, or I am humiliated." The teenagers on the card do not have the wisdom that age engenders. They do not see that each of them is an important individual with their own combination of unique skills. This is represented by their distinctive colored costumes and designs. Each figure in the card has condensed his whole concept of self-worth into a game of sticks! This is all-or-nothing thinking, and it is very damaging to self-esteem.

Think about it: Could you ever attain being the richest, most beautiful, eternally young, perfect-bodied, artistic genius? Oh, and the smartest person in the world—the best at every sport, every subject, every language, every artistic medium, and every skill set known to humans? Nobody can do that! The truth is, we each have a unique combination of gifts. You might not be the best at each skill and talent you possess; however, there is no person on the planet with your unique combination of talents, skills, and abilities.

When the Five of Wands appears, catch yourself if you are playing the game of big sticks! It's ridiculous! You don't have to win at everything to be worthy. You are special and unique, and you radiate a beauty that is all your own. Nobody does you like you. My favorite entertainer, Judy Garland, used to say, "Always try to be a first-rate version of yourself, as opposed to a second-rate version of somebody else."[27]

---

26. Fiebig and Burger, *The Ultimate Guide to the Rider Waite Tarot*, 86. The authors of this book were the first to make me realize that these were *adolescents* competing in a struggle.
27. Petersen, "Liza Minelli on the Phil Donahue Show 1991," https://youtu.be/GruxXQo8MqI. On a television interview with Phil Donahue, Liza Minnelli recounts this lesson her mother, Judy Garland, taught her growing up.

Five of Wands Reversed

If the Five of Wands appears reversed, it alerts you to people who may be targeting you with negativity because of their perception that somehow you are better than them. People with wounded egos often look at others who project self-confidence or kindness as threats. For them, being kind implies that you aren't enduring your own struggles. This isn't always the case, but insecure people often assume it's so. When confronting people with low self-esteem, it's important that you don't let your ego get triggered when they treat you in a less-than-kind manner. Immature behavior like this says more about them than it does about you. Keep being excellent for yourself. You will attract those of like mind and will repel those you don't really want around anyway.

At its most basic level, the Five of Wands reversed could represent immature adolescents or adults who are acting in an immature manner. Try to not engage in tit-for-tat behavior. If you are dealing with an immature individual, try not to personalize it. They will most likely enjoy the conflict they pulled you into. Recognize that this unfortunate individual has a lot of growing to do. Try to remember a time when you were still learning or growing to facilitate a sense of compassion.

Don't participate in ego struggles brought on by the comparison game. There is no need to struggle or prove something to others who are obviously wounded. It's time to keep your eyes on your own paper. Be at peace within yourself.

SIX OF WANDS

Excellence.

The Six of Wands represents gaining attention through excellence. This card reminds you that nobody does *you* like you! Everybody has a gift, talent, or personal strength that they really excel at. This card advises you not only to embrace your talents, but to display them unapologetically. Only you have your unique recipe of abilities. The best way to improve your life is to love yourself fully, and this includes loving the gifts that you bring.

Were you taught that it's immodest and rude to call attention to your gifts? (A huge epidemic where I'm from in the Midwest!) Do you diminish your abilities and belittle your talents so others don't think you are "better" than them? Are you speaking up and getting compensated appropriately for the work that you do?

The man on the Six of Wands is the center of a triumphant procession. He is elevated by his peers because of his gifts. His regal bearing shows that he is completely comfortable with his self-confidence. He isn't being arrogant; he is simply owning what makes *him*, him. The others in the procession all wear the same style of hat and carry their own wands. Only the rider's wand is wreathed with glory. He is standing out, and he isn't afraid of it. His horse is richly dressed; this guy is not afraid to put on a show. Most people love it! It appears that he saved the town or is a marvelous celebrity. However, if you look closely behind the man riding the horse, there is another face in the crowd. This face holds an expression of jealousy and envy.

It's a sad fact that the people who shine brightest will often be the targets of others who are insecure with their own abilities. Sometimes this fear of being targeted causes talented people with extraordinary gifts to hide their gifts. And yet, your light really isn't about others. If you are following your passion and loving every moment of it, then it won't matter at all what others think. If you truly believe in your value, then there should be no question that you should embody your best self. If you are afraid to be yourself because of backlash from others, then you probably have some serious self-loving to get to! In the end, it's not about what others think about you, but what you truly believe about yourself. Do you feel worthy enough to reveal the real you?

The Six of Wands encourages you to fully embrace your talents, abilities, and worth. It's time to stop throwing yourself under the bus to appease the wounded egos of the weak. Supportive people will love when you are confident. You will attract other individuals who are comfortable in their own skin. The people who are repelled by your light will go away. And good riddance! Follow your inner compass and stop conforming to what the herd wants you to be.

So, raise your standards! Stop apologizing for yourself to make others feel better. Increase your prices if they are way too low. Let your thoughts be known (respectfully). Call attention to your talents and promote yourself. Go for that promotion. Stop being a follower and lead your own life!

Time to get back out there and be your own best cheerleader! The cream always rises to the top.

Six of Wands Reversed

If the Six of Wands appears reversed, you are put on notice to identify any erosion to your self-confidence that you might be experiencing. Like the reversed picture, don't let the opinions of others (the crowd on top) take precedence over the belief you have in your own gifts and abilities (the wreathed wand at the bottom). What others think or say about you does not matter as much as what you think and believe about yourself.

It can be encouraging to receive the validation of others, but never place yourself in a position of dependency on it. An authentic feeling of validation can only come from within. Anything else is a fleeting imitation. It doesn't matter what others think about your talents if you are happy with what you are creating. Create the life *you* want. The only validation you truly need is your own. The Six of Wands reversed could also be advising you that it is time to proceed with your goals even if you don't feel completely sure of future success. You can't win the race without having a horse in it.

SEVEN OF WANDS

Nonconformity.

The Seven of Wands signifies standing up for your integrity and individuality. When you let your personal honor code inform your decisions, you will find yourself on the high road. Taking this road isn't always the easiest path, but it is the one that will make you shine. The Seven of Wands encourages you to think as an individual and avoid devolving into groupthink. This could mean not engaging in gossip to appease a wounded ego. It could also mean not going along with something that violates your sense of right and wrong just to gain the acceptance of others.

Do you stand up for what is right, good, and just? Are you able to take the high road and not engage in slander and gossip? Can you rise above the lower human impulses for bickering, pettiness, and the ego's need to be always right?

The man on the card is defending his position on the high road. He is on the hilltop, above all the rest. His face exudes grim determination to stand up for what is right. You can't see the other individuals attacking him on the card. You don't need to. They are all the same. They are more interested in banding together to fit in while targeting those who stand out. The man at the top of the hill is in the best position. He is "King of the Mountain," and no one will dislodge him. If you look closely, the man is wearing two different kinds of shoes. This shows that he is a nonconformist. Wearing two different shoes has made him a target by those who choose uniformity. This mob doesn't know who this guy thinks he is! How dare he stand apart from them, thumbing his nose at their conformity. The group below feels good sharing a brain, but the man on the hilltop is true to his own unique path. This distinguishes him as an individual with personal strength and honor.

We might like to think that only teenagers self-consciously care about what others think. However, every human feels a desire to be accepted and belong. Unfortunately, many adults engage in way too much negativity to gain the acceptance of their "tribe." This manifests as gossip, groupthink, throwing others under the bus, racist or homophobic jokes, and rejection of people who appear different. We all like to believe we are good people, but chronically engaging in these sorts of behaviors can rob "good people" of their integrity and individualism.

Every now and then, you hear someone who shines with integrity say, "I'm not going to engage in this conversation." Or, "I actually really like her; she is quite nice if you get to know her." It isn't because people with integrity believe they are better. It is because they embrace compassion and know the sting of unfair rejection firsthand. We admire these people because they have courage and take a stand. The most admirable people do not engage in what is beneath their dignity. Take a stand for what's right. The Seven of Wands encourages you to embrace your unique vision and individuality.

Seven of Wands Reversed

If the Seven of Wands appears reversed, it advises you to let go of the false belief that it's you against the world. This card also asks if you are injecting an attitude of struggle and exasperation into your tasks. The Seven of Wands reversed can indicate that there are many demands being made upon you mentally, physically, and emotionally at this time. This card often appears when there is the anticipation of conflict, which is making you tense. How can you proactively release some of the stress you are experiencing?

Sometimes the basic meaning of this card is to stop pushing so hard to make life do what you want. Call your attention to your neck and shoulders. Are they tense, raised, or tight? It's time to breathe deep relaxation into these muscles and let them drop. Bracing for life situations before they've happened will often ensure that they are more difficult to experience. Instead, accept life as it reveals itself to you. Even the difficult moments need to be accepted. Say yes to what is happening. Accept it. It will change your posture from tension to transcendence. The more you resist life as it is, the more unnecessary suffering you will subject yourself to.

Another meaning for the Seven of Wands reversed is that you aren't allowing yourself to be open or vulnerable with others. No one is an island. Perhaps you need to accept help from others when it's offered or even ask for it. You may need to remember that you are connected and not alone.

If you have no evidence for a possible threat from others, try not to approach your interactions with an unnecessary guard up. The keyword for this card is acceptance. Acceptance of yourself, acceptance of others, and acceptance of what is changing.

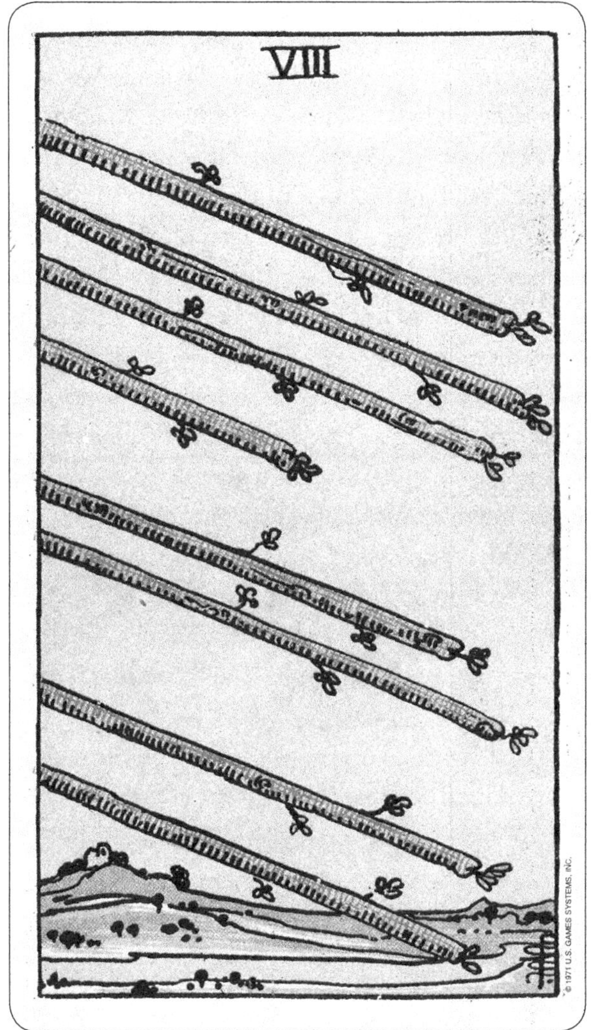

EIGHT OF WANDS

Momentum.

The Eight of Wands represents movement, progress, and momentum. Events begin to move faster when this card appears. The Eight of Wands also rules information and communication. Answers to questions become available. Once-stuck issues become unstuck, whether about a personal goal, an awaited answer, or your state of mind.

Is it time for you to confront something in your life that feels stuck and get it moving again? Is it time to act on your personal goals? Are you procrastinating about something instead of just getting the job done?

The imagery of the Eight of Wands in the Rider-Waite-Smith tarot is the only card without a human (or human part) illustrated on it. There is an impersonal quality to this card. Eight sticks are hurtling through the air; what is that supposed to tell you?! The lack of people symbolizes that progressing events should not be taken personally. It also advises you to move forward on what makes rational sense instead of letting anxiety stall you. Although all the wands are moving swiftly, they are not disorganized. There is a clear sense of direction.

A river appears on the bottom of the card, symbolizing that you need to move with life's currents instead of fighting against them. The small house on the hill signifies looking at things from a higher perspective. Take the rational view when confronting this issue. Make the logical choice.

This card can also appear to tell you to just get the job done! Write the emails, finish the task, stop procrastinating, do a Hail Mary, and take that personal risk! Ask yourself, "Am I letting anxiety about something impede my progress on this issue? Do I need to speak up and confront something so that I can overcome it?"

Don't be surprised if once-stuck parts of your life begin to pick up speed. Summon your motivation and get it done. No excuses, no whining, and no more letting anxiety run the show. Avoidance results in depletion of personal power. Today, strength comes from confronting and acting.

Let this fresh breeze at your back propel you forward. This is a very favorable card for getting events to finally move toward your target. Ride this momentum toward success.

Eight of Wands Reversed

The Eight of Wands reversed represents a flurry of activity. There are deadlines to meet, tasks to complete, bills to pay, events to be present for. All the while, life is still going on in the background. Family needs attention, mini crises need to be averted, unexpected events require immediate flexibility. All this activity can cause breathing to become shallower and anxiety levels to become elevated.

The eight staves on this card are all racing through the air. They will meet their mark more effectively if the skies are clear. The element of Air is a symbol for the mind. This card is a reminder to connect with the element of Air through deep breathing. Deep breathing has the positive effect of immediately creating calm. This will help you regain clarity. Often, we don't stop to alleviate our anxiety by partaking in this one simple act.

When the Eight of Wands appears reversed, it asks you to take a time-out. Slow down. Take a break from the frantic dash and relax. Calm down; all will get done on the list, but you need to address your center right now. Check in with your center and ask how it's feeling. Do you need to let go of something that unrelentingly races around in your head or heart? Can you be kind to yourself today and not cruel? It's time to take several deep, nourishing breaths and exhale all that stress away.

There! Doesn't that feel better?

Being productive doesn't mean being tense, irritable, and stressed out. In fact, this makes you far less effective. Today, lower your stress level by treating yourself to a break. Even a little one. You can give yourself fifteen little minutes, right? Do this, and you will accomplish all your tasks with grace and ease.

NINE OF WANDS

Boundaries.

The Nine of Wands illustrates that you win at the game of life each time you stand up for yourself. This can mean creating boundaries with others who want to control you or take you down a peg. It can also mean confronting your own self-limiting attitudes and expectations. The Nine of Wands symbolizes that a personal victory is achieved each time you stand up for your dignity, worthiness, and self-respect.

Do you have trouble standing up for yourself because you fear creating conflict? Is it difficult for you to feel proud of your strengths and accomplishments? Is your greatest adversary the sabotaging voice in your own head?

The man on the Nine of Wands has defended himself against all comers for twelve rounds. He is bandaged, showing that it wasn't easy and he endured a few blows. He has created a fence with the eight wands standing behind him. He has established a boundary. The mountains in the distance form yet another boundary. Boundaries are the theme of this card. Each wand the victor has acquired was hard-won and is a trophy of his accomplishment. He is bumped and bruised, but he is still standing. He is standing up for his honor. He is standing up for his achievements and his worth. Much like the Hermit, he leans on a staff, which represents wisdom through experience. Even unpleasant experiences offer a gift. Nothing is going to take this man down. He has too much dignity to allow that to happen. He has proven his worth to *himself.*

The Nine of Wands represents pride, but not the sort that lashes out to defend a wounded ego. This sort of pride is the dignity one feels in building their own world with blood, sweat, and tears. Be proud of the scars that life sent you in the past. They made you a survivor.

Even though things may not have always come easy up until now, the school of hard knocks has made you formidable. The only possible opponent left to defeat may be coming from within. Stand up to the shadow that tells you you aren't smart enough, talented enough, good enough, successful enough, thin enough, or strong enough.

This card appears when it is time to place boundaries up for the protection of all you've worked for. Perhaps it's time to stop meekly saying "yes" when your heart is screaming "NO!" It is okay to go against the expectations of others by being honest. It's time to stand up to bullies and manipulators with clear boundaries. Embrace the part of you that is strong and stand up for what you know is right.

Be honest and clear with yourself and others. If you take a stand, you will win.

Nine of Wands Reversed

If the Nine of Wands appears reversed, it indicates that you may need to release a chip on your shoulder. The Nine of Wands always indicates hard-fought victories, but when it appears reversed, it can also indicate hard feelings as well. Feeling angry that your life is not easy is a self-limiting belief. If we stayed comfortable and conflict-free throughout our lives, we would never grow or improve. In fact, we would deteriorate. This card calls your attention to any resentments you may harbor, including those born out of a sense of the unfairness of life. Identifying with your setbacks and grievances rather than aligning with your empowerment can be psychically crippling.

At the heart of this card is a valuable lesson: *Nobody gets a free pass in this life*. Everyone has work to do on themself. Everyone will experience, grief, pain, sadness, and loss at some point. Everyone has their own struggles to overcome, and that includes people with advantages you feel you don't have. You may look at others and think they have it easier, but do you really know all their personal struggles and losses or the ones they have yet to experience? This card asks you to stop comparing the challenges you've experienced in life with the perceived advantages of others. Be proud of your personal struggles and the personal victories you've achieved as a result. Honor them as invaluable teachers.

There is no need to resent the scars you've acquired. They are beautiful reminders of how you became powerful. No more whining, making excuses, or blaming others for the place you find yourself on your path. Accept your challenges and turn them into opportunities. This will transform your perspective from perpetual victimhood to personal empowerment.

TEN OF WANDS

Service.

The Ten of Wands represents being of service to others for the success of "the whole." This includes the whole family, whole organization, or whole community. The Ten of Wands reminds you that it is never a waste of time to make your best effort, especially if it is improving the lives of others. Although your burdens may feel heavy at times, take heart. The efforts you are exerting now will ensure a brighter future. What goes around comes around!

At times, do you feel like the man on the card, struggling and straining with the tasks on your shoulders? Do you express your love for others by your actions more than your words? Are your efforts being pooled to benefit not only you, but others as well?

The man on the Ten of Wands is hard at work. He is returning from the fields with a great harvest, but the work is not easy. He is almost at the finish line. The task is almost done. At first glance, this card might elicit feelings of stress and exhaustion. But if you look closer, you see why the man is struggling. His huge house looms in the background. Its size suggests that he doesn't live alone, but rather has a large family living there, depending on him. Although we can't see the man's face, I'd like to think he wears a determined smile. He puts his head down and pushes forward. He knows that his work matters and is valued by the whole. Without him, everything would fall. There would be no house, no money, no food, no loving and safe environment for his children to grow in. His service is his greatest expression of love. Although his present moment feels tough, he is ensuring a greater future for everyone. This is the dream of every family, to leave the next generation more stable than the one before.

Some burdens in life can feel hard to carry. Unexpected events happen. Things just get dropped in your path. Someone you love might need help. This is just part of life. There is nobility in serving the whole, but only if everyone in the whole is also doing their part. Serving shouldn't be confused with codependency. The people you are helping need to be able to demonstrate that they are also helping themselves. Even people you care about need to demonstrate (if they are able to) that they are willing to carry their own bundle of sticks!

This card also has a harvest theme to it. This indicates that the toil, work, and service you put into your long-term goals will provide a bountiful harvest. The Ten of Wands has a Saturnine quality. It indicates that if you do the hard work and endure the discomfort, you will eventually enjoy the reward.

Ten of Wands Reversed

If the Ten of Wands appears reversed, it asks you to take a break from your burdens and enjoy the harvest. Recognize how your efforts have helped the whole.

Then find some time just for you! If you've been working hard for a better tomorrow, you've already proven your service. Working toward a more stable future isn't worth it if you are too exhausted to appreciate it. Look around and fully enjoy your comfortable home and the delicious foods you eat. Share these moments with people you care about. Taking a break will ensure that you have the energy to be there for others in the future.

Lay down your burdens and lighten up. Life is not all work and drudgery. Look around you. Be present and aware of all the wonderful things that you can see in front of you. You manifested those! Be proud of the work you do and treat yourself well today. After all, even the titan Atlas got a break from carrying the burdens of the world on his back. This card also advises you to take care of your body and release any tension that has been building up. It's time for a hot bath, massage, or relaxing nap. Take care of your health. Give your body what it needs.

Finally, the Ten of Wands reversed can represent that you crossed the finish line. Good for you! Something that you have been struggling to carry can now be put aside. It may be difficult at first, but you must learn to lighten up again.

PAGE OF WANDS

Aspiration.

The Page of Wands symbolizes aspiration. Although he has not yet reached the heights of his older family members—the Knight, Queen, and King of Wands—he still possesses their same magnetic qualities within himself. The Page of Wands represents that you too embody the same strengths you admire in the people you look up to.

Who are your role models? What qualities do they possess that you wish you embodied more? How would your life be different if you could tap into more of that kind of energy?

The Page of Wands is richly dressed for his adventure in Egypt. He was inspired by his older brother, the Knight of Wands, to overcome his insecurity and bravely explore the world. He wears a vibrant yellow tunic, the most optimistic color. The Page of Wands wears the same red plume in his cap as the Fool, linking him with optimism, unlimited potential, and new beginnings.

The Page of Wands holds a staff that is much taller than him. It almost looks like a measuring rod. It's from his father, the King of Wands, and he hasn't quite grown up to it yet. His height in relation to the staff symbolizes that he is in a state of growing. The wand the Page holds also reminds him of his role models: the Knight, Queen, and King of Wands. He is mesmerized by the Knight's courage for adventure, the Queen's charisma, and the King's wisdom. He doesn't feel bad about himself by comparing their talents to his own. This is because he recognizes the force behind *their* talents is also found within himself.

The very fact that you admire certain qualities in others is because *you have those qualities in common*. Much like the Page, you may still be finding out how to make these qualities your own. Don't try to compare yourself to the abilities, talents, and achievements of others. Instead, look at the force behind those talents, and you will see that you are strengthening those same attributes within yourself.

For example, anyone who really knows me knows that I absolutely adore Judy Garland. I marvel at her talent, but more importantly, I love her fearless authenticity on stage. She took risks and performed concerts until shortly before she died, all the while struggling with deep personal insecurities and a cruel tabloid press that wanted to rip her apart every day to sell magazines. This would hurt her deeply, but she would overcome it with a joke and get others to laugh with her. She would get on stage knowing that people were judging her for her personal struggles. However, she still had the courage to sing straight into the hearts of her audience. By vulnerably sharing her shadows in the open, she helped her audiences (whom she adored) heal their own troubles with a song.

Now, I'll never be a singer. However, I find myself working on being more vulnerable and fearless every day. I also learned from Judy to trust and believe in my talents. Being sensitive and helping others is a privilege. I can't let the fear of being ridiculed for being gay, being a tarot reader, or being different keep me from opening my heart. Some days I'm more courageous than others, but I still aspire to transcend my own shadows with kindness.

Acknowledge the qualities you admire most in your heroes and recognize that you share this magic in common. You are kindred souls. The Page of Wands always encourages you to grow. You may not feel like you are filling your shoes in your current phase, but you are progressing.

The Page of Wands can also represent an exciting, passionate, and dynamic young person who is just beginning to realize their full potential. They exhibit true talent and brilliance in the area of their focus. The Page can also represent a skilled artist in the performing arts. Pages can represent the young-at-heart of any gender.

Page of Wands Reversed

If the Page of Wands appears reversed, he signifies that you must be patient while cultivating your talents. The Page of Wands is crackling with creativity. He is a fiery character whose mind can often be found thirty steps ahead of his present location. When the Page of Wands appears reversed, he reminds you to slow down and enjoy being present with what you are learning. He might also indicate that you need to take a more methodical approach to achieving your goals. Don't let your mind race and wander without discipline. You have tremendous talent and creative energy available, but they need to be refined and focused.

The Page of Wands reversed also warns against the feeling of not quite measuring up. Beware of comparing yourself with the achievements and accomplishments of others. You are on your own track and have a lifetime of lessons specifically meant for you. Comparing yourself to others is futile. Look to qualities you admire in others to *inspire* your passion, not undermine it.

If the Page of Wands reversed represents another person, he could be an individual who has tons of raw energy that needs an outlet. The Page of Wands reversed can also represent a well-meaning individual with a short attention span. This person may go along with the crowd if there are stronger personalities around. Also, they may need to be wary of trying to pose as someone else. Encourage this individual to not obsess about what others are achieving or doing.

KNIGHT OF WANDS

Adventure.

The Knight of Wands symbolizes the urge for freedom, exploration, and adventure. He is the traveler of the tarot. He is pictured here visiting Egypt. He understands that by removing himself from the humdrum routines of day-today life, he can gain a wider perspective of who he really is. A passionate, confident, and adventurous spirit.

When is the last time you halted routine and explored outside your home or work? Do you need a spontaneous vacation or a small getaway to regain perspective? Do you go to the same old restaurants and walk the same old streets every day in your community?

The Knight of Wands is a bold figure. His little brother, the Page of Wands, has a small red plume in his cap, representing the spark of adventure that accompanies new beginnings. The Knight's blazing red plume is full. His horse rears up with uncontained energy and excitement. His passions spur him onward toward new lands. The Knight of Wands doesn't sit around and think. He acts! He urges you to get out of your routines and expose yourself to something new. The world is wide, open, and waiting for you to experience it.

The Knight of Wands has long been associated with travel. Travel broadens the mind. It frees us from monotony and allows us to explore environments where people don't know our personal history. By exploring new places, you are on a journey of discovering yourself. When you return from a trip, your mind looks at the life you left behind with renewed clarity. It's called "leaving the bubble."

Not everyone can take big trips to exotic locations, but you can still go to places that allow you to connect with new people. Once there, you will realize that you aren't so different after all. By seeing yourself as others see you, you might find that you are more interesting than you thought.

Reclaim your spontaneity. Go on an outing beyond your normal perimeters. Visit a restaurant with foods you haven't tried. Talk to people who don't look like you. Get excited and plan a large trip if you need a vacation. There is no excuse for being bored or boring when this Knight appears.

The Knight of Wands can symbolize the feeling that you have been traversing through a metaphorical desert. This has been testing your endurance and willpower. The only way to arrive at the oasis is to keep going. Don't stop.

The Knight of Wands can also represent an adventurous person who loves travel, movement, and freedom. He is hard to pin down, but he is the most marvelous company. Never try to trap the Knight of Wands through guilt, obligation, or pressure, or he will bolt. Knights can represent youngish adults of any gender. Knights are usually people who are phasing out of one way of life and into another.

Knight of Wands Reversed

If the Knight of Wands appears reversed, he often represents scattered energy. He is truly the jack-of-all trades and wants to do a little bit of everything. The problem with this is that very little gets done. When the Knight of Wands reversed appears, he may symbolize a need to limit your major goals down to one or two things. This will ensure that they have a better chance of being completed. This card often represents unfinished business.

The Knight of Wands reversed can also represent a period when it is hard to control fiery passions. He can be hotheaded and may not always think about what needs to be done before diving right in. Although this is great during an emergency, it causes quite a bit of turbulence during everyday life.

Stop, breathe, and think before proceeding when this card appears.

When the Knight of Wands reversed represents another person, he may be flighty or noncommittal. He is not very good with deadlines or pressure from others. He acts now and thinks later. Upright or reversed, the Knight of Wands is rarely cruel. However, he does need to direct his boundless energy toward something constructive.

QUEEN OF WANDS

Shine brightly without apology.

The Queen of Wands is the archetype of what we all want to be. Strong, self-confident, charismatic, and self-assured of our worth. Wands in the tarot symbolize growth. This shows us that the Queen of Wands was not always so self-confident. She had to overcome a fear of what others would think of her if she were to truly be herself. This is a hard lesson in courage. Rejection from others can hurt.

Are you truly confident in who you are? Do you hide your enthusiasm to avoid the embarrassment you might feel if someone were to ridicule you? Do you have issues concerning shame or self-consciousness?

Front and center, seated before the Queen's throne, is her black cat. For centuries, black cats were considered evil and unlucky by the masses. People who owned black cats were also persecuted as witches. The Queen of Wands loves black cats. She loves them so much that she put her favorite black cat in the spotlight on her card. It's as if she's saying to the world, "I don't care what the peasants with pitchforks think of me; I love black cats."

The Queen of Wands encourages you to stop fearing what other people will say or think about you. Stop hiding your light! Have courage and be who you are! The lions on the Queen's throne symbolize courage and majesty. The Queen's crown is adorned with leaves, reminding us of the World card. She has fully graduated into her regal authority. The Queen of Wands holds a sunflower, which also appears on the Sun card (the best card in the deck). Sunflowers always face the sun. They open their petals in the direction of the sun's radiant light and represent our need to turn toward the light within ourselves. What are you struggling to like about yourself? Think of how invincible your self-esteem would become if you embraced it.

The Queen of Wands exemplifies the positive characteristics of the astrological sign of Leo. Many Leos are famous for their ability to put on a show and to shine with star quality. By embracing your Authentic Self, you will emit a light that others will notice immediately.

The Queen of Wands had to *learn* to be comfortable with herself. By learning to love and accept herself, she became open to the possibility of being loved by others for her truth. She takes the risk to smile and reach out to others before they greet her. She shows her subjects that she can see their light clearly, because she went through the process of discovering her own. The Queen of Wands never brags about her accomplishments. She allows her results to speak for themselves. She shines brightly, even if some of her cousins in the Pentacles suit think she's impractical, eccentric, or even crazy.

Many people adore the Queen of Wands. However, some people are a little threatened by her *realness*. There are even a few people who hate her for her best qualities. The Queen of Wands doesn't worry about any of that. Being targeted simply means she's relevant.

When the Queen of Wands represents a person, she is charismatic, outgoing, and gregarious. She is also a trustworthy friend, counselor, or confidant. The Queen of Wands is often exuberant and entertaining and raises the energy of any room she walks into. Queens can be mature individuals of any gender who wield strong feminine power.

Queen of Wands Reversed

If the Queen of Wands appears reversed, she usually accompanies a lack of self-confidence. Upright or reversed, the Queen of Wands is the guardian of where your self-esteem can be found. The Queen of Wands reversed can indicate a need to come out of hiding. Take a risk and allow others to see you. Like the black cat on the card, you might not always be liked by everyone. Follow the black cat's example and treat this fact with nonchalance. You don't want people like that around you anyway! Stop hiding what makes you special.

The Queen of Wands is the actress of the tarot. She teaches that sometimes you must "fake it till you make it!" Take a chance on believing in yourself, and you will probably exceed your expectations. Even if you don't feel 100 percent sure about your abilities, do the thing you are afraid to do anyway. You will rarely look back with regret when you approach life with courage, no matter the result. Give it your all, even if there are no guarantees.

When the Queen of Wands reversed represents another person, she can symbolize someone who is struggling to regain her self-esteem. Try to be supportive. The Queen of Wands reversed knows what it is like to endure the pain of rejection. She may struggle with her body image or a belief in her talents. To overcome this, she should avoid seeking external validation as a replacement for self-acceptance. Counseling, yoga, exercise, or any other form of self-improvement could greatly increase her self-confidence.

KING OF WANDS

Trust in your own competency.

The King of Wands is the wise counselor of the tarot. He came up the hard way and has survived many trials by fire. Because of his experiences, he speaks with gravity and wisdom. The King of Wands represents the part of you that is wise and competent. He teaches you to trust in yourself. You haven't let everything fall apart up until this point, so why panic and assume that suddenly you'll drop the ball now? The King reminds you that if you don't trust in your own competency and abilities, you are betraying the very part of yourself that helped you survive. This part of you deserves some respect!

Do you have trouble trusting yourself, no matter how well you do your job or run your affairs? Are you someone who came up the hard way and has some uneasiness about not having some of the perceived advantages of others? Have you proven to yourself time after time that you are competent and *still* don't believe it?

The King of Wands doesn't command people to respect him. Others need only look at him to realize his quality. The King is a tall figure in the Wands suit. If the King were to stand, he would appear much taller than the wand he wields. Although he carries himself with dignity and regal bearing, this king was not born royal. He was a soldier and came up through the ranks the hard way. He earned the respect of his men by winning battles and saving the kingdom on more than one occasion. His competent leadership naturally caused others to follow. When the former King died without an heir, the people named this proven warrior "the King of Wands."

As a King, the throne he is seated on is naturally emblazoned with lions. However, the King carries another powerful emblem that speaks to his familial roots: the "lowly" lizard, seated right next to him.

Lizards are survivors. They can live in the hottest climates by moderating their body temperature. They can literally "take the heat." This symbol reminded this King's "lowborn" ancestors for generations to not allow emotions to get too hot or too cold. This quality always helped the King while assessing himself and others.

The "noble" soldiers in the army used to laugh at the lizard on this Soldier-King's banner. To the upper echelons, lizards were dirty or, even worse, evil. Lizards were *definitely* not royal. For many years as a young man, the King felt shame about the lizard being on his family's crest. Like the lizard, it meant that he too was lowborn. However, now the King proudly places the lizard alongside the royal lion emblem. The King has gained maturity and wisdom. He now understands that coming up as a lizard gave him valuable gifts that he wouldn't have gained had he been born into the "lion's club."

Today, it's time to acknowledge that like the King, you are competent. You belong and deserve a seat at the table in front of you. You've worked hard to get here. Don't look at others and assume they are better because they have more money, a greater position, better schooling, more *this*, or more *that*. You don't know their real-life or private struggles! Everyone has difficult things they are working on, even the most well-to-do. Like the King, you will also have to battle the inner shadow that causes you to doubt yourself and your place in this world. This inner saboteur will tell you to retreat because you aren't as good as someone else. Tell that malicious voice to take a hike! It's disrespecting your inner lizard.

In truth, there is no practical way to compare lizards to lions. This is a false equivalency. Each animal brings its own gifts. However, just because the lizard's gifts are not as immediately apparent, that does not mean it should be underestimated or dismissed.

Respect your inner lizard today. It may not be as glamorous as the lions you see on the shields of others, but it is the reason you've survived, and it deserves to be honored.

If the King of Wands represents a person, he is a survivor from humble beginnings whose advice you can trust. The King of Wands could be an entrepreneur or a person whose power was earned. He is passionate and outgoing but is not ruled by passion alone. He is deliberative and thinks through problems in order to arrive at the best solution. Always trust the advice of a person represented as the King of Wands. Kings can be mature people of any gender who are leaders or figures of authority.

King of Wands Reversed

If the King of Wands appears reversed, he arrives at a time when you may be starting to doubt your competency, gifts, and abilities. This usually occurs when your focus is directed outwardly and the connection with your authentic Inner Self feels diminished. Sometimes this card appears as a reminder to stop comparing yourself to the achievements of others. Remember the false equivalency of comparing lions to lizards?

New opportunities are arriving that require you to tap into your deepest strength. This can be scary. Fear of new experiences can lead to doubt in your ability to succeed. If you are beginning to doubt your talents, abilities, or strengths, remind yourself of your power. Remember all the times you pushed past former barriers and succeeded. Reacquaint yourself with the strongest version of yourself that you can remember from the past. That person is still you, no matter how far your experiences have taken you from that time in your life. The King of Wands reversed asks you to truly remember who you are.

In truth, you do have the ability to respond wisely to whatever situation is presenting itself. Do not let your fears undermine your sense of self-confidence. The King of Wands is a tough character, upright or reversed. He is a survivor who always finds a way to succeed. In truth, he is a symbol for the same qualities that reside within you. The King of Wands encourages you to be more assertive and less passive.

The King of Wands reversed may also describe an individual who has survived against great odds but has somehow forgotten their strength. Sometimes this occurs because of a perceived setback or disappointment. This individual needs to be reminded that just because something failed before, that does not mean it won't succeed in the future. The message from the King of Wands reversed is to keep trying and never give up!

PART 3
HOW TO USE THE CARDS

Now that we've looked at the diverse archetypes of the Major and Minor Arcanas in depth, we can finally get to the fun part: doing readings! Each card is like a brilliant pigment of color. When blended together, they can create vibrant new hues and entire landscapes. A reading that resonates is truly a masterpiece. It marries imagery with reality. A good reading can provide amazing clarity to a situation that once felt amorphous and elusive. Learning how to blend tarot symbolism comes with experience. The most important guide for this process will be your own intuition.

The following chapters will provide a variety of spreads to get the most out of your tarot deck. However, this list of spreads merely scratches the surface of what you can do on your own. Try to invent your own tarot spreads. Craft them around a specific area of concern or a truth that you want brought to light.

I will also cover significator cards and how to use them in a reading. If you are unfamiliar with significator cards or don't know the first thing about how to choose one, then read on!

Finally, I will provide some tips and tricks for how to read other individuals (sometimes called "querents") effectively. Many readers choose to only read for themselves, and that is perfectly fine. Tarot is a marvelous tool for journaling, self-exploration, meditation, and many other forms of Spirit work. If you do decide to bravely read for others, the tips provided may be of use to you. They are some of the most important lessons that I have learned over the years, and they inform my tarot practice to this day.

Let's get started!

VII
© 1971 U.S. GAMES SYSTEMS, INC.
VII
THE CHARIOT.
© 1971 U.S. GAMES SYSTEMS, INC.

CHOOSING A SIGNIFICATOR

Many tarot readers begin their readings by selecting a "significator." A significator is a card that is chosen from the tarot deck to represent the "querent" (the person getting the reading). I usually pick one of the Court cards (Page, Knight, Queen, or King) to be a significator; however, you can choose any card so long as it shares a common trait with the querent. You can designate a significator based on gender, age, personality, or astrological correspondence. The important thing is that the significator card represents a unique, symbolic characteristic of the person getting the reading.

Before beginning a tarot reading, I ask my client what their astrological Sun sign is. The Sun sign in astrology is what you look at in the paper when you read your horoscope. In astrology, the twelve zodiac signs are separated by four elements: Earth, Air, Fire, and Water. Each element has three astrological signs associated with it. The Earth signs are Taurus, Virgo, and Capricorn. The Air signs are Gemini, Libra, and Aquarius. The Fire signs are Aries, Leo, and Sagittarius. The Water signs are Cancer, Scorpio, and Pisces.

The Minor Arcana of the tarot is also separated by the four elements. Earth is represented by the Pentacles suit, Air is represented by Swords, Fire is represented by Wands, and Water is represented by Cups.

Some people insist on picking Kings and Knights to represent men and boys, and Queens and Pages to represent women and girls. However, gender identity is not so black-and-white. Always select a significator based on the gender the querent identifies most with. If you are unsure, just ask them: "As a Leo, what card do you think better represents you—the King of Wands or the Queen of Wands?" Some men prefer to be represented as Queens and some women see themselves as Kings. In this case, the customer is always right!

For example, if I were going to read for an adult who identifies as female, I would select a Queen to represent that individual. If the individual were an Air sign, I would choose the Queen of Swords. If they were an Earth sign, I would select the Queen of Pentacles. For a young man, I usually pick a Knight. For a mature man, I would pick a King. Pages are gender-neutral. Pages can be children, young girls, young boys, or even people who don't identify as a specific gender.

Astrological identity is flexible, too. You may meet a client who tells you, "My Sun sign is technically Aries, but I really don't feel like one. I have a Libra rising and resonate more with Libra." In this case, I would select a card that represents Libra from the Swords suit. You can also pick a Major Arcana card to represent an astrological sign irrespective of age or gender. Here are the astrological correspondences from the Major Arcana:

- *Aries:* The Emperor
- *Taurus:* The Hierophant
- *Gemini:* The Lovers
- *Cancer:* The Chariot
- *Leo:* Strength
- *Virgo:* The Hermit
- *Libra:* Justice
- *Scorpio:* Death
- *Sagittarius:* Temperance
- *Capricorn:* The Devil
- *Aquarius:* The Star
- *Pisces:* The Moon

Another reason that I prefer to select a significator is for numerological correspondence. There are seventy-eight cards in a tarot deck. By setting aside one card to represent the querent, you are left with seventy-seven. In numerology, double-digit numbers that hold two of the same number are called "Power Numbers" (11, 22, 33, 44, 55, 66, 77, 88, etc.). The number seven has a long history of being associated with divination. The ancient Greek God of divination was Apollo. He was venerated every seventh day after the new moon. Apollo's famous Oracle at Delphi only operated on the seventh day of the month (for only nine months out of the year). For me, sevens are very powerful when performing any sort of divination.

There are many fine readers who do not choose a significator. It is totally a matter of preference. Do what works for you!

ACE
© 1971 U.S. GAMES SYSTEMS, INC.
III
THE EMPRESS.
© 1971 U.S. GAMES SYSTEMS, INC.

TAROT SPREADS

The pictorial images of the tarot are the soul of any reading; however, tarot spreads are the skeleton. Spreads provide structure, sequence, and context for card interpretation. Tarot spreads can range from just using one card to using all seventy-eight cards in the deck. Each position in a tarot spread will define and focus what the imagery of the card is pertaining to. Spread positions in a reading set definitive perimeters for how a card's symbolism should be viewed. For example, a card that appears in the "past" position in a spread will tell you that the card's imagery should be interpreted through the lens of past actions or events that have already happened.

The human brain naturally organizes data and is geared toward identifying patterns. This serves to make the information clearer and easier to process. Tarot spreads serve to organize the imagery of the cards into a structure that makes interpretation simple and effective.

The following spreads can be utilized to structure your card interpretation and can relegate meanings to specific areas of concern. Although the following spreads are ones that I have found to be most effective, you can always experiment and invent new tarot spreads for yourself.

When designing your own spread, you can organize each position to represent time (past, present, future) or to illuminate an area of concern (love, money, career opportunities, etc.). Each reader eventually comes to find a system of spreads that work best for them. Many tarot readers adjust existing spreads with their own preferences. Feel free to make your own adjustments to the following tarot spreads I've provided. The important thing is that you define what a card in a particular position pertains to before the cards are laid out.

THE CARD OF THE DAY

A Card of the Day spread consists of only one card. For this spread, no significator is needed. This method of interpretation is an easy way to begin learning tarot over time. The card selected will highlight where your energy is best focused for the day ahead. It will also provide valuable insight into what issues you are presently working through in your life. The Card of the Day can highlight where you are growing and what may need more attention or healing. Many readers pick a Card of the Day before they begin their day to see what's in store. It can be fascinating to look back at the end of your day at the card you chose in the morning. Hindsight will reveal how the symbolism contained within that card worked its way through your day.

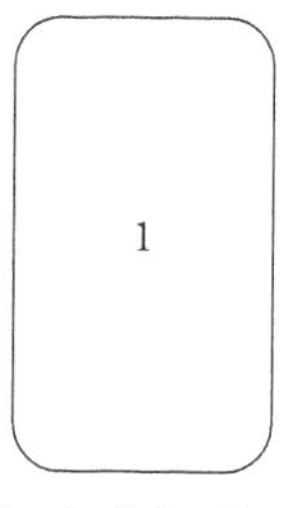

Card of the Day

To select a Card of the Day, find a sliver of time when you can relax, focus, and breathe. When you are ready, hold your deck of cards and center yourself. I find that taking three deep breaths allows me to calm my mind enough to read tarot symbolism effectively.

Slowly inhale through your nose over an eight-second count. Hold your inhalation for another eight seconds. Purse your lips into the shape you make when drinking out of a straw. Exhale through this resistance over another eight counts. Repeat this process twice more. Try not to rush or skip the breathing process. You will likely get more insight into the card if you approach your reading calm and centered.

Begin shuffling your tarot deck. While shuffling, you can ask, "What does my best self want me to see today?" Or, "What do I need to keep in mind to improve my life's direction?" While shuffling, try to release your expectations about what you hope to see. Resist the temptation to judge some cards as good and others as bad. Every card in the deck holds great magic and healing potential. When you are ready, let your intuition guide your hand to select the right card. Your inner knowing will not make a mistake. When you turn over the card and view it for the first time, simply say, "Thank you. I accept what you are showing me."

The card you choose will have a strong significance today; however, you may need to look deeper into the imagery to receive its real message. Just because you pick a brightly colored, happy-looking card, that does not mean the day will transpire without a hitch. Conversely, receiving a card that you perceive as negative does not mean that your day will be horrible or that you should just stay under the covers at home.

Take a moment to look at the picture on the card before looking up someone else's definition. Is there something that really catches your eye in the image? What does that symbol make you feel? How could this card relate to your greatest concerns lately?

The imagery of the Card of the Day does not necessarily reveal *how* your day will go, but rather *what* your intuition wishes you to see about what you are learning. If you are completely stumped about the card's meaning, feel free to look it up in this book. If a certain sentence jumps out while reading the chapter, that is your message!

SIMPLE THREE-CARD SPREAD

The Three-Card spread is an easy way to receive a quick view of the past, present, and likely future. As with the previous spread, receiving a "dark" card to symbolize your present or future does not indicate doom or failure. Rather, this card could indicate an obstacle you need to overcome, or something that you need to make peace with, before you can proceed.

To begin the Three-Card spread, quiet your mind and take three deep breaths. Think about an area of concern in your life. Shuffle your cards, calmly keeping this question in mind. When you are ready, lay three cards out in a row to gain insight into the question at hand. Try not to judge the cards you receive at face value, even if they startle you. Use the definitions provided in this book to aid you when confronting symbolism that makes you uncomfortable. Many people shut down if they don't see an image that reinforces what they want to see. Always with the tarot, you must look deeper. Read the cards through the lens of the situation you are asking about. How might the symbols that appear apply to your situation? Let your own intuition guide you to other observations you have. Try to apply the symbolism in a way that empowers you. I like to place all three cards facedown on the table before turning them over one at a time. This allows me to systematically read each card on its own merit, without being distracted by the imagery on the other cards. Stay open and nonresistant to the messages you receive. Once all three cards are revealed, try to identify what they have in common or if there is a pattern that seems to connect each card.

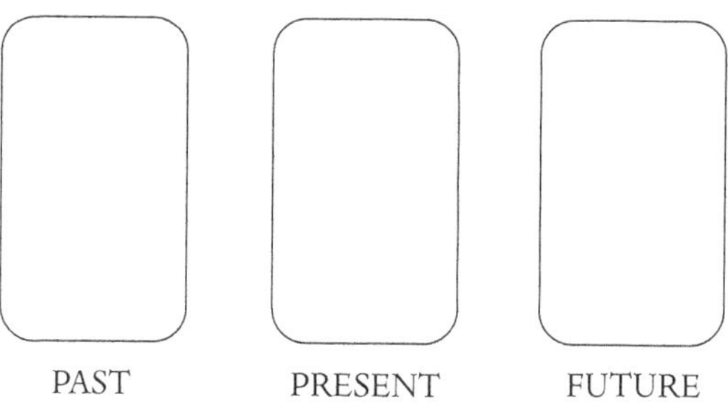

Simple Three-Card Spread

Card 1. The Past: *What have I already learned about this situation?*

This card reveals lessons you have learned and experiences you have successfully completed. This card will show the pathway you've already traveled concerning your question. Bright cards will reveal strengths that you have already developed to apply to your present concern. Darker cards will indicate trials or tribulations you have overcome or something that happened before that needs to be healed. The past card can also indicate what you need to let go of in order to proceed.

Card 2. The Present: *What am I presently experiencing or learning?*

This card reveals lessons you are presently learning or challenges you are overcoming. This image shows what your Inner Self wants you to pay attention to right now. Remember, the present is where your personal power resides. Understanding how this card's imagery applies to the question at hand will empower you to make the best decision.

Card 3. The Likely Future: *Where is this situation headed if I continue down this path?*

The future is never predestined. It is constantly shifting based on the choices we presently make. The future card will reveal where the energy is flowing. This card will provide you with insight about where this situation is most likely heading. If this card depicts a challenge, there will be a hidden symbol on the card that will reveal how to avoid or overcome it.

TRANSCEND YOUR FEARS SPREAD

This five-card spread can assist you in transcending your fear, finding your courage, and hearing the voice of your inner wisdom. Begin by choosing a significator. It is important that the significator you choose resonates with you and exemplifies what is *best* about you. If you are having trouble picking a significator for this spread, go through all the cards faceup and select the card that embodies how you feel about yourself *at your best.* Once you have selected the perfect card, place it faceup on the table before you. Gaze at the image and take a deep breath. Relax, and say to yourself, "This is the real me."

Take the remaining cards facedown and begin to shuffle them. Think about what has been giving you the most anxiety lately. What have you been obsessively worried about? What have you been internally struggling with? Breathe deeply, and when you are ready, begin to lay the cards out as follows:

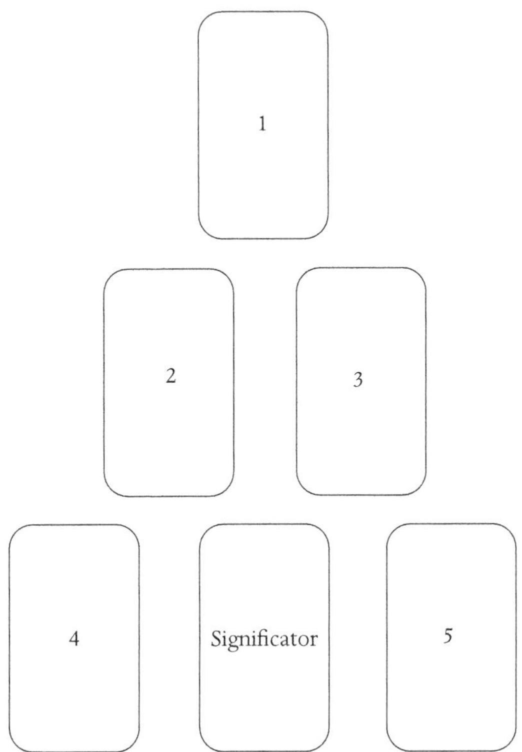

Transcend Your Fears Spread

Card 1: *What have I learned from my fear in the past?*

This card will reveal what your fear has taught you in the past. This card highlights lessons learned and strength you may have already found through your life experiences.

Card 2: *Where can I presently find my courage?*

This card reveals where your courage is currently emerging. It can also reveal the vault within your heart where your hidden courage is sealed away.

Card 3: *What expectations do I need to hold or release?*

In the case of a positive card, you'll want to hold this expectation close to your heart. In the case of a challenging card, this is an expectation that it's time to let go of. What you carry with you will affect how you habitually feel.

Card 4: *What am I learning to accept so that I no longer feel stuck?*

This card reveals a truth you must come to terms with in order to progress. This is what you must fully integrate currently to transcend your inner saboteur.

Card 5: *What advice is my inner wisdom giving me to transcend my fears?*

This card represents what the deepest wisdom within you wants you to hear. Hearing this advice will allow you to make peace with yourself and move forward.

BRING SHADOWS TO LIGHT SPREAD

This spread can reveal what your inner shadow is holding on to at this time. It will also show what your Spirit is bringing to light. If you are feeling confused by amorphous feelings of discomfort or anxiety, this spread will help you identify what those feelings are connected to. This spread will also show you what part of your life desperately needs your love at this time. As with the previous spread, pick a significator. The significator you choose should exemplify what is *best* about you. If you are having trouble picking a significator for this spread, go through all the cards faceup and select the card that embodies how you feel about yourself at your best. Place your significator card in the center of the table before you.

Take several deep breaths and relax. Take the remaining cards facedown and begin shuffling them. Think about your inner life. Let your awareness slowly sink deep within your Spirit, into the sea of your unconscious thoughts. Know that you are protected and safe, feeling these primordial waters. When you are ready, lay out the cards as follows:

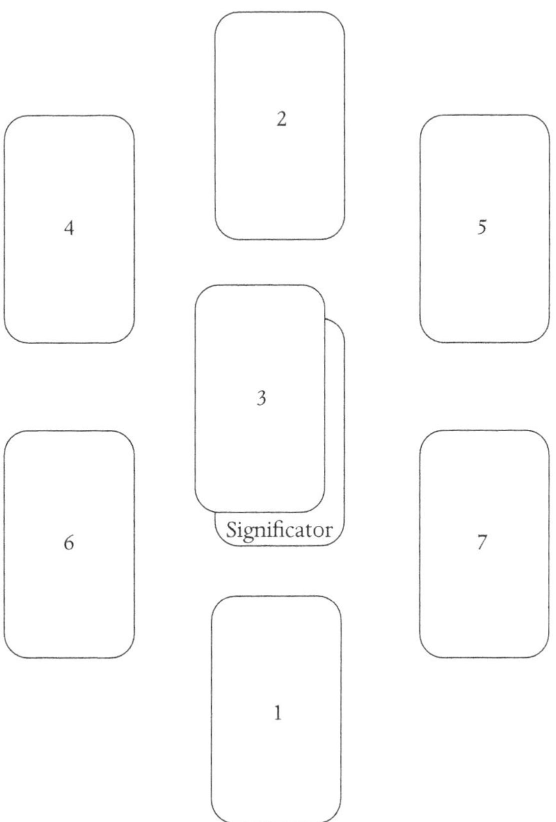

Bring Shadows to Light Spread

Card 1: *What part of my life feels submerged in shadow?*

This card represents what is affecting you unconsciously beneath the surface. This information wishes to be understood and brought to light.

Card 2: *What part of my life is returning to the light?*

This card reveals what is bubbling up from your Spirit to the surface. In the case of a challenging card, it is something your Spirit is releasing. In the case of an uplifting image, it is a sign of what you are becoming.

Card 3: *What wisdom am I gaining from my present circumstance?*

This card highlights the lesson you are learning from the external world.

Card 4: *What currently needs to feel supported?*

This card reveals where your energy needs to be strengthened and reinforced. It will also show what lesson has been neglected and needs to be accepted for progress to occur.

Card 5: *What wisdom will I gain from listening to the voice within?*

This card reveals the skills you will master if you listen to the wisdom from within.

Card 6: *What opportunities are being presented to me?*

This card shows what area of your life will show the most growth if you can heed the call of your inner wisdom.

Card 7: *Where do I need to direct my love right now?*

This card reveals where your love can be applied to bring about resolution.

THE CELTIC CROSS SPREAD

The Celtic Cross has become *the* workhorse spread for many tarot readers over the last century. For many of us, this is the first tarot spread we encounter. There are many variations of this spread, and it is up to the reader to decide which version works best for them. The following variation of the Celtic Cross spread is my own. Sir Arthur Edward Waite describes this spread in his *A Pictorial Key to the Tarot.*[28] If you would like to read his original approach to this spread, then I would advise reading his work. The following variation of this spread is the one I have been working with for many years with great success. I have altered some of the original card positions to make more sense chronologically. If you have been using this spread successfully in a different manner, then do what works best for you.

The Celtic Cross can be effectively utilized to gain insight into events that will be occurring in the coming months. The "outcome card" can give you a glimpse of major events that are still to come in roughly three to six months' time.

To begin, select a significator card from the deck to represent the querent. Place it on the table in front of you. Have the querent shuffle the remaining seventy-seven cards. (If you are uncomfortable with another person touching your cards, then you will do the shuffling.) While shuffling, I ask my clients to

28. Waite, *A Pictorial Key to the Tarot,* 299–305.

relax and think about their life... think about everything that has been going on lately. When it intuitively feels like the cards are ready (or that the client is done shuffling), give the client the option of cutting the deck. After this, lay out the cards in the following manner:

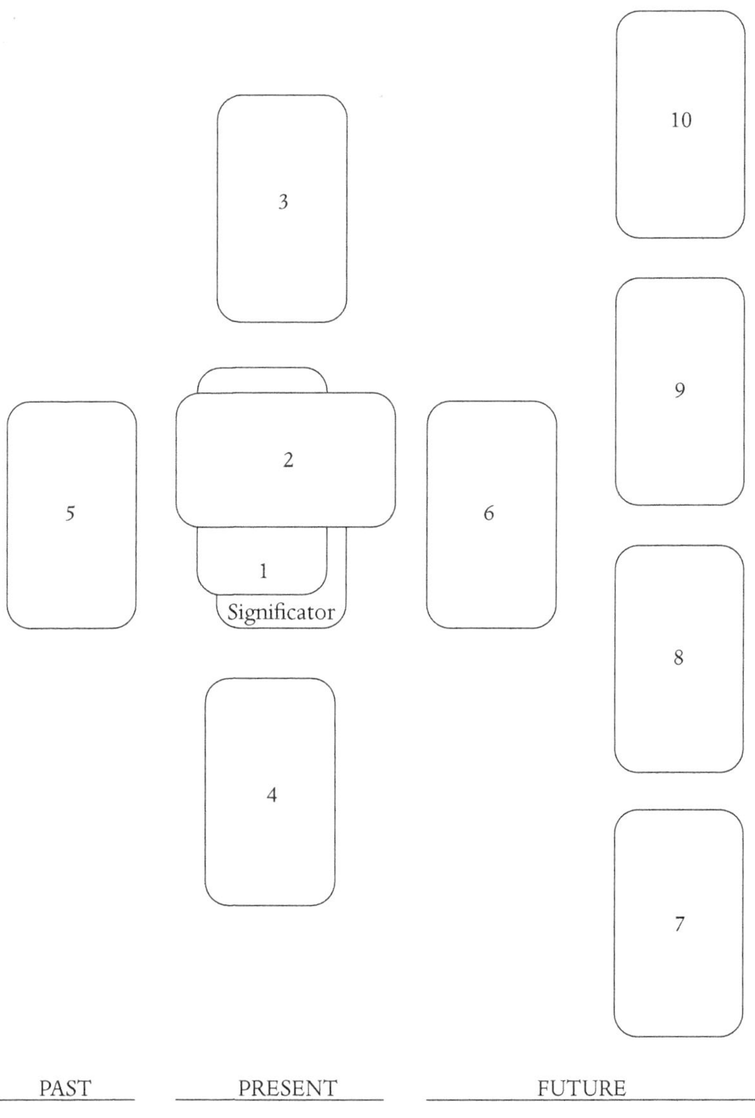

Celtic Cross Spread

Card 1: The Present. *What is currently happening in my life?*

The first card is laid directly on top of the significator. It represents your general present situation. For me, the first card is the most important card in a reading. It sets the stage for all the cards that follow. It is a lens to view all the other cards through. This card will reveal challenges you are currently facing, lessons you are learning, or strengths you possess in the present moment. This card gives a general snapshot of your present life.

Card 2: What Crosses You. *What is either helping or hindering me?*

The second card is laid horizontally over the first card and significator (forming a cross). This card reveals difficulties that must be overcome or positive attributes that you now possess to meet your challenges. I like to read the first two cards as follows: "Card 1 reveals that '*X*' is happening, but Card 2 is coloring this situation in this way…" You can also read both the upright and reversed meanings for Card 2, since it falls on its side. This can add more nuance and meaning to the crossed card. Choose the meaning that seems to resonate with your instincts.

Card 3: What Is Currently on Your Mind. *Where are my thoughts currently dwelling?*

This card will reveal your current mental state. It will show either what you are thinking about or what currently needs your focus. This card does not reveal what is *happening*, but rather what is currently going on in your head.

Card 4: Your Current Foundation. *How stable is my current foundation?*

This card will reveal if your current path is stable or shaky. This card can also represent a situation that has just happened and may be affecting your current outlook. If a challenging card appears here, it may illuminate something that must be confronted to reestablish firm footing.

Card 5: The Past or Now Passing. *What is in my past?*

This card reveals what you've already experienced. It highlights significant past events that shaped who you are today. The past card can tell you what you must leave behind. It also reveals how the past is affecting your current behavior.

Card 6: The Very Near Future. *What is happening in the next few weeks?*

This card reveals what will most likely arise in the next few weeks. When forecasting the future, keep in mind that the future can be changed by altering your present choices. This card will also reveal your state of mind during events that will soon come to pass.

Card 7: The Next Few Months. *What is happening in the next several months?*

This card reveals how the next several months are likely to go. It will also highlight major challenges or opportunities that will present themselves. The number that appears on this card can aid you in forecasting timing (a card numbered ten could indicate ten months from now... or the month of October). This card reveals what scenario is most likely to happen based on your current trajectory.

Card 8: Your Closest Relationships in the Future. *What is occurring in my closest relationships?*

This position highlights your closest relationships over the next year. This could include your family, best friends, or significant other. This card can also indicate the role you are playing for others and how they view you. It reveals who might need your attention or support. A darker card can highlight a relationship challenge or an issue you will help a loved one through in the coming months.

Card 9: Your Feelings in the Future. *How will I be feeling in the coming months?*

This position has also been called "Your Hopes and Fears." It doesn't reveal what will *happen*, but rather how you are *feeling*. A challenging card will reveal difficult emotions you are working through. This position always highlights experiences that are occurring internally. If asking about a relationship, this card will reveal the emotional condition of the relationship if it continues down its current path.

Card 10: The Final Outcome. *In the end, what's most likely to happen?*

This card reveals how your current situation will most likely resolve. If a challenging card appears, it does not necessarily mean that you are doomed to a bad outcome. It could be offering you an insight into what you must confront before enjoying a positive outcome. Many of the tarot's challenging cards provide mirrors into our own shadows, which need to be confronted and healed. The outcome card can also show what you will be working on next.

At this point of the reading, I usually ask the querent if they would like to ask some questions. They can ask for further clarification on something that resonated with them in the initial spread, or they can ask about something that wasn't initially addressed in the reading. Either the reader or querent can choose extra cards to answer singular questions. I usually select three cards to answer a specific question. You can either read them as past, present, and future (see Three-Card Spread), or you can blend the symbolism of all three cards to get a more nuanced view of the situation they are asking about.

For example, you've just finished interpreting the Celtic Cross spread for someone, and they liked their reading. Now your querent wants more clarification about a relationship with a man she just met. She asks you, "Can you tell me more about this man I've just started seeing?" You select three cards. Let's say they are the Page of Cups, the Tower, and the King of Pentacles. I would interpret this to mean that the man she is asking about is creative and passionate and expresses his feelings with ease. He may even have an artistic side. There is also a childlike quality to this man, and part of him will probably remain childlike forever (Page of Cups). The second card indicates a shaky time in his current life when he is confronting unavoidable realities and going through tremendous change (the Tower). However, the future holds good potential after the storm clears. He appears stable, patient, and nurturing (King of Pentacles). He will most likely be a financial success. I would then advise this client to enjoy her budding relationship, but to take care. The Tower card indicates a sense of instability presently. There are changes afoot for this man, and he may need some time to reestablish a sense of stability. When answering a person's questions, try not to focus on the negative. Just because the Tower appeared, that does not mean the relationship is a total loss. Blend the messages from all the cards to accurately describe the relationship.

Please note, when asking questions of the tarot, avoid asking the same question twenty different ways in the hopes of getting an answer that matches up with your expectations. Nothing derails the energy of a positive reading more than desperation or obsession. I've found the tarot will not cooperate as an effective or accurate tool if you repeatedly ask questions like, "When's he coming back?" after you've already received the answer ten times that *he's gone*! Try to formulate your questions positively, such as, "What do I need to work on to attract better relationships?" "How can I be a better partner?" "What do I need to focus on to make progress in my financial life?" Formulate your questions to empower *yourself*. In the end, you are only in control of *your* responses to situations, not somebody else's.

THE EXTENDED CELTIC CROSS SPREAD

The following spread is a variation of the Celtic Cross that I came up with many years ago. Although the original Celtic Cross was great for quick readings, I found that my sessions were ending too soon, and I was unable to glean enough information from just ten cards to really get an expansive perspective for the people I was reading. The Extended Celtic Cross uses twenty-eight cards (including the significator). It has been my workhorse spread for over twenty years. I find this spread to be very effective for a more nuanced view of not only what is happening in a client's external life, but also the inner forces that are shaping their experiences.

If you know the Celtic Cross spread, then the extended version will be very easy to understand. Instead of just one card for each spread position, there are three. Positions 1 and 2 of the Celtic Cross spread (Present and What Crosses You) are combined into one position. When all the cards are laid out, there will be nine separate groups of three cards each. The first two cards in each pile of three are laid on top of each other vertically. The third card in each group is laid over the first two cards horizontally (each spread position has a crossing card). The crossing card (third card of each group) will reveal what is happening in the external world for the querent and what effect it has on the part of their life the spread position pertains to. The second card (middle card in each group) shows how the querent's emotions are affected or what is just beneath the surface. The first card of each group (bottom of each pile) reveals the deeper lesson being learned or what their Spirit is whispering to them. This card reveals the situation at the deepest level. It highlights the unconscious attitudes that are helping or hindering the querent's personal growth. Positive cards will show strengths and challenging cards will reveal obstacles that need to be overcome.

When interpreting the three cards in each position, think of them as three different ways of describing the same situation. Notice how the images blend through patterns and commonalities. Court cards that cross each spread position are likely referencing other people in the querent's life. Court cards in the first two positions (under the crossing card) could be bringing up qualities or attributes the querent possesses that can aid them with what the spread position refers to. This spread is an excellent tool for learning how to blend tarot card meanings in relation to one another. With practice, this spread will increase your fluency with combining tarot imagery.

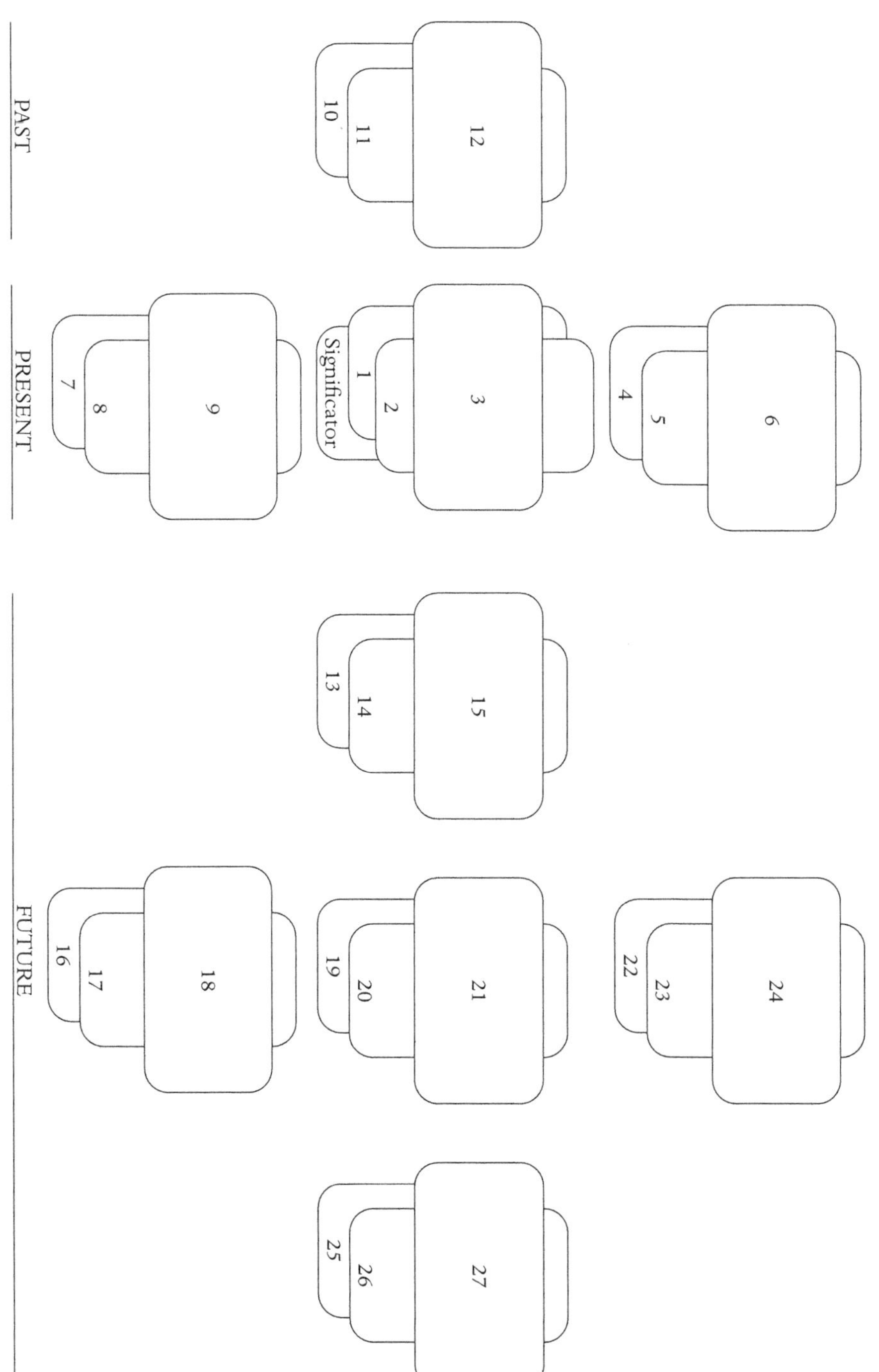

Extended Celtic Cross Spread

Present (Cards 1, 2, and 3): *What is currently happening in my life?*

These cards reveal challenges you are currently facing internally and externally. They also reveal how you are holding up to life presently. This card gives a general snapshot of your life as it is right now. Note that the What Crosses You position now appears in every grouping of cards.

What is currently on your mind (Cards 4, 5, and 6): *Where are my thoughts currently dwelling?*

These cards will reveal everything swirling around in your mind. They will highlight whether you are thinking positively or negatively. The crossing card will reveal external issues that you are thinking about. The cards in this position do not reveal what is *happening* to you, but rather what is presently going on in your head.

Your current foundation (Cards 7, 8, and 9): *How stable is my current foundation?*

These cards will reveal if your current path is stable or unstable. They can also represent a situation that has just happened and is affecting your current outlook. If challenging cards appear here, they may illuminate what needs to be confronted to reestablish firm footing. The crossing card will reveal how to overcome the obstacles currently on your path.

The past or now passing (Cards 10, 11, and 12): *What is in my past?*

These cards reveal what you've already experienced. They highlight significant past events that shaped who you are today. These cards can also tell you what you must surrender before moving forward. They will also show how the past is affecting your current behavior. The bottom of the first three cards can reveal pivotal moments that unconsciously affect you from the past. The middle card will show what your emotional experiences have been like. The crossing card can reveal past challenges or external influences that previously affected your life.

The near future (Cards 13, 14, and 15): *What is happening in the next few weeks?*

These cards reveal what will most likely arise in the next few weeks. When forecasting the future, keep in mind that the future can be changed through present choices. These cards can also indicate your state of mind during events that will soon come to pass. The crossing card will reveal what is happening in your external world over the next few weeks.

The next few months (Cards 16, 17, and 18): *What is happening in the next several months?*

These cards reveal how the next several months are likely to go. They will also highlight major challenges or opportunities that will present themselves within the next six months. The number that appears on the crossing card can aid you in forecasting timing. These cards reveal how the next few months will unfold if you continue down the same path. The crossing card will highlight external influences that you will be confronting. The two cards beneath the crossing card will reveal what you are experiencing internally.

Your closest relationships in the future (Cards 19, 20, and 21): *What is happening with my closest relationships?*

This position highlights your closest relationships in the coming months. This can include your family, colleagues, best friends, or significant other. This position can also indicate the role you are playing for others and how they view you. These cards can also reveal who might need your attention or support. The crossing card will always refer to someone else. Darker-looking cards can highlight relationship challenges. Court cards will always provide clues as to which of your loved ones this section is referring to.

Your feelings in the future (Cards 22, 23, and 24): *How will I be feeling over the next few months?*

This position in the spread can also be called "Your Hopes and Fears." This position doesn't reveal what will *happen* to you, but rather how you are *feeling* in the next several months. Challenging cards will reveal difficult emotions you are working through. Positive cards will show what you feel good about. This position always highlights experiences that are occurring internally. If asking about a relationship, these cards will reveal how you will end up feeling within that relationship if it continues down its current path.

The final outcome (Cards 25, 26, and 27): *In the end, what's most likely to happen?*

These cards reveal how your current situation will most likely resolve. If challenging cards appear, it does not necessarily mean that you are doomed to a bad outcome. They could be offering you an insight into what is preventing you from enjoying a positive outcome. Card 25 will show what your Spirit is working on. Card 26 will reveal what emotions you are working through. Card 27 will show what you will be focusing on in the external world.

•——• ✸ •——•

As with the Celtic Cross spread, this is the point of the reading when you can pull cards and ask further questions to gain more clarity.

If you are just learning tarot, it may be easier to begin learning spreads with fewer cards until you are comfortable reading them fluently. The Extended Celtic Cross spread can reveal infinite card combinations and possibilities to provide deeper insight into your inner and outer lives.

A FEW THOUGHTS ON READING FOR OTHERS

As with any skill, becoming a better tarot reader comes with experience. Try to do as many readings as you can when you are just beginning. Do consults for friends and family. Provide readings at holiday parties. Do them with people who are very different from you. *Diversity* will always take your readings to the next level. Don't be afraid of mistakes! They are going to happen and will be your best teachers for how to craft your language in the future. If you feel nervous about doing readings for people, that is a sign that you need to do more readings! Over time, you will develop your own style and cadence. Your confidence will also improve once you see how positively you can impact the lives of others.

When providing readings for others, *trust the symbolism in front of you*! A big mistake many readers make is that they waffle. They look more at the client's face, at their expressions of approval or disapproval, rather than at the answers on the table in front of them. They second-guess what they are about to say, fearing it will be "wrong." They want the validation of their querent, and the reading is no longer about seeking wisdom, but rather protecting the reader's ego.

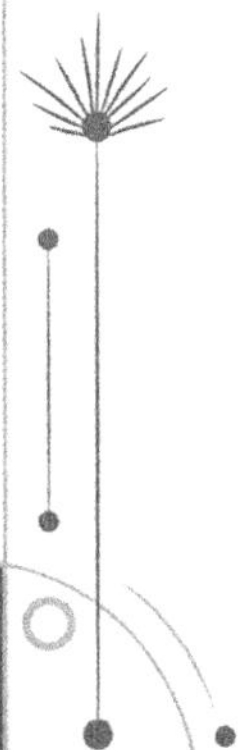

My approach to reading tarot is simple: I set my ego aside and *start talking*. Allow your words to flow forth without overthinking them. If you feel stuck, describe the symbols on the cards. Talking about the symbolism will lead you out of any mess you find yourself in. If you describe the archetypal images on the card, your message will probably hit its mark. Your client will absorb the flow of information you are providing and will make their own mental connections. It may not always make sense to you, and that is totally fine. Just talk. The information that comes out in a reading is not your information. It is your client's information. What they do with your message is up to them.

Another misconception many beginning readers have is that they need to be "all-knowing." Let me admit something to you. I may be psychic, but I'm not a mind reader! When someone sits down at my table, I usually don't know the first thing about them. I may have a first impression; however, when the reading begins, I need to set my assumptions aside. When beginning a spread interpretation, I simply start talking about the symbols that appear on the cards and how they might relate to the person's life. As I weave through the reading, the client's life comes into sharper focus. By the end of the reading, I usually have a good sense of the person I am reading. It isn't instant. I need to disseminate the layers, card by card, to get a more focused perspective. It's okay to not know everything. If you can't answer a question, simply say that you don't know. Pretending to be all-knowing is a form of hubris. It's as if you are daring the Universe to smack you down a peg or two! Try to approach your readings with a modicum of humility. Even the best predictive readers can't see everything. Some things are meant to remain unknown so that destiny can play out.

Try not to allow your client to constantly interrupt you while you are reading. It disrupts the flow of information. Tactfully tell them that you need to finish your thought or you will lose the message. Reassure them that they will be able to ask questions at the end of your spread interpretation. As you read the symbolism, trust what you are saying. Trust the imagery in front of you. A good reading is already built into the archetypes spread before you.

Maintaining healthy boundaries is important to retain your sanity. I am instantly repelled by desperation from obsessive clients. It usually reveals an underlying emotional issue that one tarot reading is probably not going to solve. If a person needs emotional help beyond your education and expertise, refer them to the appropriate professional. Unless you are a legitimate medical doctor or licensed therapist, you should not be providing a diagnosis for your client. Also, you don't have to read everyone. Reserve the right to refuse service to people who are obsessive or just frankly give you the creeps. Trust your instincts and let your inner Emperor speak up. You can always say no. You get to choose the people you share your gift with.

Finally, be ethical. As a reader, you are going to be entrusted with people's secrets and sensitive information. Be trustworthy and make good decisions. Never lie to your client to make you or them feel better. Be honest, but try to deliver your truth with compassion. Do not use readings to manipulate others or to suggest something that you know to be morally dubious. Keep your ego in check. Nobody likes pomposity. Try not to brag about how you delivered a shocking but sensitive truth to your client or made them cry with how "on point" you were. It just looks amateurish. Most importantly, do not purposefully frighten or scare your client. Fear-based readings drag the energy down to a lower vibration. Readings are about serving the higher good. Speak honestly about issues that arise, but never use your words as weapons to shock or harm the person who is trusting you with their hopes and sensitive heart.

VII
© 1971 U.S. GAMES SYSTEMS, INC.
XII
THE HANGED MAN.
© 1971 U.S. GAMES SYSTEMS, INC.

CONCLUSION

I am so grateful for our journey together through the hills and valleys of the tarot. It is a path you can traverse for a lifetime, and yet still arrive at exciting new landscapes. With tarot, there will always be something to learn. It is my hope that you continue to use the tarot as a positive force in the world and let your own inner wisdom speak clearly to you. Never fear the images that reveal themselves to you. They are *symbols.* They can always be perceived constructively, if you so choose.

Like the gentle Queen of Cups, prize your intuitive gifts. Your sensitivity makes you strong, unique, and fascinating. Oracles, seers, shamans, and medicine people have been shaping the human experience from the start. Our messages can always be perceived, gently nudging the trajectory of history. When we use our gifts to serve, we can speak to what is best and wisest in humanity.

People have always needed oracles. No matter how linear or literal our society tries to become, there is always a yearning for its wisest messengers: special individuals who speak a symbolic language, deeper than mundane artifice.

You are one of those amazing people.

Be proud of that.

Blessings,
Elliot Adam

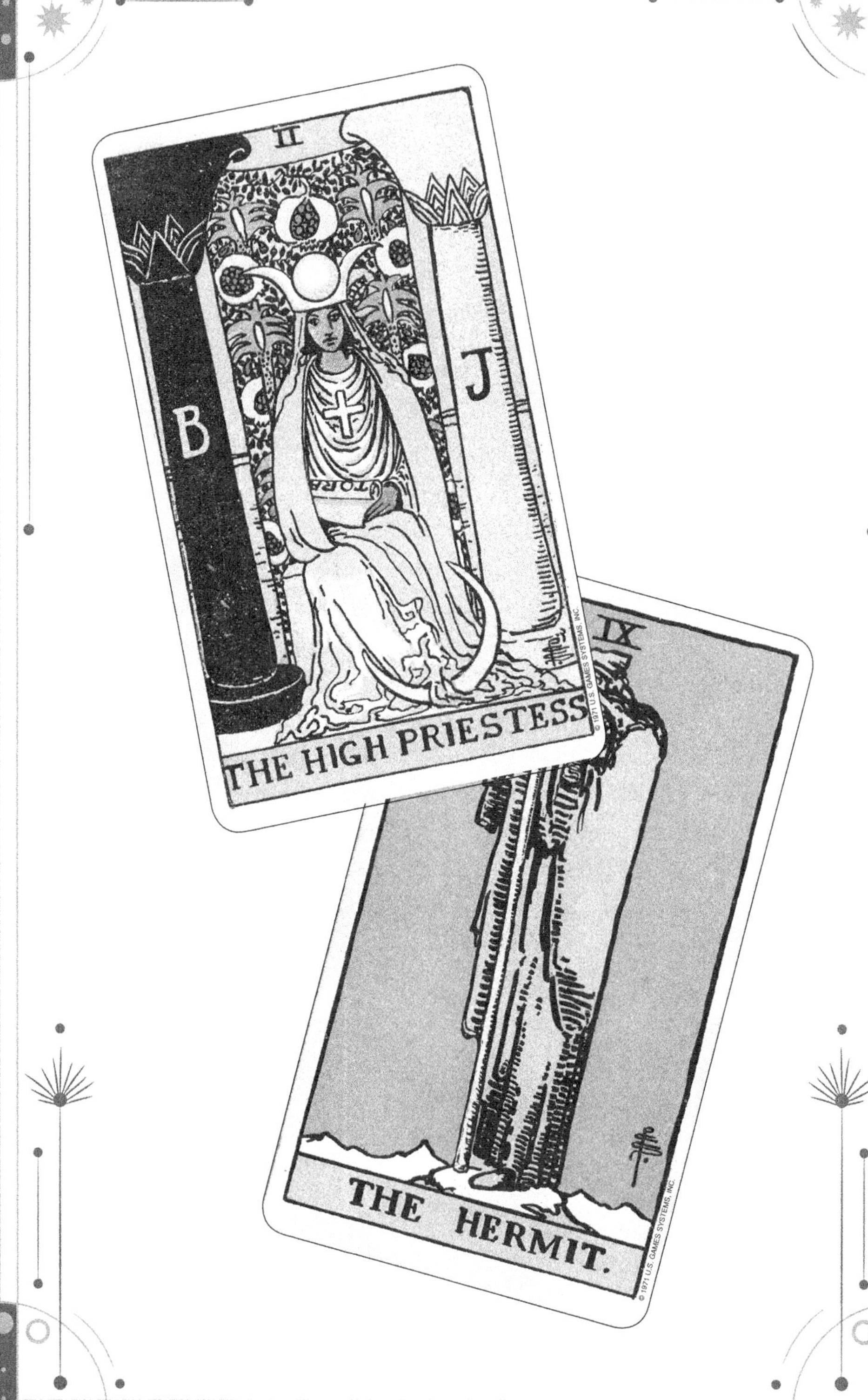
II
B
J
TORA
THE HIGH PRIESTESS
© 1971 U.S. GAMES SYSTEMS, INC.
IX
THE HERMIT.
© 1971 U.S. GAMES SYSTEMS, INC.

APPENDIX: QUICK TAROT READING REFERENCE GUIDE

QUICK GUIDE

0 The Fool

(Upright) Take a chance. Positive new beginnings. Optimism. Don't be afraid of looking stupid; try. Something in its beginning phase.

(Reversed) Release fear of falling and failing. Be teachable and open to learning new things. Be brave and make the attempt.

1 The Magician

(Upright) Focus on what you want. Take control of the situation. Tune in to your Higher Self. Use your head, not your heart. Communicate. Make up your mind. Set your intentions.

(Reversed) Allowing your thoughts to run on autopilot. Clean out your mental attic. Notice what kind of thoughts might be limiting you at this time. Focusing on the parts of yourself that make you feel capable and confident.

2 The High Priestess

(Upright) Wisdom. Trust your instincts. Inner knowing. Strong intuitive abilities. Transcend your fears and touch what is limitless within. Make time for Spirit.

(Reversed) Recurring signs and symbols. Synchronistic events that will guide your way. Patterns. Examine the situation from a different perspective. Get another perspective.

3 The Empress

(Upright) Fertility, abundance, and growth. Nurture what you love. A message of relief. Nurturing yourself and others. Love. Embracing the sacred feminine.

(Reversed) Time to nurture something that's been neglected. Issues that may stem from your mother. The false fear that you won't have or be enough. An insecurity that needs to be dealt with honestly.

4 The Emperor

(Upright) Assertion. Power. Boundaries. Stable foundations. Speak up for yourself. Be willing to fight for yourself and your goals. Protecting your space. Maturity. Embracing the sacred masculine.

(Reversed) Identify what feels unstable and address it. Stop avoiding conflict. Do what must be done. Take charge. Improve your self-esteem through action.

5 The Hierophant

(Upright) Seeking the Sacred. Spiritual epiphanies and revelations. Overcoming fear of connecting with the Divine. Prayer. Communion with divinity. Asking for what you need.

(Reversed) Challenge inflexibility. Don't be too rigid. Dealing with stubborn people. Be the bigger person. Connect with your better angels.

6 The Lovers

(Upright) Love. Harmony restored. Looking on others with unconditional love. Transcendence through love. Balance internal and external needs. Cooperation. Compromise.

(Reversed) A need to restore harmony in yourself or in a relationship. Don't rush to anger or impatience; ask for more information. Fall back in love with your life. Heal relationships by starting with yourself.

7 The Chariot

(Upright) Victory. Courage. Leaving your comfort zone. Boldly going out into the world. Your instincts will protect you. Trusting the Mystery. Be brave; it's time to move now.

(Reversed) Vacillation. The fear of making the wrong choice is preventing momentum. Get moving again. Fear of making mistakes. You won't win if you don't try. Make the decision you have been afraid to make.

8 Strength

(Upright) Self-control. Reining in out-of-control behaviors. Being gentle with yourself. Healing. Self-love. Your Higher Self knows best. Reclaiming your confidence and courage. You are stronger than you think. Taming the beast within.

(Reversed) Beginning to doubt your strength. Push yourself to persevere. Challenging limitations. Stop being so hard on yourself. Just because you aren't perfect doesn't mean you aren't worthy. Respect yourself and others will, too.

9 The Hermit

(Upright) Self-examination. Checking in with yourself. Time spent alone. Examining feelings that were put on ice. Trust your inner Wise One. Move slowly. Take your time.

(Reversed) Rejoin the land of the living. Time to reemerge. Reconnect with the world. Get out there again. Share what you have learned with others.

10 Wheel of Fortune

(Upright) Events, both good and bad, are out of your control. Detach from drama by finding your center. Can indicate good luck or good news. Sit in the eye of the storm and remain calm. Get off the emotional roller coaster.

(Reversed) Repeated life lessons. Repeated patterns. Recurring behaviors. Revisiting something that you thought you already learned. Going back to retrieve a missing part of you.

11 Justice

(Upright) Tell the truth to yourself. Absolute honesty. Clarity. Be direct but kind. Something needs balancing. Don't be afraid of the word "no." The truth shall set you free.

(Reversed) The feeling that life feels lopsided. Excess. A situation that feels unfair. Let Karma take care of it. Face the facts. Truth will restore your equilibrium. Snapping out of self-deception.

12 The Hanged Man

(Upright) Self-sacrifice. A worthy investment of energy. Pausing to gain a new perspective. Something that feels "hung up" or delayed. Wisdom. Temporary discomfort that leads to growth. Growing pains. Sacrificing something for the sake of something better.

(Reversed) Getting back on your feet again. The delay is over; time to move. Life will no longer appear upside down.

13 Death

(Upright) An inevitable change that must be accepted. Letting go. The metaphorical death of something that precedes rebirth. Stop trying to resurrect what you've outgrown. Acceptance. A major change. Don't fear the change. It's for the best.

(Reversed) Resisting changes. Trying to hold on to something that is no longer useful. Stepping out of shadows and back into the light. Clearing energy blockages. Let go; the sun will rise again.

14 Temperance

(Upright) Finding the right balance between two aspects of your life. Replenishing something that feels empty. Restoring yourself. Check in with your body. Self-care. If something has been dominating your life, do the opposite. Restoring peace and calm.

(Reversed) Feeling depleted. Excessive worries or behaviors. Need for self-care. Drink more water. Spend time near water. Eliminate stressful triggers. Be gentle with yourself.

15 The Devil

(Upright) Confronting your inner saboteur. Shadows pipe up just before your breakthrough. Confronting untruths. Facing addictive behaviors. Do not allow yourself to be manipulated. Time to slip out of the chains that have bound you in the past. By embodying your better angels, the Devil loses all power.

(Reversed) Old chains are slipping off. Something that kept you stuck is now being released. Expressing buried feelings. Bringing old traumas to light so that they heal. Not being fooled by the manipulative behaviors of others.

16 The Tower

(Upright) Catharsis. Snapping out of denial. Coming back to reality. An ending that feels painful but must happen. Facing the truth of your feelings. Major healing following a crisis. A breakthrough. Freedom from feeling trapped.

(Reversed) A period when things felt uncertain or shaky. Old, outdated structures being swept away. The hurricane has passed, and now it's time to clean up. Getting life back in order. You didn't need it anymore if it was already crumbling apart. The return of light after darkness.

17 The Star

(Upright) Transcendent wisdom. Hope renewed. Light at the end of the tunnel. Seeking what is eternal. Positive connections with evolved souls. A guide. Remember your Spirit's purpose. Working on the things that will be here long after you are. Doing something to contribute to the collective. Teaching. Connecting with amazing people, perhaps from far away.

(Reversed) Time to balance the transcendental with the practical. Balancing spiritual and mundane concerns. Balancing your inner and outer worlds. Sharing your gifts, even when you don't receive something in return.

18 The Moon

(Upright) Instincts. Intuitive pull. Checking in with your unconscious. Intuitive work. Psychic abilities. If you've been feeling "loony," an issue is trying to come to the surface from within. The hidden side of people. Depth. Allowing your emotions to flow.

(Reversed) Stop neglecting your instincts or suppressing your feelings. Feeling crazy or cut off from reality. Make time to listen to your inner needs. Time to do a reading. Stop ignoring your hunches. Your intuition is usually right.

19 The Sun

(Upright) The best card. Happy times. Optimism. The return of light. Good news. A reason to feel joyful. Magical assistance. Help is coming. Everything in this situation will turn out all right. You will eventually receive your heart's true desire.

(Reversed) Still the best card in the deck. The same meaning as the upright version, although to a bit of a lesser degree. The clouds are parting, and the sun is returning. Get out of the house and move.

20 Judgement

(Upright) Rebirth. Renewal. The phoenix rising from the ashes. Stepping out of a mental grave. New life. The "dead" parts of you are stirring back to life again. Awakening. Positive news. Accepting that you deserve better. A revelation.

(Reversed) Sleepwalking through life. Time to wake up! Be alert to or aware of what is happening. Snapping out of a trance. Time to rekindle weakened flames. A need for resuscitation. Resurrect your passion for life. A situation that feels like it's on life support.

21 The World

(Upright) Completion. Finishing a huge life cycle. Perspective. Graduation. Attainment. Mastery. Victory. An accomplishment that should not be minimized. Know your power. Looking at your whole journey. The situation has run its course. Enlightenment.

(Reversed) Resistance to finishing the job. Fear of success. Fear of finishing a project or life phase. Doing the same thing over and over. Break the cycle. Getting off the hamster wheel.

Ace of Swords

(Upright) Victory. Triumph through action. Taking the bull by the horns. Surviving. Restoring peace. Reclaiming your power. Restoration of confidence.

(Reversed) Guarding your new beginning. Protecting something that's newly instituted. Creating new habits and routines. Protecting yourself from the influence of others. Being at rest. Peace.

Two of Swords

(Upright) Feeling in-between. In limbo. Transitions. Magical time of transformation. Balance. Finding your center. A transition to a better time. Trusting.

(Reversed) Stepping out of limbo. Making a choice. Choosing a path at the fork in the road. Action after a period of stillness. Seeking closure.

Three of Swords

(Upright) Forgiveness of past betrayals. An opportunity for the heart to heal. Overcoming sorrow. Letting go of pain. Abandoning righteous indignation. Dealing with wounds. Releasing emotional burdens. Facing your wounds.

(Reversed) Becoming aware of self-inflicted wounds. Challenging negative expectations. Knowing the difference between thoughts and reality. Choosing to not continually hurt yourself with past traumas.

Four of Swords

(Upright) Peace. Rest. Alone time. Recuperation. A well-deserved break. Slow down. It can wait. Restoration. Rejuvenation. Relaxation. Finding time to breathe.

(Reversed) Restless energy. Nervous energy that needs an outlet. Avoid extremes. Step away from triggers that make you feel anxious, harried, or stressed.

Five of Swords

(Upright) Pace yourself. Don't take on too much. Stop being Superman or Superwoman. Get organized with your tasks. Do a little bit every day. Make a commitment to yourself to establish consistency.

(Reversed) Deadlines that might be causing stress. Too heavy an expectation for success. Scattered or unfocused energy that needs to be properly channeled. Eliminating stress triggers.

Six of Swords

(Upright) Movement. Moving. Travel. Transition. Leaving a problem behind. Heading toward a new life. Changes for the better. Temporary discomfort leading to happiness. A new and better life is opening to you now. Go with the flow.

(Reversed) Feeling stuck. A need to get things moving again. Procrastination. Stop fighting the waves and go with the flow. Stop resisting the discomfort that results in positive change.

Seven of Swords

(Upright) Outwitting your obstacles. Craftiness. Intelligence. Cunning. Don't get mad, get smart. View all angles of the challenge at hand. Finding the way to bypass a blockage.

(Reversed) Changes in luck. Unpredictable situations or actions. A need to be alert to the intentions of others. Be aware of manipulation if it is happening. Make your own luck. Pay attention to details. The details matter in this situation.

Eight of Swords

(Upright) Fears that need to be challenged. Stop giving up before you've given your best effort. A situation that appears hopeless isn't. You aren't defeated yet. Taking off the blindfold that keeps you stuck. Healing your sense of worth. Freeing yourself from bondage to a person, place, behavior, or thing.

(Reversed) Escaping from self-limiting thoughts. Old fears are losing their grip. Freeing yourself from worrying. Regaining perspective. It's time to know your value. Choosing to be free.

Nine of Swords

(Upright) Confronting fears and restless shadows. Seeing nightmares for what they are: dreams. Standing up to negative thinking. Insomnia. You need to change your perspective. The situation is not hopeless; your perspective is. Stand up to your shadow.

(Reversed) Waking up from the nightmare of thinking you are less than you are. Walking away from something toxic. Challenging assumptions of dread. Remembering light will follow darkness. It will go better than you fear. It usually does.

Ten of Swords

(Upright) Surrendering something. Facing what is making you anxious. Confronting shadows. Facing the fear will ensure you are no longer a victim. A serious issue that needs to be looked at honestly. If you face the issue, you will gain the power to finally release it. Acceptance, even when it is difficult.

(Reversed) The black clouds are breaking up and light is returning. Surviving a challenging ordeal. The black rain cloud that seemed to be following you is now dissipating. Sunlight is the best disinfectant. Allow your fears to be spoken into the light and release them.

Page of Swords

(Upright) Time to lower unnecessary defenses. A need to allow others in. Personalities with wounded egos. Don't take the actions of others personally; it's their issue. A person with a lot of insecurity. Allow your vulnerability to be seen.

(Reversed) Be more aware of how you are communicating. Sharp-tongued individuals. The way you speak sets the tone. Be mindful of the words you use. Let go of the need to be right.

Knight of Swords

(Upright) Rushing through life. Be kinder to your body. Tunnel vision. Relentless pursuit of success. Slow down. Schedule some time for rest. Turn off the phone and television and return to your center.

(Reversed) Manage increasing stress in a healthy manner. Be present. Challenging obsessive thoughts or thinking. Placing your focus on something more productive or healthy. Get your mind and your body to be kinder to each other.

Queen of Swords

(Upright) Bringing order to chaos through clarity and boundaries. Change the energy from being a victim to becoming the victor. Playing hardball. A strong female. Stepping into your personal authority and power.

(Reversed) A warning not to isolate yourself from others. A loner. Dealing with a person who's a bit bossy. Using your language to improve the energy. Don't allow your voice to contribute to toxicity. Time to speak up respectfully.

King of Swords

(Upright) Challenge your assumptions. Dealing with a fixed or rigid individual. Challenging stereotypes. Understanding a challenge more acutely in order to change it. Working within rigid systems.

(Reversed) Acquiring the knowledge that will lead to a breakthrough. The need for more information before making a judgement. Examining your own attitudes and responsibility in this matter. A need to be more accountable.

Ace of Cups

(Upright) Transcendent love. Renewal. Joy. Spiritual bliss. Replenishment. New beginnings. Birth. Let love be the answer. Miracles.

(Reversed) Pouring your energy into what brings you joy is never a waste. Nurturing a project, person, or yourself. Rejuvenating your Spirit. Turning toward the Sacred. Replenish yourself before giving to another.

Two of Cups

(Upright) Relationships. Important negotiations based on respect. Honest and respectful communication. Being mindful of others' pride. Respecting another's dignity. Collaboration. Discussions. Agreements. Marriage. Relationships. A partnership that is destined.

(Reversed) Beware of miscommunications. Reading the signals incorrectly. Misinterpreting another's body language or writing. Be open and curious instead of jumping to conclusions. Rising above the traps set by the ego.

Three of Cups

(Upright) Charisma. Joy. Celebration. Dynamism. Cheering up others. Raising the energy. Embracing the light. Nurturing something important to you. Improving the environment around you with positive energy.

(Reversed) Distractions that are keeping you from your bliss. A need to reconnect with your joy. Happiness is a choice.

Four of Cups

(Upright) Not accepting blessings, assistance, or miracles. Getting stuck in your head. Accept the gift being offered. Stop ruminating. Catch yourself if you are brooding. Open yourself to the good things being offered.

(Reversed) Challenge the illusion that you are alone. Recognizing if you are feeling shut down emotionally. Reconnect. Release the chip on your shoulder.

Five of Cups

(Upright) Recognizing the trance of negative thinking. A need to absorb your successes, not just your perceived failures. Changing mental channels. Positive thinking is needed. The importance of shifting your focus.

(Reversed) Viewing perceived setbacks as opportunities. Not getting what you originally wanted, but for a good reason. Letting go of perceptions of "bad" or "good" fortune. Recognizing that negative thinking is the obstacle.

Six of Cups

(Upright) Memories. The past. Recalling what made you happy before. Remembering your bliss. Something from the past is being revisited.

(Reversed) Healing the past. Forgiveness of the past. Letting go of past burdens. Releasing. Redirecting your attention to where your power resides: the present.

Seven of Cups

(Upright) Illusions. Dreams. A need for practical action. Dreams are not reality. Creativity. Escapism. Recognizing what distracts you. Mind-altering activities. If you want your dream to manifest, you must act.

(Reversed) Awakening from a trance. Not allowing yourself to run on autopilot anymore. A wake-up call. A need to be more alert. Distinguishing fantasy from reality.

Eight of Cups

(Upright) The needs of your Inner Self are calling you. A return to authenticity. Sometimes a period of depression. A journey within. Deep healing. Overcoming blockages by tapping into Source.

(Reversed) Returning to your true nature. Stepping away from external distractions. Rejecting the superficial. Acknowledging your real feelings.

Nine of Cups

(Upright) Pleasure. Wishes fulfilled. Taking your seat at the table of success. Indulgence. Using your senses. The table is set. "Life is a banquet, and most poor suckers are starving to death!"

(Reversed) Something done in excess. Overindulgence. Addictive personalities. Choosing balance. Recognizing what is taking up an excess of your time.

Ten of Cups

(Upright) Gratitude. Happy partnerships. Loving family. Good news or messages. Perspective. Seeing the world with new joy. Bliss in the home.

(Reversed) Recognizing the influence of colors on your mood and environment. Redecorating. Making changes for the sake of beauty. Opening your eyes to the wonder of the present. Being open.

Page of Cups

(Upright) Creativity. An artist. The magical inner child. A positive young person. Issues concerning pets. Communicating feeling through writing, music, or art.

(Reversed) Creative blocks resulting from neglected feelings. Stop overthinking. Too much nitpicking is a creative buzzkill. Let things get delightfully messy occasionally.

Knight of Cups

(Upright) The messenger of love. Romantic needs. Following your heart. Passion. Committing to your course. Bravely talking about feelings. Allowing yourself to be vulnerable. Following your bliss.

(Reversed) Difficult conversations that lead to healing. A need to discuss buried emotions. Releasing burdensome anxieties. Learning to trust your heart again. Open your heart again!

Queen of Cups

(Upright) Valuing feelings and emotions. Not just experiencing life through the head, but also through the heart. Seeking beauty. A nurturing woman. Compassion. Care. Accepting all emotions and experiences as teachers. Emotional wisdom and maturity.

(Reversed) Bottling up feelings. Passing through life without letting it in. A need to be reminded of beauty. Releasing old emotions that have become burdensome. Taking time to take care of the emotional needs of yourself or others. Let your feelings flow.

King of Cups

(Upright) Channeling your feelings toward progress. Emotional maturity. A trustworthy and kind man. Issues that need to be addressed with home or property. Staying strong in your feelings. Establishing roots. Emotional stability amid the waves.

(Reversed) Stay calm amid stormy seas. Not allowing yourself to get swept up in the passions of the moment. Remain calm. Removing clutter. Throwing away what you don't need anymore from your heart or environment.

Ace of Pentacles

(Upright) Prosperous new beginnings. New money. Fresh opportunities. An offer. Doorways are opening for you now. An increase in stature. A new job.

(Reversed) Procrastination may be hindering your success. Act on your goals; don't just dream about them. Don't talk yourself out of success. Get the ball rolling. Start!

Two of Pentacles

(Upright) Staying flexible. Unpredictability. Juggling finances. Remaining good-humored. Juggled different aspects of your life successfully.

(Reversed) Release fixed expectations. Too much attachment to a certain outcome. Remember your sense of humor. Learn to laugh at it all. Don't personalize chaotic events.

Three of Pentacles

(Upright) Learning. Perfecting. Studying. Teaching. Researching. Knowledge. Manifesting. Carrying out plans. Honing a skill. Remain teachable. Cooperation with others.

(Reversed) Repeated lessons. Revisiting an issue before you can progress. Impatience with the learning process. Acknowledge your progress and stop being so hard on yourself.

Four of Pentacles

(Upright) Seeking security. External position or power. Trying to find happiness through *things.* Time to remove blockages. Good financial prospects, but remember that money alone can't *make* you happy.

(Reversed) Releasing avoidance behaviors. Removing old blockages. Surrender that which is causing suffering. Giving and sharing.

Five of Pentacles

(Upright) Poverty consciousness. Confronting issues of self-worth. Giving to others with boundaries. Realizing that you are worthy of your seat at the table. A need to make better financial decisions.

(Reversed) Wasting energy on something that isn't showing a return. Stop depleting yourself on people or pursuits that are only taking. It's no longer appropriate to give yourself away. Raising your standards.

Six of Pentacles

(Upright) Generosity. Entertaining angels unaware. Help received. Kindness. The cultivation of good Karma. Hospitality. Support and opportunities offered from a benefactor.

(Reversed) Placing others on a pedestal at the expense of yourself. Looking to others to take control. Reaffirming that you are qualified and competent. Accepting help but not becoming dependent on it.

Seven of Pentacles

(Upright) Acknowledging your progress. A great deal has been accomplished, but there is still more work to do. Not quite finished with the task at hand. The promise of a good harvest. Patience.

(Reversed) Just because a thought is negative, that does not make it truer. Mistaking pessimism with being realistic. Feeling discouraged with details. The process of refining. Training your mind to believe in success.

Eight of Pentacles

(Upright) Meaningful work. Focus and determination. Serving the community through your job. Your work is your platform to make the world better. Valuing your skills. A hard worker.

(Reversed) Being mindful of the energy you are infusing your work with. A need to release resentment. Stop depleting your energy on a job that isn't fulfilling. An opportunity to change your employment. Self-work.

Nine of Pentacles

(Upright) Wealth and prosperity. Wealth consciousness. Training your focus on what you want. Sensitivity to your environment. Good financial prospects. A helpful, wealthy individual.

(Reversed) Tolerating something beneath your standards of excellence. Raising your expectations. Taking out the garbage literally and metaphorically. You deserve the best.

Ten of Pentacles

(Upright) Legacy. Working on the things that last. Financial security. Family. Community. Solidity. Investing your energy and resources wisely. Keep your eye on the long game.

(Reversed) Acknowledging your ancestors. Remembering those who came before. Looking to history for answers. Following the example of those you admire in your family. Feeling the Spirit of a relative who passed on.

Page of Pentacles

(Upright) The eternal student. Passion for learning. Practical application of knowledge. A student. A smart and kind young person. School. Teaching. Learning a new skill.

(Reversed) Feeling like you are losing passion for your interests. A need to change up the energy. Participating in activities that reignite your passion for learning. Can also emphasize reviewing the basics or relearning something.

Knight of Pentacles

(Upright) Feeling disappointment that things are not moving forward. Unfulfilled expectations based on apparent lack of progress. Getting stuck in how things appear now instead of viewing the long game. A man who has a lot of potential but just doesn't seem to be living up to it currently. Eventual success, but details need to be addressed.

(Reversed) Managing expectations. Patience. Look for evidence before making a judgement. A need for tenacity. Never give up. Often, not getting what you initially wanted leads to better things.

Queen of Pentacles

(Upright) Stable growth. Focusing on what you are manifesting. Tuning out the anxiety that may be chattering away in the background. Patience. A strong and financially stable woman. Presence. Enjoying the comforts of the moment.

(Reversed) Too much attention is being placed on anxieties. Finding calm amid uncertainty. It's okay to *not* have it all figured out yet. The grass will grow whether you worry about it or not. Relax!

King of Pentacles

(Upright) Patiently nurturing your goals. Sweet success. Commitment. Order. Prosperity. A man you can trust, especially in the realm of finances. Loving the work that you do. Being prepared. Good health and stability. Longevity.

(Reversed) Feeling overwhelmed as a result of disorganization. Identifying what is halting your progress. Removing mental clutter in the form of distractions. A need for patience and understanding.

Ace of Wands

(Upright) New inspiration. Fresh ideas. Branching into new realms of possibility. A sense of urgency. Time to act on your inspiration now. A breakthrough. Taking advantage of your opportunities.

(Reversed) Don't allow your brilliant ideas to slip away; write them down. Get the ball rolling. Speak with experts. Research your goal and the steps needed to achieve it. Don't pass up your opportunities.

Two of Wands

(Upright) Restlessness. Always desiring more, leading to a sense of being dissatisfied. Insatiability. A need to acknowledge the blessings of the present. The desire for external success. Choose to be happy today, not "one day."

(Reversed) Obsessive thinking about events that haven't happened yet. Excess worrying. A need to get another opinion. Tunnel vision. A need to be alert to the present. Nothing in life goes exactly as we plan it.

Three of Wands

(Upright) Growth. Branching out. Yearning. Life is opening to you now. New opportunities. New business prospects. A potential move. Looking toward the horizon. Your life is still a blank canvas awaiting your masterpiece. Communicating about your goals.

(Reversed) Finding joy in the present. Gratitude and joy for the life you are currently living. Watch out for mistaking something "new" for something "better." Being content in your own backyard.

Four of Wands

(Upright) Celebration. Joy. A party. Sociability. Get-togethers. Having fun. Siesta. Enjoyment. Humor. Reconnecting with friends or loved ones. A rite of passage.

(Reversed) Changing social structures. Outgrowing old friendships. Time needed away from others to get clear. Detach from drama.

Five of Wands

(Upright) Comparing yourself to others. Competitiveness. Struggle. Trying to prove yourself. Immature people. Tense working relationships. Teenagers. Unrealistic expectations placed on yourself to prove your worth.

(Reversed) People who project their insecurities onto others. Rise above pettiness or conflicts. It's best to not let your ego make the decision. Dealing with immature individuals.

Six of Wands

(Upright) Fame. Acclaim. Recognition. Success. Victory. Achievement. Promote yourself. Share your talents. Self-confidence. Ask for a raise. Seek that promotion. Bring attention to your skills and talents.

(Reversed) Don't let the opinions of others dictate how you feel about yourself. Stop seeking validation "out there." Keep your eyes on your own paper. It's time to reinforce an authentic sense of self-esteem.

Seven of Wands

(Upright) Individuality. Taking the high road. Standing up for what you know is right. Defending your position. Doing your own thing. Nonconformity. Going against the grain. Embracing your uniqueness.

(Reversed) Releasing the belief that it's you against the world. Increasing stress that needs to be surrendered. Lower your guard. Let others help. Stop being so tense. Drop your shoulders.

Eight of Wands

(Upright) Momentum. Movement. Progress. Information. Messages. Fast-moving events. A lot to process. Picking up speed. Something that needs to be addressed quickly.

(Reversed) Flurry of activity. Don't take this increased activity personally. Remember to breathe. Give yourself a break. Lower your stress and anxiety levels.

Nine of Wands

(Upright) Boundaries. You are a survivor. Not backing down when things get tough. Pick yourself up and dust yourself off. Protecting what you've achieved. Standing up to bullies. Be assertive.

(Reversed) Releasing the chip on your shoulder. Recognizing if anger is robbing you of joy. Release your frustration. Let off some steam. Realize that no one gets a free pass in life. Everyone will have their share of trials.

Ten of Wands

(Upright) Service. You are almost at the finish line. Hard work. Sometimes struggle, but for a good cause. The harvest. Rewards for your efforts.

(Reversed) Put down the burden and enjoy the harvest. Take a break. Recognizing that life is about more than work and drudgery. Taking care of your physical body.

Page of Wands

(Upright) Aspirations. Looking up to others you admire. Following the examples of your heroes. An optimistic or adventurous young person. Precociousness. Talent. You are still growing.

(Reversed) Patience when cultivating a talent. Focus scattered energy. Having your mind in too many places at once. Looking up to others but not comparing your talents to theirs. Being all right with not having a finished product.

Knight of Wands

(Upright) Adventure. Travel. Curiosity. A foreign experience. Seeing new lands. Experiencing new cultures. A passionate young man with an exciting and adventurous spirit. Following a spirit of exploration. Spontaneity.

(Reversed) Scattered energy. Limiting your major goals down to one or two. Incorporating your experiences. A need to commit to the goal at hand. Doing something with the knowledge that you've gained.

Queen of Wands

(Upright) Self-esteem. Shining unapologetically. Don't be afraid to let others see who you are. Embracing your authenticity. A unique woman who is not afraid to put on a show. Charisma. Growing into a sense of self-confidence. Looking at the bright side of things. Optimism. Radiance.

(Reversed) A need to bolster your confidence. Rediscover your courage. Come out of hiding. If you feel like a fraud, that's normal! All successful people feel this way at one point or another. Fake it till you make it!

King of Wands

(Upright) A wise counselor. Trust your competency. Respecting the part of you that helped you survive. A respected man from humble beginnings. Not letting your reactions get too "hot" or too "cold." Being proud of your roots.

(Reversed) Resist the urge to doubt yourself now. New opportunities presented require you to tap into your deepest strength. The King of Wands always finds a way to succeed. Push past your fear of not being good enough. Don't limit yourself!

BIBLIOGRAPHY

Amberstone, Ruth Ann, and Wald Amberstone. 2008. *The Secret Language of Tarot.* San Francisco: Weiser Books.

Andrews, Ted. 2013. *Enchantment of the Faerie Realm.* Woodbury, MN: Llewellyn Publications.

Dickerman, Alexandra Collins. 1992. *Following Your Path: Using Myths, Symbols, and Images to Explore Your Inner Life.* Los Angeles: Jeremy P. Tarcher, Inc.

Fiebig, Johannes, and Evelin Burger. 2016. *The Ultimate Guide to the Rider Waite Tarot.* Woodbury, MN: Llewellyn Publications.

Hollander, P. Scott. 1996. *Tarot for Beginners.* St. Paul: Llewellyn Publications.

Katz, Marcus, and Tali Goodwin. 2015. *Secrets of the Waite-Smith Tarot.* Woodbury, MN: Llewellyn Publications.

Liddell, H. G., and R. Scott. 1889. *Greek-English Lexicon.* 7th ed. Oxford: Oxford University Press.

Osbon, Diane K. 1991. *A Joseph Campbell Companion: Reflections on the Art of Living.* New York: HarperPerennial.

Pausanias. 1935. *Description of Greece.* Vol. IV, edited by Jeffrey Henderson. MA: Harvard Uniuversity Press.

Petersen, Elisabet. 2015. "Liza Minelli on the Phil Donahue Show 1991." April 10. Video, 51:31. https://youtu.be/GruxXQo8MqI.

Plato. 1999. *The Apology*. Edited by G. P. Goold. Cambridge, MA: Harvard University Press.

Pollack, Rachel. 1999. *The Complete Illustrated Guide to Tarot.* New York: Barnes & Noble Books.

———. 2008. *Tarot Wisdom: Spiritual Teachings and Deeper Meanings*. Woodbury, MN: Llewellyn Publications.

Reed, Theresa. 2016. *The Tarot Coloring Book*. Boulder: Sounds True.

Retzlaff, Nancy. 2011. *Cinderella Doesn't Live Here Anymore: How to Manifest All You Desire to Live Happily Ever After.* Milwaukee: MavenMark Books.

Sams, Jamie, and David Carson. 1999. *Medicine Cards: Revised, Expanded Edition.* New York: St. Martin's Press.

Waite, Arthur Edward. 2001. *A Pictorial Key to the Tarot.* Stanford: U.S. Games Systems, Inc.

TO WRITE TO THE AUTHOR

If you wish to contact the author or would like more information about this book, please write to the author in care of Llewellyn Worldwide Ltd. and we will forward your request. Both the author and publisher appreciate hearing from you and learning of your enjoyment of this book and how it has helped you. Llewellyn Worldwide Ltd. cannot guarantee that every letter written to the author can be answered, but all will be forwarded. Please write to:

Elliot Adam
℅ Llewellyn Worldwide
2143 Wooddale Drive
Woodbury, MN 55125-2989

Please enclose a self-addressed stamped envelope for reply, or $1.00 to cover costs. If outside the U.S.A., enclose an international postal reply coupon.

Many of Llewellyn's authors have websites with additional information and resources. For more information, please visit our website at http://www.llewellyn.com.

NOTES

NOTES

NOTES

NOTES

NOTES